Hennemann (ed.)

Global Data Strategies

Global Data Strategies

A Handbook

edited by

Moritz Hennemann

2023

BECK • NOMOS • HART

Published by
Verlag C.H.Beck oHG, Wilhelmstraße 9, 80801 München, Germany,
email: bestellung@beck.de

Co-published by
Hart Publishing, Kemp House, Chawley Park, Cumnor Hill, Oxford, OX2 9PH, United Kingdom,
online at: www.hartpub.co.uk

and

Nomos Verlagsgesellschaft mbH & Co. KG, Waldseestraße 3–5, 76530 Baden-Baden, Germany,
email: nomos@nomos.de

Published in North America by Hart Publishing
An Imprint of Bloomsbury Publishing 1385 Broadway, New York, NY 10018, USA
email: mail@hartpub.co.uk

Suggested citation:
[Author] in: Hennemann, *Global Data Strategies*, 2023, para. [#] mn. [#]

www.beck.de

ISBN 978 3 406 78294 7 (C.H.BECK)
ISBN 978 1 5099 7367 5 (HART)
ISBN 978 3 7560 1198 8 (NOMOS)

Printed in Germany by
Beltz Grafische Betriebe GmbH
Am Fliegerhorst 8, 99947 Bad Langensalza
Typeset by
Reemers Publishing Services GmbH, Krefeld
Cover: Druckerei C.H.Beck Nördlingen

CO_2 neutral
chbeck.de/nachhaltig

Table of Contents

Preface

Fellow Reader,

This Handbook delivers manifold perspectives on data strategies worldwide. Policy cycles, concepts, instruments, and effects of data strategies are mapped and analysed. The contributions focus on different parts of the world and combine different disciplinary angles. An overview of the contributions (§§ 2–9) can be found in the Introduction (§ 1 mn. 8 et seq.) to this book. Common starting point of the chapters was the Global Data Law I: Global Data Strategies Conference to which the authors contributed. The conference was held in Passau in September 2021 and was organised by the University of Passau Research Centre for Law and Digitalisation (FREDI).

I do first and foremost thank the (co-)authors for their wonderful contributions which made this Handbook possible – especially bearing their manifold other obligations in mind. Furthermore, I am more than grateful for my wonderful team at the University of Passau. Their motivation and effort brought the conference and this Handbook to life. Johanna Hähnle, Academic Research Assistant at FREDI, deserves my greatest thanks for her esteem dedication in leading the coordination of various activities, especially – and always kindly – “managing” authors and contributions. Furthermore, I do thank Dr. Patricia Boshe, Senior Researcher at FREDI, as well as Josefine Ehrlicher and Timo Hoffmann, Academic Research Assistants at the Chair for European and International Information and Data Law, for supporting the review and final editing process. Dr. Boshe also took over the lead for the Global Data Law II: African Data Protection Laws Conference held in Accra in September 2022. In addition, I do also thank our excellent student research assistants, Matthias Biller, Josefine Dittmar, Franziska Fahl, Johanna Heidbrink, Julia Lebmann, Johannes Schwarzbauer, and Clemens Spirkl, who took the main burden of formatting. Finally, Hildgund Kulhanek deserves our applause for her always thorough, helpful, and focussed support from the publisher’s side.

We do sincerely hope that you, fellow reader, will enjoy the following chapters. We look forward to your feedback and thoughts. Please drop us an email to fredi.digitalisierung@uni-passau.de.

Sincerely yours,
Moritz Hennemann

List of Abbreviations

Act 843	Data Protection Act, 2012
AfCFTA	African Continental Free Trade Agreement
African Charter	African Charter on Human and Peoples' rights
AI	Artificial Intelligence
AIDA	Special Committee on Artificial Intelligence in a Digital Age
API/APIs	Application Programming Interface(s)
Art.	Article
AU	African Union
B2B	Business to Business
B2C	Business to Consumer
B2G	Business to Government
BD&S	Big Data & Society
BfDI	Bundesbeauftragte für den Datenschutz und die Informationsfreiheit
BIDE	Beijing International Data Exchange
BMJV	Bundesministerium der Justiz und für Verbraucherschutz
BRI	Belt-and-Road Initiative
BTLJ	Berkeley Technology Law Journal
CAC	Cyberspace Administration of China
CBPR	Cross-Border Privacy Rules
CCPA	California Consumer Privacy Act
CEMAC	Economic and Monetary Community of Central Africa
cf	compare
Ch	Chapter
CII	Critical Information Infrastructure
CNIL	Commission Nationale de L'informatique et des Libertés
CNPD	Commission Nationale pour la Protection des Données
COM	Commission
CPC	Communist Party of China
CPPA	California Consumer Privacy Act
CPR	Common Pool Resource
CPRA	California Privacy Rights Act
CR	Computer und Recht
DA	Data Act
DestinE	Destination Earth
DFFT	Data Free Flow with Trust
DFS	Digital Financial Services
DGA	Data Governance Act
DMA/DMA, draft	Digital Markets Act (current)/Digital Markets Act 2020 (draft)
DPA	Data Protection Act 2012
DPC	Data Protection Commission
DPD	Data Protection Directive
DSA/DSA, draft	Digital Services Act (current)/Digital Services Act 2020 (draft)
DSR	Digital Silk Road
e.g.	for example
EAC	East African Community
EC Regulations	Electronic Communications Regulations from 2011
ECA	Electronic Communications Act 2008
ECCAS	Economic Community of Central African States
ECJ	European Court of Justice
ECOWAS	Economic Community of West African States

Ed./Eds.	Edition/Editions/Editor/Editors
EDPB	European Data Protection Board
EEA	European Economic Area
EHDS	Health Data Space
EMIs	Electronic Money Institution
Environ Plan D	Environment and Planning D: Society and Space
EOSC	European Open Science Cloud
ESCO	European Skills, Competences, Qualifications and Occupations
EU	European Union
FERPA	Family Educational Rights and Privacy Act
FFD	Free Flow of non-personal Data
FTC	Federal Trade Commission
GAFA	Google, Apple, Facebook, Amazon
GDPR	General Data Protection Regulation (EU)
GPLR	Global Privacy Law Review
GRUR	Gewerblicher Rechtsschutz und Urheberrecht
GSMA	Global System for Mobile Communications Association
HFCAA	Holding Foreign Companies Accountable Act 2020
HIPPA	Health Insurance Portability and Accountability Act
HKEX	Hong Kong Stock Exchange
IAPP	International Association of Privacy Professionals
ICT	Information and Communications Technology
ICT4AD	The Ghana ICT for Accelerated Development Policy
IIJA	Infrastructure Investment and Jobs Act
INC	Incorporated
IoT	Internet of Things
IPO	Initial Public Offering
ITIF	Information Technology and Innovation Foundation
KI	Künstliche Intelligenz (= Artificial Intelligence)
Law & Contemp. Probs	Law & Contemporary Problems
LGDP	Lei Geral de Proteção de Dados (Brazilian General Data Protection Law)
Ltd	Limited
MIIT	Ministry of Industry and Information Technology
ML	Machine Learning
MLPS	Multi-Level Protection System
MMR	Multimedia und Recht
mn.	margin number
MNO	Mobile Network Operator
MPIIC	Ministry of Public Infrastructure, Industries and Commerce
MTNDPF	Medium-Term National Development Policy Frameworks
n	(foot)note
n. d.	no date
N.Y.U. J. Int'l L. & Pol.	New York University Journal of International Law and Politics
NFDI	National Research Data Infrastructure/Nationale Forschungsdaten-infrastruktur e. V.
NFIDS	National Financial Inclusion and Development Strategy
NJW	Neue Juristische Wochenschrift
No.	Number
NPC	National People's Congress
Nw. U. L. Rev	Northwestern University Law Review
NYSE	New York Stock Exchange

NYU	New York University
NZKart	Neue Zeitschrift für Kartellrecht
OD-PSI	Open Data and Re-use of Public Sector Information
OECD	Organisation for Economic Co-operation and Development
OP	Office of the European Union
p./pp.	page/pages
PCAOB	Public Company Accounting Oversight Board
Philos. Technol.	Philosophy & Technology
PII	Personal Information Interests
PIPL	Personal Information Protection Law 2021
PPDS	Public Procurement Data Space
PPRA	Protection of Pupil Rights Amendment
RabelsZ	Rabels Zeitschrift für ausländisches und internationales Privatrecht
RDi	Recht Digital
RECs	Regional Economic Communities
RSP	Resolutions on topical subjects
SADC	Southern African Development Community
SAMR	State Administration for Market Regulation
SC	State Council
SEC	Security Exchange Commission
sec.	section
SMEs	Small and Medium-Sized Enterprises
SOEs	State-Owned Enterprises
SPC	Supreme People's Court
SPD	German Social Democratic Party
SPP	Supreme People's Procuratorate
Stan. Tech. L. Rev.	Stanford Technology Law Review
Tech	Technology
TILEC	Tilburg Law and Economics Center
U.S./US	United States
UN	United Nations
VLOPs/VLOPS	Very Large Online Platforms
ZD	Zeitschrift für Datenschutz
ZEuP	Zeitschrift für Europäisches Privatrecht
ZfDR	Zeitschrift für Digitalisierung und Recht

List of Contributors

Anna Bernzen is Assistant Professor of Law at the University of Regensburg, Germany.

Sena Afua Dei-Tutu is a Lecturer at the University of Ghana School of Law, Ghana.

Urs Gasser is Professor of Public Policy, Governance and Innovative Technology and serves as Rector of the Hochschule für Politik (HfP) and Dean of the TUM School of Social Sciences and Technology Munich, Germany.

Nikolas Guggenberger is Assistant Professor of Law at the University of Houston Law Center, United States. He also holds an appointment at the Cullen College of Engineering's Electrical and Computer Engineering Department.

Moritz Hennemann is Professor of Law and Director of the Research Centre for Law and Digitalisation at the University of Passau, Germany.

Timo Hoffmann is PhD Candidate at the University of Passau, Germany.

Daniel Schnurr is Professor of Machine Learning and Uncertainty Quantification as well as head of the Research Group Data Policies at the University of Regensburg, Germany.

Winfried Veil is Senior Policy Advisor at the Federal Ministry of the Interior and Community, Department DG I 4 (Data Policy, Data Strategy, Open Data), Berlin, Germany.

Franziska Weindauer is Senior Policy Advisor Digital Policy at the German Federal Chancellery, Berlin, Germany.

Anna Zeiter is Associate General Counsel and Chief Privacy Officer at eBay Inc., Bern, Switzerland.

Zhenbin Zuo is PhD Candidate at the University of Cambridge, United Kingdom.

§ 1 GLOBAL DATA STRATEGIES: AN INTRODUCTION

Content

Data strategies are inherently global. Data streams are able – for good or bad – to 1
flow around the globe within milliseconds. Data streams form data ecosystems of various kinds. They stretch from the security sector to economies, from the research sector to non-governmental actors, and from diverse private to many public sectors. Data is in many forms and for many purposes of value. The availability and the use of data ecosystems has consequently an intense geopolitical dimension.[1] Data ecosystems are an informational infrastructure of societies – carrying codified information, enabling data pooling and sharing as well as data analysis. Thereby, data ecosystems are able to foster individual, collective, and common goods. This ability is also strongly connected to the specific characteristics of data in general and informational goods especially – non-rival, non-exclusive and highly contextual.

A. One Global Data Strategy?

Societies and states as well as supra-national and international institutions have to 2
decide if and in which way they frame, steer, and limit data ecosystems. This decision goes along with manifold calibrations on different levels and for various different, but often interdependent sectors. A decision on data governance is rarely taken at a specific moment in time, but is a constant process of societal and regulatory evolution. Such an evolution of policies and instruments is inevitable. Codified information – as part of a greater knowledge – is a societal resource that constantly changes, evolves and – with respect to the technological advances of the last decades and centuries – grows – as does the need for data orders for data formats, data places, and data spaces.[2] The different known and unknown settings data is and might be used in make data governance not only a highly dynamic regulatory field, but a highly complex one. It is the *regulatory* task to finetune the lines between a variety of aims – some detached, some concurring, and many conflicting – and find adequate regulatory frames for data formats, data places, and data spaces. The *strategic* task is to envision – ideally research- and

[1] *Cf* e.g. Liu, *Studies in Comparative International Development* 2021, 45.

[2] Data Law as such (where Data Protection Law only forms a part of it) is a rather newly established legal discipline, *cf* Streinz in: Craig/de Búrca (eds.), *The Evolution of EU Law*, 3rd ed., 2021, 902–936, Steinrötter, *RDi* 2021, 480.

evidence-informed[3] – the use and non-use of data within the respective society and – ideally – to the benefit of the commonwealth.[4]

3 There is not one global data strategy. Against the current geopolitical background,[5] there cannot and will not be. Perspectives on – inter alia – data sovereignty[6], data location[7], data attribution[8], data access[9], data quality, data monetarisation[10], data contractualisation[11], data trade[12], data (mis)use, and data inequality[13] are too different. More importantly to note is, however, that there shall not be a 'one size fits all'-global data strategy. Cultural, regulatory, and economic settings require – for many good reasons – diverse, pluralistic, and pluriversal approaches towards data and data governance.[14] Furthermore, the structural and infrastructural side of data governance should not be neglected. Data governance is in various ways interlinked with and dependent on data standards on the one hand and the 'hardware' side of data generation and data processing on the other hand – and levels of data standardisation and data infrastructure are different in various (urban and rural) regions for many reasons.[15]

4 On this basis, different approaches from the Global West to the Global East and from the Global North to the Global South have already evolved. Other and new approaches will hopefully continue to evolve – and stimulate the competition for strategic and regulatory ideas.[16] A 'one size fits all'-global strategy (agreement) within the next years might foreclose this 'market' too early. We have already seen in the last years that instruments of specific actors might create a strong (and not always innovative[17] and beneficial[18]) drive towards them.[19] On the regulatory level, the General Data Protection

[3] Gasser in: Burri (ed.), *Big Data and Global Trade Law*, 2021, 195.

[4] See especially the case studies by Struett/Aaronson, *The Global Data Governance Project: 52 case studies*, 2021.

[5] *Cf* Alison/Klyman/Barbesino/Yen, *The Great Tech Rivalry: China vs the U.S., Avoiding Great Power War Project*, 2021, and Pottinger/Feith, *The New York Times* 30 November 2021.

[6] *Cf* e.g. Chander/Sun, *University of Hong Kong Faculty of Law Research Paper No. 21021/041* 2021.

[7] Chander/Lê, *Emory Law Journal* (2015), 676; Svantesson, *OECD Digital Economy Papers No. 301*, 2020; Cory/Dascoli, *ITIF* 2021.

[8] *Cf* e.g. Zech, *Zeitschrift für Geistiges Eigentum* 2017, 317; Amstutz, *AcP* 2018, 438; Drexl et al., *Max Planck Institute for Innovation and Competition Research Paper No. 16-10* 2016; Kerber, *International Review of Intellectual Property and Competition Law* 2016, 759.

[9] Drexl, *NZKart* 2017, 339 and 415; Grünberger in: BMJV/MPIIC (eds.), *Data Access, Consumer Interests and Public Welfare*, 2021, 253; Hartl/Ludin, *MMR* 2021, 534; Ducuing, *Network Industries Quarterly* 2019, 21. *Cf* also Specht-Riemenschneider in: BMJV/MPIIC (eds.), *Data Access, Consumer Interests and Public Welfare*, 2021, 401.

[10] *Cf* e.g. Crémer/Montjoye/Schweitzer, *Competition policy for the digital era: Final report*, 2019.

[11] *Cf* American Law Institute and European Law Institute (eds.), *ALI-ELI Principles for a Data Economy – Data Transactions and Data Rights (ALI-ELI Principles)*, 2017–2021; *cf* for data licence agreements Schur, *GRUR* 2020, 1142; Hennemann, *RDi* 2021, 61; Czychowski/Winzek, *ZD* 2022, 81.

[12] Chander/Schwartz, *University of Chicago Law Review* 2023, 49.

[13] *Cf* Fischer/Streinz, *Columbia Journal of Transnational Law* 2022, 829.

[14] *Cf* Abebe et al., *Narratives and Counternarratives on Data Sharing in Africa*, 2021, as well as Boshe/Hennemann/von Meding, *Global Privacy Law Review* 2022, 56. *Cf* also Salaymeh/Michaels, *RabelsZ* 2022, 116.

[15] See Erie/Streinz, *NYU Journal of International Law and Politics* 2021, 1. *Cf* on data standardisation Gal/Rubinfeld, *NYU Law Review* 2019, 737.

[16] *Cf* e.g. Boshe/Hennemann/von Meding, *Global Privacy Law Review* 2022, 56.

[17] *Cf* e.g. Gal/Aviv, *Journal of Competition Law and Economics* 2020, 349. See also Purtova, *Law, Innovation and Technology* 2018, 81.

[18] Mannion, *Vanderbilt Journal of Transnational Law* 2020, 685.

[19] Schwartz, *N.Y.U. Law Review* 2019, 771.

Regulation (GDPR)[20] and its global reception is probably the prime example in this regard. The GDPR has been very influential in many countries (as the Data Protection Directive (DPD)[21] was)[22] and a result of the famous *Brussels Effect* (*Bradford*)[23]. Nevertheless, at least by now, alternative data protection approaches are developed. Conceptual framings reach from 'Strasbourg'[24] to 'Beijing'[25]. Countries are setting counterpoints to the EU approach. California and its California Consumer Privacy Act (CCPA)[26] and its California Privacy Rights Act (CPRA)[27] is here the prime example.[28] A bi-partisan draft of an American Data Privacy and Data Protection Act is heavily discussed – offering some hope of a true competition of regulators. A Global Cross-Border Privacy Rules (CBPR) Forum has been initiated[29] – briefly after an agreement in principle on a Trans-Atlantic EU-U.S. Data Privacy Framework[30].

5 A competitive approach to the market of strategies does not, however, mean that a competition in substance is always the aim.[31] Strategies do have to balance the accepted degree of cooperation and competition within and between societies. The most fundamental domain of data cooperation is the framework for data transfers from one country to another.[32] Enabling or limiting data transfers means defining the territorial outreach of a data ecosystem and its potential. This is – at the ground – a question of trust towards another state, region, or society. It is obvious, but noteworthy that the level of trust is linked to and dependent on the data (and the data analysis) in question. Research data, especially health and climate data, flows hopefully more freely – to the benefit of global challenges – than, for example, security-sensible data. With respect to the manifold (unknown) possibilities to analyse a specific set of data (and derive intelligence from it), it seems rather clear that societies do and will have to negotiate about acceptable trade-offs of any cooperative and of any competitive approach within the fields of data governance. A maximisation of specific goals (or values) is nor realistic nor sensible. Rather the degrees of freedom[33] must be defined and calibrated as well as

---

[20] Regulation (EU) 2016/679 on the protection of natural persons with regard to the processing of personal data and on the free movement of such data, and repealing Directive 95/46/EC (General Data Protection Regulation).

[21] Directive 95/46/EC of the European Parliament and of the Council of 24 October 1995 on the protection of individuals with regard to the processing of personal data and on the free movement of such data (Data Protection Directive).

[22] Greenleaf, *Privacy Laws & Business International Report* 2021, 6; Hennemann, *RabelsZ* 2020, 864; Hennemann/Lienemann/Spirkl (eds.), *University of Passau Institute for Law of the Digital Society Research Paper Series No. 22-15* 2022; Boshe/Hennemann/von Meding, *Global Privacy Law Review* 2022, 56.

[23] Bradford, *Northwestern University Law Review* 2012, 1.

[24] Bygrave, *Computer Law & Security Review* 2021, 105460.

[25] Erie/Streinz, *NYU Journal of International Law and Politics* 2021, 1.

[26] California Consumer Privacy Act of 2018, Cal. Legis. Serv. Ch. 55 (A.B. 375) (WEST).

[27] California Privacy Rights Act of 2020, available at https://leginfo.legislature.ca.gov/faces/codes_displayText.xhtml?division=3.&part=4.&lawCode=CIV&title=1.81.5 (last accessed 13 December 2022).

[28] *Cf* Chander/Kaminski/McGeveran, *Minnesota Law Review* 2021, 1733.

[29] Global Cross-Border Privacy Rules Declaration, available at https://www.commerce.gov/global-cross-border-privacy-rules-declaration (last accessed 13 December 2022).

[30] European Commission, European Commission and United States Joint Statement on Trans-Atlantic Data Privscx Framework, available at https://ec.europa.eu/commission/presscorner/detail/es/ip_22_2087 (last accessed 13 December 2022). *Cf* also European Data Protection Board, *Statement 01/2022 on the announcement of an agreement in principle on a new Trans-Atlantic Data Privacy Framework*, 2022.

[31] *Cf* again Pottinger/Feith, *The New York Times* (30 November 2021).

[32] *Cf* in this regard as the most prominent proxy the ECJ judgements ECJ Case C-362/14 Maximillian Schrems v Data Protection Commissioner [2015] ECLI:EU:C:2015:650 – Schrems I and ECJ Case-311/18 Data Protection Commissioner v Facebook Ireland Ltd and Maximillian Schrems [2020] ECLI:EU:C:2020:559 – Schrems II. See also Schwartz/Peifer, *Georgetown Law Journal* 2017, 115.

[33] Möllers, *Freiheitsgrade*, 2020.

constantly evaluated and adjusted. *Data realpolitik* is strongly needed[34] and forms the fundament for any strategic approach.

B. The Strategic Turn

6 To this end, we have seen a strategic turn towards data and data governance over the last years and decades[35].[36] Various data strategies have been developed. For Europe, this process does not start[37] (and definitely does not end) with the EU Data Strategy of 2020[38], but the document has been a prominent driver of strategic and regulatory debates since then[39] – inside and partly also outside the European Union. The structural approach towards European Data Spaces is underway.[40] To the same token and for example, the African Union has just published its AU Data Policy Framework.[41] China, on the other side, is putting a heavier effort into data sovereignty – linking this rather multifaceted term[42] especially to data localisation.

7 The G7 digital ministers, on the other hand, have recently pointed to the promotion of a data free flow with trust[43], highlighting inter alia prospects of international data spaces.[44] Germany – as G7 president – highlighted: '[W]e want to promote the free flow of data with trust across borders, counter digital inequality, strengthen security on the internet, advocate good governance in cyberspace, facilitate fair competition and improve connectivity. In doing so, we also want to work to harness the potential of the digital transformation for a sustainable way of life and economy even more effectively while making digital progress itself more sustainable and inclusive.'[45] The Declaration on the Future of the Internet, signed by more than 60 states, highlights

[34] Hennemann/Specht, *Tagesspiegel Background Digitalisierung & KI* 27.06.2022.

[35] *Cf* Organisation for Economic Cooperation and Development (OECD), *Guidelines Governing the Protection of Privacy and Transborder Flows of Personal Data*, adopted on 23 September 1980 and revised on 11 July 2013.

[36] *Cf* in detail the contribution by Gasser/Hennemann (§ 2 below).

[37] See already European Commission, *Building a European Data Economy*, COM(2017) 9 final.

[38] European Commission, *A European Strategy for Data*, COM(2020) 66 final.

[39] See e.g. Picht/Richter, *GRUR Int.* 2022, 395. *Cf* especially the (partly already successful) push for a Data Act and Data Governance Act by the European Commission (European Commission, Proposal for a Regulation of the European Parliament and the Council on harmonised rules on fair access to and use of data (Data Act), COM(2022) 68 final; Regulation (EU) 2022/868 of the European Parliament and the Council of 30 May 2022 on European data governance and amending Regulation (EU) 2018/1724 (Data Governance Act)). On the Data Act see Bomhard/Merkle, *Recht Digital* 2022, 168; Hennemann/Steinrötter, *NJW* 2022, 1481; Leistner/Antoine, *IPR and the use of open data and data sharing initiatives by public and private actors*, 2022; Specht-Riemenschneider, *GRUR* 2022, 937; on the Data Governance Act see Hennemann/von Ditfurth, *NJW* 2022, 1905; Graef/Gellert, *TILEC Discussion Paper No. DP2021-006* 2021; Richter, *ZEuP* 2021, 634.

[40] *Cf* the proposal for a European Health Data Space by European Commission, Commission Staff Working Document on Common European Data Spaces, SWD(2022) 45 final. *Cf* also the proposal for the European Health Data Space, see https://ec.europa.eu/health/publications/proposal-regulation-european-health-data-space_en.

[41] African Union, *AU Data Policy Framework*, 2022, available at https://au.int/en/documents/20220728/au-data-policy-framework (last accessed 13 December 2022).

[42] *Cf* Chander/Sun, *University of Hong Kong Faculty of Law Research Paper No. 21021/041* 2021.

[43] See also World Economic Forum, *Data Free Flow with Trust (DFFT): Paths towards Free and Trusted Data Flow, White Paper*, 2020; Ducuing, *Technology and Regulation* 2020, 57; Le Chapelle/Porciuncula, *We need to talk about data: Framing the debate around free flow of data and data sovereignty*, 2021; BfDI, *G7 Datenschützer und Privacy-Behörden wollen DFFT voranbringen*, Press Release 10/2022.

[44] G7 Digital Ministers' Track – Annex 1, *G7 Action Plan for Promoting Data Free Flow with Trust.*

[45] G7 Germany, *Policy Priorities for Germany's G7 Presidency in 2022*, 2022.

similarly the goal 'to realize the benefits of data free flows with trust based on our shared values as like-minded, democratic, open and outward looking partners'[46].

C. Of Fundamentals, Economics, Strategies, and Law & Economics: A Brief Overview

Having the on-going global debates in mind, this Handbook tackles and is willing to contribute to the discourse on data strategies – may they be national, regional, supranational, or international from different angles. Starting point forms a contribution by *Urs Gasser* and myself on *Unlocking the Potential of the Data Age: Key Tasks and Challenges of Data Strategies*[47]. The chapter (only) sets the brief scene for the following chapters. It highlights data and policy life cycles. Thereby, the chapter points to the conceptional tasks data strategies have, engages with the 'wicked problems' data strategies are facing (and trying to solve), and underline the sometimes neglected dimension of strategy implementation. *Daniel Schnurr* provides the indispensable economic background to the debate. His chapter on *Global Data Economics: Principles, Strategies and Policies*[48] lays the fundament for the policy debates surrounding data generating, data transfer, and data use in economic settings. *Schnurr* points to the facets of data value, elaborates on the special characteristics of data, and highlights central challenges. He concluded with recommendations on the design of data strategies. 8

With regard to respective debates, this volume offers four different perspectives on (the evolvement of a) data strategy – from Europe to the U.S., from Africa to China. All contributions offer a diverse picture of the existing (and of potential) data strategy, data policy, and data governance instruments. *Winfried Veil* and *Franziska Weindauer* accompany the reader into the *EU and German Data Strategies – Aspiration and Reality*[49]. The authors especially point to coherences and incoherencies of the European and German approaches. *Veil* and *Weindauer* characterise the strategies as 'in many ways too contradictory' and unsuited to deconflict different policy goals.[50] However, they also note that 'both strategies are neither failed attempts nor unnecessary'. The EU is regarded as 'trendsetters by propagating new paradigms such as data access or data spaces'. *Nikolas Guggenberger* unfolds the current state of a *US Data Strategy*[51]. He analyses the Federal Data Strategy and its (meant) limits and widens the perspective to other complementary forms of legal and non-legal data governance – from privacy and competition law to industrial and infrastructure policy. On the basis of his analysis, *Guggenberger* sees no realistic setting for a comprehensive data US data strategy[52]. These insights are complemented by *Zhenbin Zuo's* account on *China's Data Strategies: Institutionalisation, Activation, and Layering*[53] – also based on his empirical research[54]. The chapter starts his analysis of the Chinese approach(es) by pointing to processes of 'institutionalisation', especially with respect to data security, data protection, and competition law. On this basis, *Zuo* discusses (potential) forms of 'activation' (e. g. 9

[46] U.S. Department of State, *Declaration for the Future of the Internet.*
[47] *Cf* below § 2.
[48] *Cf* below § 3.
[49] *Cf* below § 4.
[50] *Cf* below § 4 F.
[51] *Cf* below § 5. See also https://strategy.data.gov/2021/action-plan/.
[52] *Cf* below § 5 D.
[53] *Cf* below § 7.
[54] *Cf* Zuo *Journal of Cross-disciplinary Research in Computational Law* forthcoming.

data property, data common, or 'party managed data'), before he turns to processes of 'layering' (data cycles, local habitats, and sustainable design). *Sena Dei-Tutu* and *Timo Hoffmann* contribute a regional analysis by *Assessing Ghana's Data Protection Framework Within the Context af Africa's Data Governance Strategy: Trends, Direction and Prospects*[55]. The chapter puts a special focus on Ghana which also serves an example for a national perspective of an African country[56], but also enlarges its perspective by engaging with the Malabo convention[57] on the one hand and the recent AU Data Policy Framework[58] on the other hand.

10 On the basis of the kaleidoscope of approaches, we turn to other – for good and bad – driving mechanisms and forces within and by data governance: interdependencies between law and economies as well as between law and power. The contribution by *Anna Zeiter* and myself is engaging with a corporation's practice in managing the various different applicable data protection laws in a globalized setting. *The Regulatory Level Playing Field(s) – Global Compliance Efforts of and Global Standard-Setting by International Corporations*[59] undertakes to group different legislative playing fields and highlights the process that corporations – for different reasons – try to reach a practicable "globally harmonised" *de facto* standard – establishing and forming *data regimes*[60]. *Anna Bernzen* is tackling a topic of utmost importance – 'data colonialism'[61]. The chapter on *'Data Colonialism'? – Big Data's Adverse Impact on the (Global) South*[62] unfolds the debate surrounding the concepts of and the realities described by the term. To that end, she undertakes an analysis of the suitability of the term and points to adverse effects by datafication, appropriation, and profit generation. Based on her analysis, *Bernzen* presents potential reactions to 'data colonialism' – highlighting processes of 'nationalising' data, ideas of a property right to data, and the establishment of data trusts.

Bibliography

11 Abebe et al., *Narratives and Counternarratives on Data Sharing in Africa*, 2021, available at https://arxiv.org/abs/2103.01168 (last accessed 13 December 2022)

Alison/Klyman/Barbesino/Yen, *The Great Tech Rivalry: China vs the U.S., Avoiding Great Power War Project*, Belfer Center for Science and International Affairs, Harvard Kennedy School 2021, available at https://www.belfercenter.org/sites/default/files/GreatTechRivalry_ChinavsUS_211207.pdf (last accessed 13 December 2022)

American Law Institute and European Law Institute (eds.), *ALI-ELI Principles for a Data Economy – Data Transactions and Data Rights (ALI-ELI Principles)*, 2017–2021, available at https://europeanlawinstitute.eu/fileadmin/user_upload/p_eli/Publications/ALI-ELI_Principles_for_a_Data_Economy_Final_Council_Draft.pdf (last accessed 13 December 2022)

Amstutz, Dateneigentum, 218 *AcP* 438 (2018)

---

[55] *Cf* below § 6.

[56] See also on Ghana the in-depth analysis by Hoffmann, *University of Passau Institute for Law of the Digital Society Research Paper Series No. 22-01* 2022.

[57] African Union Convention on Cyber Security and Personal Data Protection, available at https://au.int/sites/default/files/treaties/29560-treaty-0048_-_african_union_convention_on_cyber_security_and_personal_data_protection_e.pdf (last accessed 13 December 2022).

[58] See above n 6.

[59] *Cf* below § 3 n 8.

[60] *Cf* the seminal work of Fischer-Lescarno/Teubner, *Regime-Kollisionen – Zur Fragmentierung des globalen Rechts*, 2006.

[61] Seminal work by Couldry/Mejias, *Television & New Media* 2019, 336.

[62] *Cf* below § 9.

BfDI, *G7 Datenschützer und Privacy-Behörden wollen DFFT voranbringen*, Press Release 10/2022, available at https://www.bfdi.bund.de/SharedDocs/Pressemitteilungen/DE/2022/10_G7-Communique.html (last accessed 13 December 2022)

Bomhard/Merkle, Der Entwurf eines Data Acts: Neue Spielregeln für die Data Economy, *Recht Digital* 168 (2022)

Boshe/Hennemann/von Meding, African Data Protection Laws – Current Regulatory Approaches, Policy Initiatives, and the Way Forward, 3(2) *Global Privacy Law Review* 56 (2022)

Bradford, The Brussels Effect, 107 *Northwestern University Law Review* 1 (2012)

Bygrave, The 'Strasbourg Effect' on data protection in light of the 'Brussels Effect': Logic, mechanics and prospects, 40 *Computer Law & Security Review* 105460 (2021), available at https://www.sciencedirect.com/science/article/pii/S0267364920300650 (last accessed 13 December 2022)

Chander/Kaminski/McGeveran, Catalyzing Privacy Laws, 105 *Minnesota Law Review* 1733 (2021), available at https://www.commerce.gov/news/press-releases/2022/04/statement-commerce-secretary-raimondo-establishment-global-cross-border (last accessed 13 December 2022)

Chander/Lê, Data Nationalism, 64 *Emory Law Journal* 676 (2015)

Chander/Schwartz, Privacy and/or Trade, 90 *University of Chicago Law Review* (forthcoming 2023), available at https://papers.ssrn.com/sol3/papers.cfm?abstract_id=4038531 (last accessed 13 December 2022)

Chander/Sun, Sovereignty 2.0, 2404 *University of Hong Kong Faculty of Law Research Paper No. 21021/041* (2021), available at https://papers.ssrn.com/sol3/papers.cfm?abstract_id=3904949 (last accessed 13 December 2022)

Cory/Dascoli, How Barriers to Cross-Border Data Flows Are Spreading Globally, What They Cost, and How to Address Them, *ITIF* (2021), available at https://itif.org/publications/2021/07/19/how-barriers-cross-border-data-flows-are-spreading-globally-what-they-cost/ (last accessed 13 December 2022)

Couldry/Mejias, Data Colonialism: Rethinking Big Data's Relation to the Contemporary Subject, 20(4) *Television & New Media* 336 (2019), available at https://journals.sagepub.com/doi/abs/10.1177/1527476418796632?journalCode=tvna (last accessed 13 December 2022)

Crémer/Montjoye/Schweitzer, *Competition policy for the digital era: Final report*, European Commission (2019), available at https://ec.europa.eu/competition/publications/reports/kd0419345enn.pdf (last accessed 13 December 2022)

Czychowski/Winzek, Rechtliche Struktur und Inhalt von Datennutzungsverträgen – Datenwirtschaftsrecht III: Der Vertrag über ein neues Elementarteilchen?, 81 *ZD* 2022

Drexl et al., Data Ownership and Access to Data – Position Statement of the Max Planck Institute for Innovation and Competition of 16 August 2016 on the Current European Debate, *Max Planck Institute for Innovation and Competition Research Paper No. 16-10* (2016), available at https://papers.ssrn.com/sol3/papers.cfm?abstract_id=2833165 (last accessed 13 December 2022)

Drexl, Neue Regeln für die Europäische Datenwirtschaft? Ein Plädoyer für einen wettbewerbspolitischen Ansatz – Teil 1 und 2, *NZKart* 339 and 415 (2017)

Ducuing, Beyond the data flow paradigm: governing data requires to look beyond data, *Technology and Regulation* 57 (2020), available at https://techreg.org/article/view/10995/11969 (last accessed 13 December 2022)

Ducuing, Mandating Data Sharing to Establish Data as an Infrastructural Resource, 21 *Network Industries Quarterly* 21 (2019)

Erie/Streinz, The Beijing Effect: China's "Digital Silk Road" as Transnational Data Governance, 54 *NYU Journal of International Law and Politics* 1 (2021)

European Data Protection Board, *Statement 01/2022 on the announcement of an agreement in principle on a new Trans-Atlantic Data Privacy Framework*, 2022, available at https://edpb.europa.

eu/system/files/2022-04/edpb_statement_202201_new_trans-atlantic_data_privacy_framework_en.pdf (last accessed 13 December 2022)

Fischer-Lescarno/Teubner, *Regime-Kollisionen – Zur Fragmentierung des globalen Rechts*, 2006

Fischer/Streinz, Confronting Data Inequality, 60(3) *Columbia Journal of Transnational Law* 829 (2022)

G7 Digital Ministers' Track – Annex 1, *G7 Action Plan for Promoting Data Free Flow with Trust*, Federal Ministry of Transport and Digital Infrastructure (BMDV), available at https://bmdv.bund.de/SharedDocs/DE/Anlage/K/g7-praesidentschaft-final-declaration-annex-1.pdf?__blob=publicationFile (last accessed 13 December 2022)

G7 Germany 2022, *Policy Priorities for Germany's G7 Presidency in 2022*, 2022, available at https://www.g7germany.de/resource/blob/998352/2000328/6cb78b73c9f000183e69738c255d9cc9/2022-01-21-g7-programm-en-data.pdf?download=1 (last accessed 13 December 2022)

Gal/Aviv, The Competitive Effects of the GDPR, 16 *Journal of Competition Law and Economics* 349 (2020)

Gal/Rubinfeld, Data Standardization, 94 *NYU Law Review* 737 (2019)

Gasser, Futuring Digital Privacy, in: Burri (ed.), *Big Data and Global Trade Law*, Cambridge University Press 2021, pp. 195–211, available at https://www.cambridge.org/core/books/big-data-and-global-trade-law/futuring-digital-privacy/D6F968FA6C40F8EF557BBFB1CD333281 (last accessed 13 December 2022)

Graef/Gellert, The European Commission's Proposed Data Governance Act: some initial reflections on the increasingly complex EU regulatory puzzle of stimulating data sharing, *TILEC Discussion Paper No. DP2021-006* (2021), available at https://papers.ssrn.com/sol3/papers.cfm?abstract_id=3814721 (last accessed 13 Dezember 2018)

Greenleaf, Global Tables of Data Privacy Laws and Bills, 7th ed., 169 *Privacy Laws & Business International Report* 6 (2021), available at https://papers.ssrn.com/sol3/papers.cfm?abstract_id=3836261 (last accessed 13 Dezember 2018)

Grünberger, Data access rules: The role of contractual unfairness of (consumer) contracts, in: BMJV/MPIIC (eds.), *Data Access, Consumer Interests and Public Welfare*, Nomos 2021, pp. 253–286

Hartl/Ludin, Recht der Datenzugänge, 7 *MMR* 534 (2021)

Hennemann, Datenlizenzverträge, 2 *RDi* 61 (2021)

Hennemann, Wettbewerb der Datenrechtsordnungen, 84 *RabelsZ* 864 (2020)

Hennemann/Lienemann/Spirkl (eds.), Mapping Global Data Law. Part I: Data Protection Legislation, *University of Passau Institute for Law of the Digital Society Research Paper Series No. 22-15* (2022), available at https://www.jura.uni-passau.de/fileadmin/dokumente/fakultaeten/jura/lehrstuehle/hennemann/Mapping_Global_Data_Law/Kartensatz_August_2022_v1.6.pdf (last accessed 13 December 2022)

Hennemann/Specht, Datenrealpolitik ist gefragt, *Tagesspiegel Background Digitalisierung & KI* (27.6.2022), available at https://background.tagesspiegel.de/digitalisierung/datenrealpolitik-ist-gefragt (last accessed 13 December 2022)

Hennemann/Steinrötter, Data Act – Fundament des neuen EU-Datenwirtschaftsrechts?, 21 *NJW* 1481 (2022)

Hennemann/von Ditfurth, Datenintermediäre und Data Governance Act, 27 *NJW* 1905 (2022)

Hoffmann, Data Protection Act(ion) – Report on the Law of Data Disclosure in Ghana, *University of Passau Institute for Law of the Digital Society Research Paper Series No. 22-01* (2022), available at https://papers.ssrn.com/sol3/papers.cfm?abstract_id=4037928 (last accessed 13 December 2022)

Kerber, Governance of Data: Exclusive Property vs. Access, 47 *International Review of Intellectual Property and Competition Law* 759 (2016)

Le Chapelle/Porciuncula, *We need to talk about data: Framing the debate around free flow of data and data sovereignty*, Internet and Jurisdiction Policy Network 2021, available at https://www.internetjurisdiction.net/uploads/pdfs/We-Need-to-Talk-About-Data-Framing-the-Debate-Around-the-Free-Flow-of-Data-and-Data-Sovereignty-Report-2021.pdf (last accessed 13 December 2022)

Leistner/Antoine, *IPR and the use of open data and data sharing initiatives by public and private actors*, European Union 2022, available at https://www.europarl.europa.eu/RegData/etudes/STUD/2022/732266/IPOL_STU(2022)732266_EN.pdf (last accessed 13 December 2022)

Liu, The Rise of Data Politics: Digital China and the World, 54 *Studies in Comparative International Development* 45 (2021)

Mannion, Data Imperialism: The GDPR's Disastrous Impact on Africa's E-Commerce Markets, 53 *Vanderbilt Journal of Transnational Law* 685 (2020)

Möllers, *Freiheitsgrade*, 2020

OECD, Guidelines Governing the Protection of Privacy and Transborder Flows of Personal Data, adopted on 23 September 1980 and revised on 11 July 2013, available at https://legalinstruments.oecd.org/en/instruments/OECD-LEGAL-0133 (last accessed 13 December 2022)

Picht/Richter, EU Digital Regulation 2022: Data Desiderata, 5 *GRUR Int.* 395 (2022)

Pottinger/Feith, The Most Powerful Data Broker in the World Is Winning the War Against the U.S., *The New York Times* (30 November 2021), available at https://www.nytimes.com/2021/11/30/opinion/xi-jinping-china-us-data-war.html (last accessed 13 December 2022)

Purtova, The law of everything, Broad concept of personal data and future of EU data protection law, 10 *Law, Innovation and Technology* 81 (2018)

Richter, Europäisches Datenprivatrecht: Lehren aus dem Kommissionsvorschlag für eine „Verordnung über europäische Daten-Governance", 29 *ZEuP* 634 (2021)

Salaymeh/Michaels, Decolonial Comparative Law: A Conceptual Beginning, 86 *RabelsZ* 116 (2022)

Schur, Die Lizenzierung von Daten – Der Datenhandel auf Grundlage von vertraglichen Zugangs- und Nutzungsrechten als rechtspolitische Perspektive, 11 *GRUR* 1142 (2020)

Schwartz, Global Data Privacy: The EU Way, 94 *N.Y.U. Law Review* 771 (2019)

Schwartz/Peifer, Transatlantic Data Privacy Law, 106 *Georgetown Law Journal* 115 (2017)

Specht-Riemenschneider, Data access rights – A comparative perspective, in: BMJV/MPIIC (eds.), *Data Access, Consumer Interests and Public Welfare*, 2021, pp. 401–438

Specht-Riemenschneider, Der Entwurf des Data Act: Ein großer Wurf in die falsche Richtung?, 13 *GRUR* 937 (2022)

Steinrötter, Gegenstand und Bausteine eines EU-Datenwirtschaftsrechts, 10 *RDi* 480 (2021)

Streinz, The Evolution of European Data Law, in: Craig/de Búrca (eds.), *The Evolution of EU Law*, 3rd ed., 2021, pp. 902–936

Struett/Aaronson, *The Global Data Governance Project: 52 case studies*, 2021, available at https://cpb-us-e1.wpmucdn.com/blogs.gwu.edu/dist/c/3127/files/2021/01/The-Global-Data-Governance-Project-Jul23.pdf (last accessed 13 December 2022)

Svantesson, Data Localisation Trends and Challenges: Considerations for the Review of the Privacy Guidelines, *OECD Digital Economy Papers No. 301* (2020), available at https://www.oecd-ilibrary.org/docserver/7fbaed62-en.pdf?expires=1647463200&id=id&accname=guest&checksum=FFCA9BE79F45C3292A48D204C46A3A33 (last accessed 13 December 2022)

U.S. Departments of State, *Declaration for the Future of the Internet*, available at https://www.state.gov/declaration-for-the-future-of-the-internet (last accessed 13 December 2022)

World Economic Forum, *Data Free Flow with Trust (DFFT): Paths towards Free and Trusted Data Flow, White Paper*, 2020, available at https://www3.weforum.org/docs/WEF_Paths_Towards_Free_and_Trusted_Data _Flows_2020.pdf (last accessed 13 December 2022)

Zech, Building a European Data Economy – The European Commission's Proposal for a Data Producer's Right, 9 *Zeitschrift für Geistiges Eigentum* 317 (2017)

§ 2 UNLOCKING THE POTENTIAL OF THE DATA AGE: KEY TASKS AND CHALLENGES OF DATA STRATEGIES

Content

Data strategies are emerging around the globe. Various proposals, documents and initiatives are bubbling up at different stages, ranging from drafts to already well implemented strategies, crafted by different stakeholders, including national governments[1], regional entities[2], international organizations, and the like. Data policy is, however, neither a well-scoped nor a well-defined space. It is fair to say that the data policy landscape is very much in flux. Against this background, this contribution will reflect on the role of these strategies that are in the making based on the authors' own involvement in such efforts and a series of personal observations. It starts with a few big-picture observations about the recent emergence of relatively comprehensive or at least systematically oriented public sector data strategies. It then offers a set of observations regarding data governance, which can be seen as one core element of such strategies, but often also predates and transcends them. The article paints this picture with broad strokes, acknowledging that many important nuances within each set of observations exist. 1

A. The Strategic Turn

The first observation concerns the notion of 'strategy'. Since early 2000, and with an accelerating pace over the past ten years, an enhanced awareness of the role of data in societies can be identified globally. The increased awareness of the role of data is partly connected to the relatively new big data phenomenon. Governments and international organizations around the globe have systematically engaged in a broad range of questions related to data. These efforts were mostly sectoral-orientated by addressing 2

[1] *Cf* e.g. *Data Strategy of the Federal German Government*, 27.1.2021, and U.S. Government, *Federal Data Strategy Framework – Mission, Principles, Practices, and Action*, 2020. See for more detail the contributions of Veil and Weindauer (Europe and Germany) sub § 4, Guggenberger (U.S.) sub § 5, Dei-Tutu (Africa) sub § 6, and Zuo (China) sub § 7 in this volume.

[2] *Cf* e.g. European Commission, *A European strategy for data*, COM(2020) 66 final. See Paal/Kumkar, *ZfDR* 2021, 97 and again Veil/Weindauer sub § 4.

data policy issues in health, education, transportation and the like.[3] Sometimes approaches were already (more) general by holistically and systematically looking across sectors, stakeholders and spheres. Both types were usually accompanied with a promise of action to unlock the promises of data for societies.

3 Strategic views on data, under different terms, are not an entirely new phenomenon. Despite the increased awareness and activity today, the importance of data has to some extent been recognized as a constant element in public policy – as it is the case for notion of strategy-making in the public sector.[4] Since the 1970s, data as a resource-to-be-managed received governments' attention. For instance, the birth of modern data protection regulation in response to initiatives aimed at the creation of 'national data banks' in the 1970s, proposals concerning the 'Information Superhighway' in the 1980s, documents with respect to the rise of the internet as well as frameworks regarding access and use of public sector information in the 1990s and in the following decades mark previous phases of governance. These developments correspond with the notion that societies/states constantly (and ever since) gather and evaluate information[5] in search for *patterns*[6] as a prerequisite for (informed) decision-making.

4 In recent years, technological progress gained speed. Especially *big data*, including its interaction with artificial intelligence[7], has led data processing to new dimensions.[8] This is first true with regard to the velocity and volume of data, and second and even more importantly with regard to the capability to analyse, to find patterns, and, most importantly, to interfere 'data from data' – the latter at least minimising old(er) narratives of (only) 'individual' data.[9] Consequentially, governments have begun to elevate the topic of data and corresponding policies to the level of a cross-cutting national issue of broader strategic relevance.[10] Today, the creation, collection, access, and use of data transcends previously distinct sectors within the government – as the processing of data spans in a multidimensional manner across public and private spheres, builds upon various data ecosystems, and is inherently intertwined with the infrastructural level[11] and with

[3] Probably most prominent the Regulation (EU) 2016/679 on the protection of natural persons with regard to the processing of personal data and on the free movement of such data, and repeating Directive 95/46/EL (General Data Protection Regulation).

[4] McNabb/Lee, *Public Sector Strategy Design*, 2020.

[5] For the interplay between data and information *cf* Oster, *JZ* 2021, 167.

[6] Nassehi, *Muster*, 3rd ed., 2019.

[7] *Cf* Special Committee on Artificial Intelligence in a Digital Age [rapporteur: Axel Voss], *Draft Report on artificial intelligence in a digital age*, 9.11.2021, EP 2020/2266(INI). *Cf* generally Lee, *AI Superpowers*, 2018.

[8] *Cf* for example Tang, *Data Capital – How Data is Reinventing Capital for Globalization*, 2021 as well as the contributions to an anthropology of data in Douglas-Jones/Walford/Seaver (eds.), *JRAI* 27, 2021, Special Issue 1.

[9] For a sharp account see Solow-Niederman, *Information Privacy and the Inference Economy*, 10.9.2021, https://papers.ssrn.com/sol3/papers.cfm?abstract_id=3921003. *Cf* also Hummel/Braun/Dabrock, *Philos. Technol.* 34, 2021, 545 (572); Kerber, *IIC* 2016, 759 (762).

[10] See in this regard for instance the in-depth analysis by the German Data Ethics Commission, *Opinion* (December 2019), 79 *et seq. et passim.*

[11] See with regard to China Erie/Streinz, *The Beijing Effect: China's 'Digital Silk Road' as Transnational Data Governance*, 1.4.2021, https://papers.ssrn.com/sol3/papers.cfm?abstract_id=3810256; *cf* also Fisher/Streinz, *Confronting Data Inequality*, NYU School of Law, Public Law Research Paper No. 21–22, https://papers.ssrn.com/sol3/papers.cfm?abstract_id=3825724. Special Committee on Artificial Intelligence in a Digital Age [rapporteur: Axel Voss], *Draft Report on artificial intelligence in a digital age*, 9.11.2021, EP 2020/2266(INI), 23 (no. 97): '[n]otes that the EU's digital infrastructure is underdeveloped, with just 25 % of people in the EU being able to connect to a 5G network, compared to 76 % of people in the US; observes that the EU in general lacks high-performance digital infrastructure with interoperable data spaces, affordable energy supply, high transmission rates and volumes, reliability and short delays (…).'

standard-setting procedures[12]. The wider strategic context is also shaped by the very distinct characteristics of data. To name just a few of the most central: Data is first and foremost non-rival. It might flow easily from country to country. The use and consequentially the valuation of data (sets) is highly contextual (or even undefinable). Further, state entities and other actors might pursue new ways of accessing data.[13] These parameters are transforming the strategic (and regulatory) pillars in various sectors. It has for example been rightly argued that data's externality, data-related commitments to specific state actors, and data valuation are transforming traditional international economic relations.[14]

Against this background, it is clear that not only the competitiveness of economies, but 5
of entire states and societies is at stake.[15] Consequently, data-related questions are situated in a competitive geopolitical context.[16] Data strategies as important instruments in response to these dynamics and shifts form an integral part of data geopolitics and data diplomacy[17] – shaping data (use) between the 'free flow of data' and 'data sovereignty'[18]. These additional elements and their interactions make it harder to create sound policy as these strategies must simultaneously deal with opportunities for economic growth and development and also address challenges like privacy security and so forth.

B. Tackling the 'Wicked' And Flying in the Dark

Strategies generally range from reactive to visionary, typically with a mix of enabling, 6
constraining, and levelling components – and are often formulated in the context of transformations and in support of (strategic) changes in value-generating core pro-

[12] *Cf* Gal/Rubinfeld, *NYU L. R.* 94 2019, 737 as well as – with respect to AI – Special Committee on Artificial Intelligence in a Digital Age [rapporteur: Axel Voss], *Draft Report on artificial intelligence in a digital age*, 9.11.2021, EP 2020/2266(INI), 13 (no. 37).

[13] See e.g. – pointing to public data commons – Zygmuntowski/Zoboli/Nemitz, *Internet Policy Review* 2021, 10 (3).

[14] With respect to China see Liu, *The Rise of Data Politics: Digital China and the World*, St Comp Int Dev 56, 2021, 45; *cf* also Shaffer, *World Trade Rev* 20, 2021, 259.

[15] *Cf* for instance with regard to the African continent Bryant, 24 *Stan. Tech. L. Rev.* (2021) 389; Boshe/Hennemann/v. Meding, *GPLR* 2022, 56.

[16] *Cf* Arner/Castellano/Selga, *The Transnational Data Governance Problem* (8.10.2021), https://papers.ssrn.com/sol3/papers.cfm?abstract_id=3912487. *cf* for the prospect of a (future) rule by data Pistor, *Law & Contemp. Probs* 83 (2020), 101; with respect to AI see Special Committee on Artificial Intelligence in a Digital Age [rapporteur: Axel Voss], *Draft Report on artificial intelligence in a digital age* (9.11.2021), EP 2020/2266(INI), 9 (no. 8): '(…) [T]here is therefore a race for AI leadership within the global tech race; (…) countries that master AI will gain key advantages (…).' and 20 (no. 79): 'Observes fierce AI competition that involves not only the two frontrunners, the US and China, but also countries such as Canada, India, Israel, Japan, Russia, South Korea and the UK (…).'

[17] *Cf* inter alia Barker in: Piallat (ed.), *Der Wert der Digitalisierung*, 2021, 415 *et seq.*; Hennemann, Datenrealpolitik – Datenökosysteme, Datenrecht, Datendiplomatie, *IRDG-Research Paper Series* No. 22-18 2022.

[18] *Cf* for instance De La Chapelle/Porciuncula, *We Need to Talk About Data: Framing the Debate Around Free Flow of Data and Data Sovereignty*, Internet and Jurisdiction Policy Network (2021), https://connect.internetjurisdiction.net/zs/WsB8Ty; Ducuing, *Technology and Regulation* 2020, 57; Aaronson, *Data is disruptive: How data sovereignty is challenging data governance* (August 2021), https://www.hinrichfoundation.com/research/article/digital/data-is-disruptive-how-data-sovereignty-is-challenging-data-governance/. *Cf* also – with respect to the GDPR – Special Committee on Artificial Intelligence in a Digital Age [rapporteur: Axel Voss], *Draft Report on artificial intelligence in a digital age* (9.11.2021), EP 2020/2266(INI), 31 (no. 145): 'proposes (…) the replacement of the concept of data minimisation with the concept of data sovereignty, which would allow users to make sovereign decisions about the use of their data (…)'.

cesses.[19] This is especially the case in the public sector, but also in other sectors, and applies to data strategies as well. Data strategies can be read as part of a government's coordinated response to the fundamental socio-technological shifts associated with digital transformation processes. As already mentioned, it is generally acknowledged that data plays an increasingly important role across sectors, industries, and stakeholders. Respective strategies are understood as a tool to catalyse (or even 'finalise') the digital transformation – addressing both the promise and perils of data ecosystems and big data environments.

7 To this end, data strategies typically highlight opportunities when it comes to data in the context of research and innovation, economic growth and development, better public service and policies, and for a fairer society.[20] In addition to elements aimed at enabling and empowering – including citizen's agency through strengthening data literacy – data strategies also address and introduce constraints, for instance in the context of security, privacy, discrimination, and autonomy.[21] They typically also include elements intended to create a level playing field through mechanisms such as data portability, interoperability, and other means to ensure data availability and accessibility[22]. Bridging public and private spheres as ('two way') citizen-to-citizen, business-to-business, state-to-state, private-to-state[23], and state-to-private[24] data exchanges (and further combinations thereof) are additional means towards this goal. To a growing extent, these approaches mirror a general conceptional shift away from property towards data access as well as towards a classification of personal and non-personal data as an (strategic) asset. To this end, strategies highlight *data spaces* in order to underline the common ground of different actors (and the need to an integrated approach).[25] The European Union, for instance, points to an industrial (manufacturing) data space, a Green Deal data space, a mobility data space, a health data space, a financial data space, an energy data space, an agriculture data space, data spaces for public administration, and a skills data space.[26]

8 When it comes to addressing and managing corresponding challenges, for instance in the realm of the economic effects of data protection law, data strategies can build on a wealth of research and experience from diverse disciplines.[27] For example, there is

[19] *Cf* Wauters, *Strategic management in the public sector and public policy-making: friend or foe?*, 2019, pp. 38 *et seq.* https://www.researchgate.net/publication/333774591_Strategic_management_in_the_public_sector_and_public_policy-making_friend_or_foe.

[20] *Cf* European Commission, *A European strategy for data*, COM(2020) 66 final, 1 *et seq.*

[21] *Cf* inter alia European Commission, *A European strategy for data*, COM(2020) 66 final, 10 *et seq.*

[22] *Cf* inter alia European Commission, *A European strategy for data*, COM(2020) 66 final, 6 *et seq.* as well as Special Committee on Artificial Intelligence in a Digital Age [rapporteur: Axel Voss], *Draft Report on artificial intelligence in a digital age* (9.11.2021), EP 2020/2266(INI), 33 (no. 160 *et seq.*).

[23] *Cf* for state access to private economy data Richter, *ZRP* 2020, 245, *cf* also Elkin-Koren/Gal, *U. Chi. L. R.* 86 (2019), 403.

[24] *Cf* WTO, *E-commerce talks: two 'foundational' articles cleaned; development issues discussed* (13.9.2021), https://www.wto.org/english/news_e/news21_e/jsec_12sep21_e.htm: 'The open government data article encourages members to expand the coverage of government data made available for public access and use. It requires members to endeavour, to the extent practicable, to ensure that government data they choose to make digitally and publicly available meets particular characteristics, and to endeavour to avoid imposing certain conditions on such data.'

[25] European Commission, *A European strategy for data*, COM(2020) 66 final, 21 *et seq.*; SWD(2020) 295 final, 7.

[26] European Commission, *A European strategy for data*, COM(2020) 66 final, 22 *et seq.* et 26 *et seq.*; SWD(2020) 295 final, 7.

[27] *Cf* for the economics perspective in this volume *Schnurr* sub § 3; *cf* for instance for a Law & Economics perspective on the GDPR Gal/Oshrit 16 *Journal of Competition Law and Economics* (2020) 349; generally, with respect to privacy and innovation Lev-Aretz/Strandburg, 22 *Yale J. L. & Tech* (2020) 256; with respect to data standardization Gal/Rubinfeld, *NYU L. R.* 94 (2019), 737; with respect to

evidence that more data standardisation and data interoperability can lead to more innovation and more competition[28], but also elevate privacy and security concerns.[29] Data sharing instruments might enhance innovation, but must be carefully calibrated – especially when data is (compulsory) shared with public entities.[30] Evidence-based policymaking is therefore a standard call[31] – and more evidence to make better policies is certainly desirable. As governments start to draft data strategies and also involve in varying degrees with stakeholders, civil society and technical communities, companies and the like, it is fascinating to observe what elements of these strategies actually are supported by evidence. Given the magnitude of policy instruments, the evidence base is mixed in our view. In some areas, plenty of evidence as to what types of policy interventions may achieve a certain policy outcome exists. In other areas, important empirical questions remain open, for instance with regard to the effectiveness or relative costs of certain measures at a given stage of technological or market development. The appropriate timing of policy interventions concerning the many interconnected, yet analytically distinct aspects combined in comprehensive data strategies is often particularly difficult to determine and not clear-cut.[32]

Data policy is and will remain a 'wicked' problem – empirically as well as **9**
normatively[33] and data strategies are inevitable 'wicked' policymaking. Consequently, future-oriented actions aimed at promoting data sharing or data usage, to name just two common elements of data strategies, are by design accompanied by various degrees of uncertainty. The policy field has to deal with both 'known unknowns' and 'unknown unknowns' concerning technological, market, legal, and behavioural developments and future disruptions. It must be accepted that the efficacy of any data policy intervention might alter and be limited over time. Here as elsewhere, data policy-making is (and must be) partly regulation into an open future.[34]

C. Too Broad To Succeed? – Contextuality vs. Consistency

Several national data strategies have recently been enacted or proposed by govern- **10**
ments in Europe and abroad. Respective strategies tend to cover a broad array of different types of data and application contexts. Moreover, policy measures put forward in such strategies at times simultaneously address national, provincial, and local levels of government, organs of state or public enterprises, the private sector, and the general public. In addition, respective discourses are framed in different regulatory

---

governance-by-data Elkin-Koren/Gal, *U. Chi. L. R.* 86 (2019), 403; with respect to data (protection) law's contribution to challenge market power Paal, *Global Privacy Law Rev* 2 (2021), 8.

[28] *Cf* with regard to personal data portability Krämer, 17 *Journal of Competition Law and Economics* (2021), 263.

[29] *Cf* Gal/Rubinfeld, *NYU L. R.* 94 (2019), 737.

[30] *Cf* Elkin-Koren/Gal, *U. Chi. L. R.* 86 (2019), 403.

[31] Special Committee on Artificial Intelligence in a Digital Age [rapporteur: Axel Voss], *Draft Report on artificial intelligence in a digital age* (9.11.2021), EP 2020/2266(INI), 33 (no. 161).

[32] *Cf* inter alia Streinz in: Craig/de Búrca (eds.), *The Evolution of EU Law*, 3rd ed., 2021, Ch. 29 [p. 5].

[33] Seminal Churchman, *Management Science* 14(4) (1967), B141.

[34] *Cf* Heldt/Hennemann, *Die Goldenen Zwanziger Jahre der Technikregulierung*, Tagesspiegel Background Digitalisierung & KI (15.7.2021), https://background.tagesspiegel.de/digitalisierung/die-goldenen-zwanziger-jahre-der-technikregulierung.

settings[35] – inter alia with regard to fundamental rights, trade rules, intellectual property, or security safeguards.[36]

11 The variability of types of data, the application contexts, and the actors involved, however, underline the need for a careful calibration. Furthermore, data in itself is of a contextual nature. Processes of data creation, collection, access, and use are inherently bound to real life settings. Conflicting interests with regard to these processes are inevitable. Respective processes become clearly visible where different stakeholder interests collide – solving these tensions does require in the very end a (regulatory) decision to not offer data (use) for any interest. For instance, current debates about digital pandemic responses illustrate how the use of data might be highly desirable from a public health angle while creating undesirable risks from a data protection perspective. Similarly, a data strategy might seek to promote the sharing of proprietary non-personal data, but might be in tension with interests protected under trade secrets law. In other words, the contextual nature of data and how it is valued make it difficult to maintain strategic and normative coherence when moving from principle to implementation – not at least due to dynamic feedback effects of data-focused policy interventions themselves.

12 Furthermore, the relationship between data strategies and data governance is in itself complicated. Thomas Struett and Susan Aaronson have mapped over 50 different country approaches to data governance around the globe and demonstrated that there is no holistic or consistent approach in any of these countries.[37] Data governance is an umbrella term for various forms of collective regulation of matters related to the creation, collection, access, and use of data, ranging from non-regulation, institutionalized self-regulation to co-regulation between state and private actors to traditional law making by governments.[38] In important areas such as trade secrets, data governance predates the recent, big-data-induced wave of data strategy-making. While of course linked to previous cycles of tech-innovation and also interacting with technological advancements, norms governing public data, data flows in the context of trade, or data protection and privacy have a long history and create (at least in part) the backdrop against which today's data strategies are introduced and implemented.[39] Unsurprisingly, given the different origins, trajectories, and approaches underlying these and other domains of data governance, the respective objectives, approaches, and techniques are not always fully interoperable with contemporary data strategies.[40] Data protection concerns with corresponding legal path-dependencies, for instance, might make it politically challenging to include personal data in the scope of a data strategy (although

---

[35] *Cf* with respect to trade law Shaffer, *World Trade Rev* 20 (2021), 259; Yakovleva/Irion, *Int'l Data Privacy Law* 10 (2020), 201; see also – underlining the lens of (data) pollution – Ben-Shahar, *J of Legal Analysis* 11 (2019), 104.

[36] The EU Commission, for example, highlights – with references to different acts (Data Governance Act, Digital Markets Act, Act on High Value Data Sets, and Data Act) – the importance to ensure trust, regulate market power, boost public sector data, and ensure fairness, see SWD(2020) 295 final, 7.

[37] See Struett/Aaronson, *The Global Data Governance Project: 52 Case Studies* (5.5.2021), https://cpb-us-e1.wpmucdn.com/blogs.gwu.edu/dist/c/3127/files/2021/01/The-Global-Data-Governance-Project-Jul23.pdf as well as https://datagovhub.elliott.gwu.edu/2021/05/17/the-global-data-governance-mapping-project/.

[38] See for example also Micheli/Ponti/Craglia/Suman, *Big Data & Society* 7 (2020).

[39] *Supra* Streinz in: Craig/de Búrca (eds.), *The Evolution of EU Law*, 3rd ed., 2021, Ch. 29.

[40] *Cf* for instance for the GDPR Zarsky, 47 *Seton Hall Law Rev* (2017) 995 and – again – Gal/Oshrit 16 *Journal of Competition Law and Economics* (2020) 349 as well as *cf* Special Committee on Artificial Intelligence in a Digital Age [rapporteur: Axel Voss], *Draft Report on artificial intelligence in a digital age* (9.11.2021), EP 2020/2266(INI), 29 (no. 135): '(…) EU data governance is currently highly uncoordinated (…).'

the boundaries between personal and non-personal data are blurring). This factor is and will be even more important if specific path-dependencies are 'exported' by legal transplants[41] to other actors (as it was and is the case with respect to European Data Protection Law instruments being 'widely used' in African states[42]).[43]

D. Of Life and Policy Cycles

Over the past decades, both sectoral and cross-sectoral policies aimed at addressing data issues have often targeted or otherwise prioritized certain aspects of data. In the context of public sector data, for instance, access to data has been a long-standing strategic issue. In the realm of data protection, it is the collection of data that historically has been a focal point, with a recent gradual shift towards questions of data usage.[44] At least some of the prominent data strategies that were enacted or proposed take a more holistic approach by introducing a life cycle model of data. Policy instruments and measures might be tailored to address the creation of new data, incentivize the sharing of data, regulate access to data, or promote the use of data, to name just a few common elements in such comprehensive policy documents. While it might be too early to call it a sustainable trend, anecdotal evidence suggests an increased interest by policy-makers to promote the use or re-use of data and measures that target this specific phase within the broader data life cycle model. **13**

The analysis of different data strategies reveals an interesting and impressive diversity of tools and techniques available that can be deployed to address various policy objectives and preferences when it comes to the creation, dissemination, access, and use of data. For instance, both at the national and regional level recent data strategy initiatives have identified a broad range of measures that can be used to promote the sharing of data, including data sharing mandates, data intermediaries, liability shields, or tax incentives, to name just a few examples. While the array of policy instruments available is good news from a policy-making perspective and also allows for blended or mixed approaches, it is often hard to determine which instrument is best suited to address a specific data issue in a given context and a specific moment in time, and at what costs and with what effects. The question of match-making or fit between available tools and techniques in the data strategy toolkit on the one hand and a particular situation with its characteristics in terms of technologies, interest, incentives, etc. involved on the other hand often remains open or contested and deserves attention from researchers going forward. **14**

Uncertainty also flows from the interplay between proposed measures and the state of technology. Data strategies are written today and are based on the current notion of technology, but obviously technology is evolving.[45] A prime example is the GDPR and the Data Protection Directive (DPD) before. The DPD was written in pre-big data and pre-AI times – in respect to today's effects. Computing power and other aspects of the digital transformation were tackled. As the challenges changed an upgrade was **15**

---

[41] Watson, *Legal Transplants*, 2nd ed., 1993.

[42] *Cf* in this regard Boshe/Hennemann/v. Meding, *GPLR* 2022, 56.

[43] See on the global 'competition' between different forms of data protection rules (and the role of the GDPR) Hennemann, 84 *RabelsZ* (2020), 864 and the seminal work by Bradford, *Nw. U. L. Rev* (2012) 1.

[44] *Supra* for instance Streinz in: Craig/de Búrca (eds.), *The Evolution of EU Law*, 3rd ed., 2021, Ch. 29.

[45] *Cf* Special Committee on Artificial Intelligence in a Digital Age [rapporteur: Axel Voss], *Draft Report on artificial intelligence in a digital age* (9.11.2021), EP 2020/2266(INI), 17 (no. 61): '(…) [L]egislative cycles are therefore often out of sync with the pace of technological progress (…).'

required – a task that the GDPR tried to fulfil, but did not fully reach. It is therefore – not only in this context – of vital importance that there is a constant analysis how well tools fit as technologies and markets evolve, as new business models emerge, as new players enter the (future) data ecosystems.[46]

E. Learning Implementation and Implemented Learning

16 Perhaps unsurprisingly given what is known about the power of data, governments in many parts of the world have been advised by policy experts and international organizations to consider comprehensive approaches to data across all sectors and levels of government. Data strategies, which in practice of course come in different shapes and flavours, promise to be a suitable instrument for such a holistic approach. The longer-term effectiveness of these frameworks, however, will not only depend on the soundness of the policy prescription at the level of strategy. As strategies – for good reasons – do not change constantly, equally important are at least two additional capacities: the ability to implement and the ability to learn and iterate.

17 By definition, strategies offer high-level guidance typically in form of relatively abstract principles. Given the recent flourishing of policy initiatives in areas like data and technology, the challenge of good policy-making turns increasingly into an associated challenge of good policy implementation.[47] Internationally and nationally – at least in the Global North – there does not seem to be a general strategy deficit, but instead an implementation deficit (and there is already the next round of strategies with respect to AI in the (policy) loop[48]). It remains an open question who exactly will implement the many strategies, at what level within the government, and at what speed. In some cases, capacities and implementation guidance are offered as part of strategy documents – aimed at assisting states, people, businesses, and decision makers at the same time. However, closer examinations of the local implementation capacity required to turn "gold standards" into something that fits the respective environment and is tailored to the respective state of technology and market development seems to be missing. To turn strategies into reality, additional investments in human resources, skill-building, and knowledge-sharing are likely to be needed.

18 Similarly, given that data strategies are policy efforts under conditions of uncertainty, the ability to learn and iterate will be a key success factor in the future, which tends to be underestimated at the level of strategy when compared to the aspirational substantive elements in such documents. Here as elsewhere, feedback loops and mechanisms of learning need to be built into the full policy life cycle and across communities of practice. This will likely require novel monitoring capabilities, interfaces, and also next-

---

[46] *Cf* Special Committee on Artificial Intelligence in a Digital Age [rapporteur: Axel Voss], *Draft Report on artificial intelligence in a digital age* (9.11.2021), EP 2020/2266(INI), 25 (no.112): '(…) [T]he 'pacing problem' requires the EU to combine ex ante and ex post approaches by complementing its legislative toolbox with alternative governance approaches that are able to deliver much quicker, more adaptable and more effective solutions (…).'

[47] *Cf* in this regard for example Jameson/Taylor/Noorman, *Data Governance Clinics: a New Approach to Public-Interest Technology in Cities* (24.9.2021), https://papers.ssrn.com/sol3/papers.cfm?abstract_id=3880961.

[48] For example 20 EU member states have AI strategies, see Special Committee on Artificial Intelligence in a Digital Age [rapporteur: Axel Voss], *Draft Report on artificial intelligence in a digital age* (9.11.2021), EP 2020/2266(INI), 21 (no. 85).

generation coordination mechanisms across actors[49] as well as within governments.[50] Structured "lessons learned" might reduce the constant 'flying in the dark'.

F. Measuring Effects

The notion of learning is in many ways intertwined with measuring the effects of data strategies. What are the benchmarks of a successful data strategy? Some data strategies we have reviewed prescribe hundreds of actions and, at the same time, are not free of tension and are deeply contextual. Objectives and desired outcomes might vary depending on the application area, involved stakeholders, or phase in the life cycle of data. Additionally, measurement can be done in quantitative and in qualitative ways.[51] 19

Perhaps unsurprisingly given this variety, current data strategies typically do not specify metrics of success based on which the various policy interventions can be evaluated down the road.[52] In some areas, the quantitative flow of data might be an indicator of success. The use and reuse of data or certain types of data could be an indicator. For instance, if more non-personal data were shared and used in the future compared to the status quo, it might be a positive indicator where such data flows are seen as a key enabler and driver of innovation. Outgoing-transborder flows might indicate – from the outset – a relevant 'innovative value' of the domestically generated data. The same might be true with regard to the data formats originated in a specific region and used elsewhere. In other areas – for instance, where citizen empowerment through data literacy programs is the policy prescription[53] – data flows per se might not be an adequate measure to track progress. And sometimes, depending on the normative context, even the reduction of data flows might be a measure of success, for instance when it comes to commercial surveillance practices or forms of data colonialism[54] or security-sensible data. By the same token, however, one might consider innovation, economic growth, or inclusion as overarching parameters – notwithstanding the difficulty of such a measurement. The measurement of data strategies is definitely requiring much more research. 20

---

[49] *Cf* the new EU-US Trade and Technology Council, https://trade.ec.europa.eu/doclib/docs/2021/june/tradoc_159642.pdf.

[50] *Cf* for instance the proposal of 'A Bretton Woods for data' by Denham, UK Information Commissioner, https://ico.org.uk/about-the-ico/media-centre/news-and-blogs/2021/09/a-bretton-woods-for-data/ as well as the WTO negotiations for a new eCommerce Treaty, see WTO, *Negotiations on e-commerce advance, eyeing a statement at MC12* (10.11.2021), https://www.wto.org/english/news_e/news21_e/ecom_10nov21_e.htm.

[51] *Cf* in this regard OECD, *A Roadmap Toward A Common Framework For Measuring The Digital Economy* (2020), https://www.oecd.org/sti/roadmap-toward-a-common-framework-for-measuring-the-digital-economy.pdf.

[52] The European Union announced in its data strategy an 'European analytical framework for measuring data flows' for Q4/2021 (European Commission, *A European strategy for data,* COM(2020) 66 final, 24: 'This should be a durable framework that provides the tools to conduct a continuous analysis of data flows and the economic development of the EU's data processing sector, including a robust methodology, economic valuation and data flows collection mechanisms. It will serve to better understand patterns of data flows and centres of gravity, both within the EU and between the EU and the rest of the world, and can be a basis for adequate policy responses by the Commission, if necessary.').

[53] *Cf* Carmi/Yates/Lockley/Pawluczuk, *Internet Policy Rev* 9(2) (2020).

[54] *Cf* Zuboff, *The Age of Surveillance Capitalism*, 2019; Couldry/Mejias, 20 *Television & New Media* (2019) 336; Couldry/Mejias, *The Cost of Connection*, 2019.

G. Humanity

21 Finally, it is important to emphasize that data, technology, big data, AI, IoT, virtual reality, quantum computing and the like are not abstract and isolated technological phenomena. They are both embedded in society and have deep societal implications that cut across different societal systems – and therefore, ultimately, have impact on actual human beings.[55] Data strategies, for example, should not seek for innovation and economic growth as an end in itself, but to benefit all members of society and not just a few. Existing inequalities, participation gaps, and divides should not be deepened but overcome through means of good data policymaking.[56] In our view, such normative goals should be the core of every strategy. Data strategies must serve humanity – and the role of civil society will be instrumental in ensuring that data strategies will do what they promised to do. The civil society's watchdog function will again and again be important in this respect – in order to use tech responsibly and realise sociotechnical change inclusively.

H. Summary

22 The broad lines we stroke already suggest some degrees of caution when embracing data strategies as policy instruments: Whether or not these strategies will live up to the promise will ultimately depend on the degree to which contextually adequate instruments are developed and implemented, and to what extent they actually serve the individual, collective, and public interests – and ultimately benefit all members of society. The stakes could not be higher.

Bibliography

23 Aaronson, *Data is disruptive: How data sovereignty is challenging data governance* (2021), available at https://www.hinrichfoundation.com/research/article/digital/data-is-disruptive-how-data-sovereignty-is-challenging-data-governance/ (last accessed 13 December 2022)

Arner/Castellano/Selga, The Transnational Data Governance Problem, *BTLJ* (2021), available at https://papers.ssrn.com/sol3/papers.cfm?abstract_id=3912487 (last accessed 13 December 2022)

Ben-Shahar, Data Pollution, 11 *J of Legal Analysis* 104 (2019)

Bradford, The Brussels Effect, 107(1) *Nw. U. L. Rev.* 1 (2012)

Bryant, Africa in the Information Age: Challenges, Opportunities, and Strategies for Data Protection and Digital Rights, 24 *Stan. Tech. L. Rev.* 389 (2021)

Carmi/Yates/Lockley/Pawluczuk, Data Citizenship: rethinking data literacy in the age of disinformation, misinformation, and malinformation, 9(2) *Internet Policy Rev.* 1 (2020)

---

[55] *Cf* in this regard also European Commission, *A European strategy for data*, COM(2020) 66 final, 4.

[56] *Cf* also in this regard Viljoen, *A Relational Theory of Data Governance* (11.11.2020), 131 Yale Law Journal (2020), 370 as well as Wu/Verhulst/Pentland/Avila/Finch/Gupta, *Data & Policy* 3 (2021), e14.

Churchman, Wicked Problems, 14(4) *Management Science* (1967), available at https://www.jstor.org/stable/2628678 (last accessed 13 December 2022)

Couldry/Mejias, Data Colonialism: Rethinking Big Data's Relation to the Contemporary Subject, 20(4) *Telev. New Media* 336 (2019)

Couldry/Mejias, *The Costs of Connection: How Data is Colonizing Human Life and Appropriating It for Capitalism*, 2019

Craig/de Búrca (eds.), *The Evolution of EU Law*, 2021

De la Chapelle/Porciuncula, We need to talk about data: Framing the Debate Around Free Flow of Data and Data Sovereignty, *Internet and Jurisdiction Policy Network* (2021), available at https://connect.internetjurisdiction.net/zs/WsB8Ty (last accessed 13 December 2022)

Denham (UK Information Commissioner), A Bretton Woods for data (2021), available at https://ico.org.uk/about-the-ico/media-centre/news-and-blogs/2021/09/a-bretton-woods-for-data/ (last accessed 13 December 2022)

Douglas-Jones/Walford/Seaver (eds.), Towards an Anthropology of Data, 27(S1) *JRAI* 9 (2021)

Ducuing, Beyond the Data Flow Paradigm: Governing Data Requires to Look Beyond Data, *TechReg* 57 (2020)

Elkin-Koren/Gal, The Chilling Effect of Governance-by-Data on Data Markets, 86(2) *U.Chi. Law Rev.* 403 (2019)

Erie/Streinz, The Beijing Effect: China's 'Digital Silk Road' as Transnational Data Governance, 54(1) *N.Y.U. J. Int'l L. & Pol.* 1 (2021)

European Commission, *A European strategy for data*, COM(2020) 66 final, available at https://eur-lex.europa.eu/legal-content/EN/ALL/?uri=CELEX:52020DC0066 (last accessed 13 December 2022)

European Commission, SWD (2020) 295 final, available at https://eur-lex.europa.eu/legal-content/EN/TXT/PDF/?uri=CELEX:52020SC0295&from=EN (last accessed 13 December 2022)

European Parliament, Special Committee AIDA (rapporteur: Axel Voss), *Draft Report on artificial intelligence in a digital age*, EP 2020/2266 (INI), available at https://www.europarl.europa.eu/doceo/document/AIDA-PR-680928_EN.pdf (last accessed 13 December 2022)

EU-US Trade and Technology Council, Factsheet, available at https://trade.ec.europa.eu/doclib/docs/2021/june/tradoc_159642.pdf (last accessed 13 December 2022)

Fisher/Streinz, *Confronting Data Inequality*, NYU School of Law, Public Law Research Paper No. 21–22 (2021), available at https://papers.ssrn.com/sol3/papers.cfm?abstract_id=3825724 (last accessed 13 December 2022)

Gal/Oshrit, The Competitive Effects of the GDPR, in: 16(3) *Journal of Competition Law & Economics* 349 (2020)

Gal/Rubinfeld, *Data Standardization*, 94(4) *NYU Law Review* 737 (2019)

German Data Ethics Commission, *Opinion* (2019), available at https://www.bmi.bund.de/SharedDocs/downloads/EN/themen/it-digital-policy/datenethikkommission-abschlussgutachten-lang.pdf;jsessionid=DC203F5D4678E2278829F1755963361D.2_cid373?__blob=publicationFile&v=4 (last accessed 13 December 2022)

German Federal Government, *Data Strategy of the German Federal Government* (2021), available at https://www.bundesregierung.de/breg-en/news/data-strategy-adopted-1845882 (last accessed 13 December 2022)

Heldt/Hennemann, Die Goldenen Zwanziger Jahre der Technikregulierung, *Tagesspiegel Background Digitalisierung & KI* (2021), available at https://background.tagesspiegel.de/digitalisierung/die-goldenen-zwanziger-jahre-der-technikregulierung (last accessed 13 December 2022)

Hennemann, Datenrealpolitik – Datenökosysteme, Datenrecht, Datendiplomatie, University of Passau *IRDG-Research Paper Series* No. 22-18 2022, available at https://www.jura.uni-passau.de/

fileadmin/dokumente/fakultaeten/jura/institute/irdg/Research_Paper_Series/Hennemann_Datenrealpolitik_IRDG_Research_Paper_2022_11_03_No_22_18.pdf (last accessed 13 December 2022)

Hennemann, Wettbewerb der Datenschutzrechtsordnungen – Zur Rezeption der Datenschutz-Grundverordnung, 84(4) *RabelsZ* 864 (2020)

Hennemann/Boshe/v. Meding, African Data Protection Laws – Current Regulatory Approaches, Policy Initiatives, and the Way Forward 3(2) *Global Privacy Law Rev.* 56 (2022)

Hummel/Braun/Dabrock, Own Data? Ethical Reflections on Data Ownership, 34(1) *Philos. Technol.* 545 (2021)

Jameson/Taylor/Noorman, Data Governance Clinics: a New Approach to Public-Interest Technology in Cities (2021), available at https://papers.ssrn.com/sol3/papers.cfm?abstract_id=3880961 (last accessed 12 May 2022)

Kerber, Governance of Data: Exclusive Property vs. Access, 7 *IIC* 759 (2016)

Krämer, Personal Data Portability in the Platform Economy: Economic Implications and Policy Recommendations, 17(2) *Journal of Competition Law & Economics* 263 (2021)

Lee, *AI-Superpowers: China, Silicon Valley, and the New World Order*, Houghton Mifflin Harcourt (2018)

Lev-Aretz/Strandburg, Privacy Regulation and Innovation Policy, 22 *Yale J. L. & Tech* 256 (2020)

Liu, The Rise of Data Politics: Digital China and the World, in: 56(1) *St Comp Int Dev* 45 (2021)

McNabb/Lee, Public Sector Strategy Design: Theory and Practice for Government and Nonprofit Organizations, Routledge (2020)

Micheli/Ponti/Craglia/Suman, Emerging models of data governance in the age of datafication, 7(2) *BD&S* 1 (2020)

Nassehi, *Muster – Theorie der digitalen Gesellschaft,* 2019

OECD, *A Roadmap Toward A Common Framework For Measuring The Digital Economy* (2020), available at https://www.oecd.org/sti/roadmap-toward-a-common-framework-for-measuring-the-digital-economy.pdf (last accessed 13 December 2022)

Oster, „Information“ und „Daten“ als Ordnungsbegriffe des Rechts der Digitalisierung, 76(4) *JZ* 167 (2021)

Paal, Market Power in Data (Protection) Law, 2(1) *Global Privacy Law Rev.* 8 (2021)

Paal/Kumkar, Die digitale Zukunft Europas – Europäische Strategien für den digitalen Binnenmarkt, 1(1) *ZfDR* 97 (2021)

Piallat (ed.), *Der Wert der Digitalisierung: Gemeinwohl in der digitalen Welt*, transcript (2021)

Pistor, Rule by Data: The End of Markets?, 83(2) *Law & Contemp. Probs* 101 (2020)

Richter, Zugang des Staates zu Daten der Privatwirtschaft, 53(8) *ZRP* 245 (2020)

Shaffer, Trade Law in a Data-Driven Economy: The Need for Modesty and Resilience, 20 *World Trade Rev.* 259 (2021)

Solow-Niederman, Information Privacy and the Inference Economy, *Northwestern University Law Review* (2021), available at https://papers.ssrn.com/sol3/papers.cfm?abstract_id=3921003 (last accessed 13 December 2022)

Struett/Aaronson, *The Global Data Governance Project: 52 case studies* (2021), available at https://cpb-us-e1.wpmucdn.com/blogs.gwu.edu/dist/c/3127/files/2021/01/The-Global-Data-Governance-Project.pdf as well https://datagovhub.elliott.gwu.edu/2021/05/17/the-global-data-governance-mapping-project/ (last accessed 13 December 2022)

Tang, *Data Capital – How Data is Reinventing Capital for Globalization*, Springer (2021)

U.S. Government, *Federal Data Strategy Framework – Mission, Principles, Practices, and Action* (2020), available at https://strategy.data.gov/overview/ (last accessed 13 December 2022)

Viljoen, A Relational Theory of Data Governance, 131(2) *Yale Law Journal* 370 (2020)

Watson, *Legal Transplants: An Approach to Comparative Law*, University of Georgia Press (1993)

Wauters, *Strategic management in the public sector and public policy-making: friend or foe?* (2019), available at https://www.researchgate.net/publication/333774591_Strategic_management_in_the_ppubli_sector_and_public_policy-making_friend_or_foe (last accessed 13 December 2022)

WTO, *E-commerce talks: two "foundational" articles cleaned; development issues discussed* (2021), available at https://www.wto.org/english/news_e/news21_e/jsec_12sep21_e.htm (last accessed 13 December 2022)

WTO, *Negotiations on e-commerce advance, eyeing a statement at MC12* (2021), available at https://www.wto.org/english/news_e/news21_e/ecom_10nov21_e.htm (last accessed 13 December 2022)

Wu/Verhulst/Pentland/Avila/Finch/Gupta, How data governance technologies can democratize data sharing for community well-being – Corrigendum, 3 *Data & Policy* (2021), available at https://www.cambridge.org/core/journals/data-and-policy/article/how-data-governance-technologies-can-democratize-data-sharing-for-community-wellbeing/2BFB848644589873C00E22ADEA6E8AB3 (last accessed 13 December 2022)

Yakovleva/Irion, Pitching trade against privacy: reconciling EU governance of personal data flows with external trade, 10(3) *Int'l Data Privacy Law* 201 (2020)

Zarsky, Incompatible: The GDPR in the Age of Big Data, 47(4) *Seton Hall Law Rev.* 995 (2017)

Zuboff, *The Age of Surveillance Capitalism: The Fight for a Human Future* (2019)

Zygmuntowski/Zoboli/Nemitz, Embedding European values in data governance: a case for public data commons, 10(3) *Internet Policy Rev.* 1 (2021)

§ 3 GLOBAL DATA ECONOMICS: PRINCIPLES, STRATEGIES AND POLICIES

Content

A. Introduction

Rapid advances in information technology and ubiquitous connectivity of electronic devices have fuelled the digital transformation that is now reshaping industries and societies worldwide. In consequence of pervasive digitalization, data itself has emerged as an economic resource of strategic importance. This has not only been recognised by private actors, who aim to benefit from the manifold business value of data, but more recently, policymakers on national and supra-national levels have drafted high-profile data strategies. At the same time, data is the subject of controversial policy debates around the globe, as exemplified by recent antitrust cases and regulatory proposals in the European Union that devote special attention to the economic implications of data use and the ramifications for competition and innovation in digital markets. 1

For data strategies and data policies to be effective in achieving the envisioned policy goals, it is crucial to understand the special economic properties of data and their implications for economic value creation. These economic properties are directly tied to the technical requirements and advances in information technology that enable and constrain the use of data in today's digital markets. In this chapter, both technical and economic foundations are discussed with respect to what makes data a special resource for businesses and societies. Beyond these fundamental principles, this chapter also reviews recent empirical evidence and theoretical insights on the economics of data. Thereby, it is not the goal of this chapter to provide an exhaustive review of the 2 economic and technical literature, but to introduce the reader to the main issues and manifold research streams that are considered to be vital for designing effective data strategies and data policies.

3 Building on expositions of the manifold value of data and its special properties as an economic good, the main goal of this chapter is to highlight two overarching challenges that policymakers currently face when they aim to maximize economic welfare from data. First, data concentration due to data agglomeration by a few dominant digital gatekeepers raises significant concerns about competition and innovation in digital markets. Second, data fragmentation due to dispersed data creation and a lack of data exchange poses the risk that the full collective value of data cannot be achieved. Although, on the surface, these two challenges may paradoxically seem to contradict each other, they both stem from the same idiosyncratic characteristics of data as an economic good. Therefore, they present a dual policy challenge, where measures to address one of them will necessarily have ramifications for the other. Most importantly, both these challenges involve economic trade-offs that need to be navigated by policymakers when devising and implementing data strategies and data policies. Therefore, these economic trade-offs are discussed in detail with respect to the underlying economic characteristics, their implications for welfare and policy goals as well as potential approaches to balance the involved economic benefits and losses.

4 The remainder of this chapter is organised as follows. Next, in Section B, the many facets of data value are reviewed based on the recent empirical literature. Here, the focus is on user data and its business value for firms as well as its inherent and instrumental value to data subjects. In addition, new approaches to unlock the social value of data are described. Section C presents an overview of the special properties of data as an economic good. In particular, the non-rivalry of data, data-driven network effects, the complementary input structure for value creation from data, the implications of data quality and the information paradox are discussed in detail. Based on these foundations, two overarching economic challenges with respect to data strategies and data policies are described in Section D. Finally, Section E concludes by highlighting the role that data strategies can play for devising economically effective data policies.

B. The Many Facets of Data's Economic Value

5 Data embodies diverse value to different stakeholders. In the following, empirical evidence for the business value of data as well as individual consumers' data valuation is presented. In particular, studies from the economics, marketing and information systems literature are reviewed. Due to the special properties of data, individual incentives of private actors may often be insufficient to achieve the full collective or social value of data (as described in more detail in Section D. II.). Therefore, this section also discusses data altruism as a new approach to encourage data sharing for the common good.

I. Business Value of User Data: Value Categories and Moderating Factors

6 Promises of (big) data generating unprecedented business value are widespread and have by now become the conventional wisdom. However, in practice, firms and organizations frequently experience for many use cases that such value may not be readily available from any type and use of data. Therefore, both on the firm as well as

on the policy level, a more differentiated view on how and when data can create business value is required in order to devise and implement effective data strategies.

In a recent literature review, Fast, Schnurr and Wohlfarth summarize the empirical 7 evidence on the business value of user data in the internet economy.[1] User data is frequently collected by online services and may be actively provided and entered by users themselves, for example, in the case of user-generated content on social media sites. Moreover, user data may be collected by simply observing and recording users' behaviour. In this regard, a prominent example of data collection involves tracking users' online behaviour through clickstream analyses. Based on numerous individual and context-specific empirical studies, the aggregate empirical evidence demonstrates that such user data can create diverse business value across different data use cases and value categories.

Firstly, user data can be leveraged for general service quality improvements, service 8 personalization and personalized recommendations to promote customer retention.[2] This is achieved by increased user satisfaction, but also by raising users' switching costs. For example, knowledge about individual preferences and current interests can enable an e-commerce service to present users with more relevant products, which may increase satisfaction with the service. However, the experience of a faster product discovery and a more comfortable search process also raises opportunity costs of consumers to switch to a competing service, which may not have the same intimate knowledge about the same customer.

Secondly, data-driven quality improvements, service personalization and recommen- 9 der systems may have a direct positive effect on revenues in the consumer market.[3] As personalization can (i) increase users' valuation of a service, (ii) improve product fit to users' preferences and (iii) shape users' preferences in a way that is beneficial to the service provider, data can increase individuals' willingness to pay for a product or service and also increase the number of consumers. Hence, user data can have a positive effect on revenues by raising the intensive margin of consumption ('how much is a single user willing to consume'), by growing the extensive margin of consumption ('how many users are willing to use a service'), or by increasing consumers' willingness to pay and thus the price ('how much is a single user willing to spend per unit of consumption').

Thirdly, data can create business value in multi-sided markets, where platforms 10 mediate transactions and interactions between different market sides. In particular, personalised recommendations and targeted recommendations based on user data can be leveraged by platform businesses to generate higher indirect revenues.[4] For example, better tailored recommendations have been found to facilitate the discovery of (niche) products, to increase cross-selling of additional items and upselling of more profitable products, as well as to promote sales volume and variety, especially in e-commerce markets. Moreover, there is comprehensive empirical evidence that the effectiveness of targeted advertising hinges critically on firms' access to fine-grained and timely user data.

However, beyond these findings of significant and positive business value of user 11 data, the literature also reveals that the relationship between user data and business value generation is rarely monotonic.[5] Instead, there are numerous moderating factors that can diminish or even nullify the beneficial economic effects from data. Among

---

[1] Fast/Schnurr/Wohlfarth, *Journal of Information Technology* (2023), forthcoming.
[2] *Ibid.*
[3] *Ibid.*
[4] *Ibid.*
[5] *Ibid.*

others, these factors include consumers' privacy concerns, firm reputation, trust, transparency of data practices, users' perceived control over data collection and use, as well as contextual factors of personalised recommendations and targeted advertising, such as timing and placement.[6] These moderating factors highlight two important aspects with respect to the business value of user data: On the one hand, the value of data is highly context-dependent and must be assessed with respect to the specific circumstances. On the other hand, consumers themselves may attribute significant value to their personal data. In consequence, anticipated economic benefits can backfire if consumers perceive the collection and use of their data as intrusive, unfair, or adverse to their interests.

II. Consumers' Subjective Valuation of their Personal Data

12 There is a rich and growing literature on individuals' valuation of their personal data.[7] In particular, one strand of research studies has investigated subjects' willingness to accept a proposal to sell personal data and/or willingness to pay to protect their personal data from disclosure. Among the first studies, Huberman, Adar, and Fine show that individuals' monetary valuation of their personal data is closely connected to whether the disclosure of such data contains information on traits that are perceived to be individually and socially desirable or undesirable.[8] Huberman et al. find that a participant's monetary valuation for a data set with demographic information increases significantly with the individuals' respective Body Mass Index. More generally, Fast & Schnurr show that different monetary valuations for varying data types can be explained by individuals' perceived information sensitivity.[9] Thereby, information sensitivity refers to the potential negative consequences, such as psychological, physical, or material loss[10] as well as the perceived discomfort[11] that a person attributes to the disclosure of a specific data set. Thus, high information sensitivity may stem from the data collection of a specific data type or the anticipated disclosure of this data.

13 Based on an experimental study, Lin demonstrates that individuals' data valuation can be separated into two preference components: an intrinsic 'taste' for privacy and an instrumental value that depends on the anticipated economic consequences of a specific data use.[12] The intrinsic preference component varies widely across individuals as well as different categories of data and does not depend on how data disclosure affects economic outcomes. This is in line with individuals' 'privacy concerns' – a popular construct in the information systems literature – as a key driver of individuals' data valuation.[13] In contrast, the instrumental preference component arises endogenously and hinges critically on whether an individual believes that disclosure and use of a particular data set will lead to economic losses in the future.

---

[6] Several of these factors also affect consumers' individual valuation of their data and are thus further discussed in Section B. II.

[7] Godel/Litchfield/Mantovani, *Communications & Strategies*, *88*, 2021, 41; Wagner/Wessels/Buxmann/Krasnova, *Proceedings of the 51st Hawaii International Conference on System Sciences*, 2018.

[8] Huberman/Adar/Fine, *IEEE Security & Privacy*, *3*(5), 2005, 22.

[9] Fast/Schnurr, *Proceedings of the 41st International Conference on Information Systems (ICIS 2020)*, 2020.

[10] See, for example, Milne/Pettinico/Hajjat/Marko, *Journal of Consumer Affairs*, *51*(1), 2017, 133.

[11] See, for example, Li/Sarathy/Xu, *Decision Support Systems*, *51*(3), 2011, 434 and Mothersbaugh/Foxx/Beatty/Wang, *Journal of Service Research*, *15*(1), 2012, 76.

[12] Lin, *Marketing Science* 41(4) (2022) 663.

[13] See, for example, Smith/Dinev/Xu, *MIS Quarterly*, *35*(4), 2011, 989; Wagner/Wessels/Buxmann/Krasnova, *Proceedings of the 51st Hawaii International Conference on System Sciences*, 2018.

A finding that has now emerged across empirical studies with different populations indicates that frequently, some individuals exhibit very high intrinsic privacy preferences, such that their data valuation exceeds the commercial value of this data or that they refuse to disclose data at all ('privacy fundamentalists').[14] Conversely, some individuals are willing to disclose data even for prices close to zero, although the same type of data is deemed highly valuable by others ('privacy pragmatists').[15] Some studies have found that a minority of individuals may even enjoy the risk of personal data disclosure ('privacy unconcerned').[16] In a cross-country survey, Prince and Wallsten demonstrate that individuals' data valuation significantly differs between countries, which suggests that cultural factors shape individuals' subjective valuation and privacy preferences.[17] In particular, Germans generally attribute a higher monetary value to their personal data (especially financial data) compared to citizens of the United States and Latin American countries. At the same time, the relative valuations for different types of data are found to be largely similar across these countries, implying that international data protection rules could follow a harmonised pattern of relative protection for different data types. Across contexts, several studies have found that women attribute a higher value to their personal data than men and that valuation increases with age.[18] **14**

Given the empirical evidence that both firms and individuals attribute significant value to user data, the normative theory of the 'privacy calculus' postulates that individuals as rational decision-makers are willing to share their data with organizations and firms if the anticipated benefits from data sharing outweigh involved privacy risks and possible negative economic consequences.[19] According to this view, data transactions and data trades should occur if the involved parties can obtain an individual benefit from these transactions, respectively. However, it is well known that consumers often lack transparency about data collection and data disclosure. In many cases, consumers may not even be aware that they are sharing their personal data at all (e.g. if data is collected by digital tracking technologies in online environments). Moreover, privacy research has identified manifold cognitive biases and psychological paradoxes that shape human behaviour.[20] Therefore, there are strict limits to the applicability of a solely rational view. Most famously, the 'privacy paradox' captures people's tendency to state a high preference for privacy protection (indicative of a high valuation for their data), which, however, is then often contradicted by actual decisions that do not reflect these stated concerns about data disclosure.[21] **15**

---

[14] Lin, *Marketing Science* 41(4) (2022) 663; Benndorf/Normann, *The Scandinavian Journal of Economics, 120*(4), 2018, 1260. The segmentation of individuals in 'privacy fundamentalists', 'privacy pragmatists' and 'privacy unconcerned' goes back to A. Westin, which, however, has been criticised more recently (see Urban/Hoofnagle, in: *Symposium on Usable Privacy and Security (SOUPS 2014) Workshop on Privacy Personas and Segmentation (PPS)*, 2014).

[15] Benndorf/Normann, *The Scandinavian Journal of Economics, 120*(4), 2018, 1260; Fast/Schnurr, *Proceedings of the 41st International Conference on Information Systems (ICIS 2020)*, 2020; Frik/Gaudeul, A measure of the implicit value of privacy under risk. *Journal of Consumer Marketing*, 2020.

[16] Frik/Gaudeul, A measure of the implicit value of privacy under risk. *Journal of Consumer Marketing*, 2020.

[17] Prince/Wallsten, *How Much is Privacy Worth Around the World and Across Platforms?*, 2021.

[18] Fast/Schnurr, *Proceedings of the 41st International Conference on Information Systems (ICIS 2020)*, 2020; Prince/Wallsten, *How Much is Privacy Worth Around the World and Across Platforms?*, 2021.

[19] Culnan/Armstrong, *Organization Science, 10*(1), 1999, 104.

[20] Acquisti/Brandimarte/Loewenstein, *Science, 347*(6221), 2015, 509; Dinev/McConnell/Smith, *Information Systems Research, 26*(4), 2015, 639.

[21] Acquisti/Brandimarte/Loewenstein, *Science, 347*(6221), 2015, 509; Norberg/Horne/Horne, *Journal of Consumer Affairs, 41*(1), 2007, 100.

16 Furthermore, improved transparency and a higher degree of control about firms' use of personal data may even increase consumers' willingness to share personal data, although such data sharing may have detrimental consequences. Therefore, 'transparency paradoxes' as well as 'control paradoxes' can arise. In particular, the sole semblance of transparency and control can lead individuals to believe that their data is better protected, irrespective of the actual privacy risks and potential economic losses, thus paradoxically leading to more sharing of personal data.[22] For example, Tucker finds that consumers are more likely to accept the use of their data for targeted advertising after users were given seemingly more control over their data, although firms' targeting ability was unaffected by these control measures.[23] Moreover, Brandimarte, Acquisti and Loewenstein show that if people are given more control about the disclosure of their data, this reduces perceived privacy risks of such disclosure, thus increasing the propensity of individuals to share this data.[24]

III. The Social Value of Data: Data Altruism

17 Besides private economic benefits for businesses and individuals, data can also generate large social benefits. This has recently been emphasised by the notion of 'data altruism', which refers to 'data voluntarily made available by individuals or companies for the common good'.[25] Especially in the health domain, the large-scale collection of fine-grained data on individuals' behaviour and physiological measurements promises new insights and knowledge generation with the help of machine learning applications. In this context, digital platforms such as 'Open Humans' provide individuals the opportunity to donate their data (e.g. health data from fitness trackers) to various research projects (e.g. on genetics or personality research).[26] In Germany, the new Patient Data Protection Act, adopted in 2020, will allow individuals to donate digital health records to research projects on a voluntary basis.[27]

18 In many of these use cases there is only a limited or even no individual benefit of data disclosure. Thus, as implied by the term 'data altruism', unlocking the social value hinges critically on individuals' intrinsic motivation and their pro-social behaviour. Although such motives haven proven to be a powerful source of motivation for some people, there is a significant risk of free-riding by others.[28] This is because individuals can benefit from the social value of a pooled data resource without contributing data themselves and without incurring the potential costs of data disclosure (such as privacy risks or transaction costs). For example, people are likely to benefit from new insights generated by data-driven health research even if they do not contribute such research data themselves. Hence, data donations involve a collective action problem and a public good dilemma, leading to the undersupply of the socially valuable good. Recent research findings indicate that this issue may be mitigated by providing individuals with

---

[22] Acquisti/Brandimarte/Loewenstein, *Science*, *347*(6221), 2015, 509.

[23] Tucker, *Journal of Marketing Research*, *51*(5), 2014, 546.

[24] Brandimarte/Acquisti/Loewenstein, *Social Psychological and Personality Science*, *4*(3), 2013, 340.

[25] See European Commission, Proposal for a Regulation of the European Parliament and of the Council on European data governance (Data Governance Act) – COM/2020/767 final, 2020, p. 8 for the definition of data altruism; Fast/Schnurr, *Data Donations for Digital Contact-Tracing: Short- and Long-term Effects of Monetary Incentives*, 2022; Hillebrand/Hornuf, *The Social Dilemma of Big Data: Donating Personal Data to Promote Social Welfare*, 2021.

[26] https://www.openhumans.org (last accessed 20 December 2022).

[27] See § 363 PDSG.

[28] Riemer/Ciriello/Peter/Schlagwein, *European Journal of Information Systems*, *29*(6), 2020, 731.

additional extrinsic incentives such as monetary incentives.[29] However, the effectiveness of one-time compensation mechanisms diminishes significantly if the social value of data donations hinges on the continued and uninterrupted data sharing of individuals' personal information, as it is common for applications in the health domain.[30] These findings imply, again, that the behavioural aspects of data valuation and disclosure decisions are important variables when considering individuals' decision to share data. Thus, instead of sole extrinsic incentives, individuals' data contributions in public good contexts may also be promoted by non-monetary rewards, social norms, the framing of choices (such as defaults) or other 'nudging' mechanisms.[31]

C. Special Properties of Data as an Economic Good

Data as an economic good exhibits several special properties that distinguish it fundamentally from other economic goods. This is because the actual value of data stems from the information contained in a data set and firms' ability to transform such information into actionable knowledge.[32] In fact, from a more technical perspective, data is only the digital representation of signals organised by a given syntax that then must be combined with contextual meaning (i.e. semantics) to become interpretable information.[33] In practice, these different notions are frequently subsumed under the term 'data' without further differentiation. In line with this practice, this chapter focuses on the economic implications that derive from information being at the heart of data value instead of making explicit technical distinctions with respect to the aforementioned concepts of data, information and knowledge. **19**

I. Data as a Non-rival Resource

Data is a non-rival resource, meaning that data can be used simultaneously by different entities without being used up.[34] This is different from rival economic goods where the use by one entity precludes the simultaneous use by another entity. Non-rivalry implies that the same data can be shared or sold multiple times by a data creator and that the same data can be collected by firms through different channels and at different points in time. For example, demographic characteristics or the emotional state of a consumer may be inferred by online firms based on the consumer's online search queries, her audio streaming playlists, or her e-commerce purchases. **20**

Some scholars have argued that due to the non-rivalry of data, especially user data can generally be replicated by competitors and therefore does not entail a competitive advantage for firms.[35] However, even if data is non-rival in principle, this does not necessarily imply that all firms have equal access to the data sources. Instead, some **21**

---

[29] Frimpong/Helleringer, *PloS One*, *16*(11), 2021, Article e0258945; Munzert/Selb/Gohdes/Stoetzer/Lowe, *Nature Human Behaviour*, *5*(2), 2021, 247.

[30] Fast/Schnurr, *Data Donations for Digital Contact-Tracing: Short- and Long-term Effects of Monetary Incentives*, 2021.

[31] *Cf* Johnson/Goldstein, *Science*, *302*, 2003, 1338.

[32] Krämer, *Journal of Competition Law & Economics*, *17*(2), 2021, 263 (265 f.).

[33] *Ibid.*

[34] Schepp/Wambach, *Journal of European Competition Law & Practice*, *7*(2), 2016, 120; Jones/Tonetti, *American Economic Review*, *110*(9), 2020, 2819.

[35] See, for example, Lambrecht/Tucker, *Competition Policy International*, 2017, 1.

firms may be in a superior position or have specific capabilities such that they can collect data of larger quantity, higher quality or more detail.[36] Following this line of argument, data may thus promote inimitable competitive advantages despite its non-rival nature, especially if other structural factors or firms' strategies facilitate protecting data-driven value creation from competitors' imitation.[37] In particular, digital platforms that intermediate transactions between affiliated businesses and consumers regularly find themselves in an advantaged position to collect and use data, as they can observe data flows between affiliated parties on the platform without being explicitly involved in the associated transactions or interactions.[38]

22 From an economic welfare perspective, non-rivalry also implies that data should be shared and used widely to generate the maximum social benefits, as the same data can be simultaneously used for diverse purposes by multiple entities and reproduction as well as distribution costs are close to zero. At the same time, non-rivalry may negatively affect individual incentives of firms to share or even collect this socially valuable data, as is further discussed with respect to the two overarching economic challenges in Section D. This is especially the case when data is non-excludable, in addition to being non-rival, meaning that the data owner cannot exclude other entities from accessing this data. In general, non-excludable and non-rival goods give rise to the public good dilemma and free-riding problem highlighted in Section B.III. But even for excludable data, non-rivalry may lead to socially inefficient undersupply of data.[39]

II. Data-driven Network Effects

23 In many economic use cases, data is created as a by-product of usage. For example, this applies to machine-generated data, where sensors record the state of their physical environment and create a digital representation of their surrounding and its dynamic changes over time. Also, most user data is created when consumers interact with a digital service. User data may be actively and explicitly volunteered by a consumer, but a large share of user data is collected by simply observing and recording consumers' activities in the digital sphere. Thus, the usage of a firm's service is naturally intertwined with the firm's ability to collect user data. This relationship can give rise to scale advantages for firms with a large user base as well as positive feedback loops, where higher usage leads to more data and more data can then again be leveraged to attract more usage.

24 In the economics literature, this phenomenon and its competitive implications have been subsumed under the concept of 'data-driven network effects'.[40] A prominent and often cited example for data-driven network effects are online search engines that can improve the quality of their search rankings by observing users' behaviour and click-streams on the search result page. Schaefer and Sapi present empirical evidence that a larger user base enables a search engine to accelerate its statistical learning and improve its accuracy in predicting the most relevant results for a specific search query.[41] This positive network effect on quality is further reinforced, the more data a search engine

---

[36] Krämer/Schnurr/Broughton Micova, *The role of data for digital markets contestability: case studies and data access remedies*, 2020.

[37] Fast/Schnurr/Wohlfarth, *Journal of Information Technology* (2023), forthcoming.

[38] *Cf* Hagiu/Teh/Wright, *The RAND Journal of Economics*, 53(2)(2022), 297.

[39] Jones/Tonnetti, *American Economic Review*, *110*(9), 2020, 2819.

[40] Prüfer/Schottmüller, *Journal of Industrial Economics*, 69(4), 2021, 96.

[41] Schaefer/Sapi, *Complementarities in Learning from Data: Insights from General Search* (2022).

can collect about each individual user. These quality advantages from data scale are particularly noticeable for rare or new search queries that require fast statistical learning or inferences from related search queries.[42]

Prüfer and Schottmüller conceptualize data-driven network effects as a reduction in the marginal costs of innovation for a firm.[43] That is, the more user data a firm can collect the more efficiently it can invest in quality upgrades of its service. Based on this conjecture, the authors analytically show that data-driven network effects can render digital markets prone to market tipping. Similar to conventional network effects that directly depend on the number of users, data-driven network effects may thus trigger a 'winner-takes-all' dynamic, where only a single dominant market will emerge from the competitive process, whereas other competitors will be marginalised. Prüfer and Schottmüller further highlight that this dynamic is not limited to competitive dynamics within a market.[44] If data-driven network effects from one market can be leveraged to 'connected markets' – that is user data obtained in one market contains valuable information for services in other markets – this can give rise to a 'domino effect', where a data-rich firms does not only dominate a single home market, but also leverages this market power into other markets. 25

Data may often exhibit such supply-side economies of scope. That is, a firm that offers multiple services is able to deliver these services at a lower cost than two separate firms that each offer a distinct service. For example, this is the case if a firm can use data from one service as an input for another service, such as in the case of information on users' preferences, or if the analysis of a joint data set aggregated from multiple services generates additional insights over isolated analyses of the distinct data sets.[45] In the digital economy, the most popular firms have by now established integrated services ecosystems that allow them to combine data sources from diverse services and thus to benefit from data-driven economies of scope and the associated network effects.[46] 26

III. Complementary Inputs for Economic Value Creation from Data

Especially for big data, i.e. large, unstructured and heterogenous sets of data that are subject to constant changes, updates, and additions,[47] the extraction of economic value crucially depends on firms' access to complementary inputs. To infer and derive valuable information from big data sets, firms require a well developed information technology infrastructure, know-how about algorithms and data science techniques to derive relevant insights from data, as well as skilled human resources and adequate organizational capabilities.[48] 27

For example, for the manufacturing sector in the United States, Brynjolfsson and McElheran find that business performance gains from data are especially pronounced 28

[42] He/Kannan/Liu/McAfee/Qin/Rao, *13th International Conference on Web and Internet Economics*, Bangalore, India, 2017, 294.

[43] Prüfer/Schottmüller, *Journal of Industrial Economics*, 69(4) (2021), 967.

[44] *Ibid.*

[45] See, for example, Martens, *An economic policy perspective on online platforms*, 2016.

[46] See, for example, Krämer/Schnurr/Broughton Micova, *The role of data for digital markets contestability: case studies and data access remedies*, 2020.

[47] Gandomi/Haider, *International Journal of Information Management*, 35(2), 2015, 137.

[48] See also Krämer/Schnurr/Broughton Micova, *The role of data for digital markets contestability: case studies and data access remedies*, 2020; Lambrecht/Tucker, *Competition Policy International*, 2017, 1.

for firms with a well-established information technology infrastructure.[49] Moreover, the findings of the study suggest that information technology investments and the propensity of a firm to use data for business performance improvements reinforce each other. A similar complementary relationship with respect to data-driven performance improvements is found for the availability of skilled workers. Brynjolfsson, Jin and McElheran find further support for these complementary relationships.[50] In order for a manufacturing firm to benefit from the adoption of predictive data analytics, the firms must either have a high level of accumulated information technology capital, employ a skilled workforce, or focus on a specific form of production process design.

29 These results are in line with empirical findings by Müller, Fay, and vom Brocke, who show that a firm's investments in big data and analytics assets are associated with a significantly higher firm productivity.[51] According to the authors' definition, such big data and analytics assets comprise foundational database technologies, data mining software and machine learning algorithms, as well as data visualization and presentation tools.[52] Moreover, Tambe finds that productivity gains from investments in big data technology depend critically on (i) firms' access to labour markets that can supply skilled workers as well as (ii) a firm's earlier investments in data assets and data-driven decision-making practices.[53]

30 In general, investments into information technology infrastructure are associated with high fixed costs. Furthermore, establishing data analytics know-how as well as respective organizational capabilities requires significant time to develop. In consequence, economies of scale and scope frequently arise that favor large and established firms with respect to the availability and maturity of these complementary input resources. This is, for example, illustrated by empirical findings that large firms (that is, firms with a large number of employees or firms belonging to a multi-unit firm) are significantly more likely to make use of data for relevant business decisions.[54]

IV. Data Quality

31 The economic value of data depends crucially on its quality. For example, it is easy to accumulate or generate large quantities of data, which, however, could be entirely useless if the data is of poor quality (e.g. in the case of random or fake data points). In general, data quality can be defined as 'the measure of the agreement between the data views presented by an information system and that same data in the real world'.[55] In this vein, data quality is a multi-dimensional construct that can be measured and evaluated along a set of various criteria. On a fundamental level, these criteria comprise data accuracy (records of true value), data completeness (no missing records), data timeliness (no outdated records), data consistency (no contradicting records) and data deduplication (no redundant records).[56]

---

[49] Brynjolfsson/McElheran, *Data in action: data-driven decision making in US manufacturing*, 2016.

[50] Brynjolfsson/Jin/McElheran, *The Power of Prediction: Predictive Analytics, Workplace Complements, and Business Performance*, 2021.

[51] Müller/Fay/Vom Brocke, *Journal of Management Information Systems*, *35*(2), 2018, 488.

[52] *Ibid.* (p. 496).

[53] Tambe, *Management Science*, *60*(6), 2014, 1452.

[54] Brynjolfsson/McElheran, *American Economic Review: Papers & Proceedings*, *106*(5), 2016, 133.

[55] Orr, *Communications of the ACM*, *41*(2), 1998, 66 (67).

[56] Fan/Geerts, *Foundations of Data Quality Management. Synthesis Lectures on Data Management*, 2012, 3 et seq.

In this sense, the ongoing debate about the relationship between data quantity and economic value falls short when it does not sufficiently consider data quality as an important determinant of data value. Considering quality as a key driver of data's business value also suggests that firms may not only compete with respect to data access in terms of quantity, but also along the quality dimension. To this end, high-quality data can sometimes substitute the need for large-scale data in terms of quantity.[57] However, at least to some extent, larger quantities of data can also be helpful to detect and correct quality issues and increase the robustness of inferences and predictions.[58] 32

Furthermore, in practice, established firms with a large user base and well-developed complementary inputs (see Section C.III.) will often have an advantage over market entrants and start-up firms in collecting and maintaining high-quality data sets. Therefore, even though non-rivalry implies general replicability of user data by different competitors, the quality of user data that firms can collect will regularly differ significantly. For example, established firms with a large user base often have access to up-to-date and fine-granular data. Moreover, in cases where firms have been maintaining long-lasting relationships with customers, they are likely to obtain more complete data on an individual level than newly formed start-up firms. 33

In addition, observed user data that is collected without active participation of a consumer is often likely to be of higher accuracy, because in contrast to volunteered user data, this type of data is generally less prone to manipulation or errors by the underlying data subject.[59] For example, if users are directly asked for information, they may enter fake names and addresses to preserve anonymity, state biased preferences to not reveal sensitive traits or submit fake product or location reviews to hurt potential competitors. Detection of such low-quality data is much easier if data accuracy can be verified based on users' observed actual behaviour, e.g. users' geographic location based on GPS data, media consumption based on streaming data or home addresses based on e-commerce transaction data. Even in the case of anonymised data sets, individual characteristics could be revealed if data is recorded on a highly fine-granular level over time.[60] 34

Whereas data quality can be measured based on the aforementioned objective evaluation criteria, the economic value of data also depends crucially on the quality of information conveyed by the data. This information quality is highly context-dependent and subjective, as expressed by conventional definitions of information quality as 'fitness for use' or 'fitness for purpose'.[61] More formally, information quality has been defined as 'the totality of requirements for information [...] that relate to its suitability for meeting given information needs'[62] and the information quality literature has developed elaborate catalogues of respective requirements.[63] This multi-dimensional, context-dependent and subjective nature of information quality presents a major challenge for the commodification of data and thus can be viewed as a significant barrier for inter-organizational data sharing and the emergence of data markets. This is further reinforced by data being an experience good and the Arrow information paradox, which are discussed in the next section. 35

---

[57] Martens/Provost/Clark/de Fortuny, *MIS Quarterly*, *40*(4), 2016, 869.

[58] *Ibid*; Junqué de Fortuny/Martens/Provost, *Big Data*, *1*(4), 2013, 215.

[59] Krämer/Schnurr/Broughton Micova, *The role of data for digital markets contestability: case studies and data access remedies*, 2020.

[60] See, for example, De Montjoye/Hidalgo/Verleysen/Blondel, *Scientific Reports*, *3*, 2013, Article 1376.

[61] Wang/Strong, *Journal of Management Information Systems*, *12*(4), 1996, 5.

[62] Nohr in: Riekert/Michelson (eds.) *Informationswirtschaft – Innovation für die Neue Ökonomie*, 2001, 57 (60).

[63] See the seminal paper by Wang/Strong, *Journal of Management Information Systems*, *12*(4), 1996, 5.

V. Data as an Experience Good and the Arrow Information Paradox

36 The evaluation of data quality and the assessment of data value is further complicated by data being an experience good. This means that data quality can often only be assessed after a data set can be fully accessed and analysed, i.e. only after the data has been purchased or collected. This is in contrast to search goods, whose quality can be determined before the purchase, e.g. by inspection of a physical good or by the analysis of certain product features. In consequence, experience goods involve substantial information asymmetries between data holders and prospective data acquirers, which can impede the realization of economic transactions.

37 Although there exist well-known institutions and mechanisms to mitigate information asymmetries in general contexts, there are additional barriers for data trades that impede the emergence of efficient data markets. Most famously, the Arrow information paradox states, in its essence, that in order for a potential buyer to be able to assess the quality and value of a data set, the buyer must gain detailed knowledge of the contained information.[64] However, if the buyer learns this information in order to determine the quality, there is no remaining economic incentive to still purchase the data set for a positive price. Hence, sellers must balance how much information to reveal about a data set: on the one hand, potential buyers must obtain sufficient information such that they believe that they can benefit from the information contained in the data set; on the other hand, information revelation must be limited such that the acquisition of the data set remains valuable to the prospective buyer.

38 Moreover, the economic value of data is highly contextual and varies significantly across potential buyers. Even for the same buyer, the identical data may be of high economic value at some point in time but could be entirely useless at another point in time if the same information has already been learned in some other way. In consequence, mechanisms such as product reviews or general quality assurances and certificates that facilitate trading of other experience goods are much less effective in supporting market transactions of data and information goods.

D. Two Overarching Economic Challenges for Data Strategies and Data Policies

39 Among policymakers in Europe, it is now a common goal that data should be shared and used widely between individuals, private organizations, and public actors. This is illustrated by a recent wave of data strategies and data policies on the national and supranational level. For example, with respect to public sector agencies and state administrations, the revised European Open Data Directive mandates non-discriminatory access to government data and public sector information at zero or marginal costs for data re-users.[65] With respect to data of individuals, the Data Governance Act proposal aims to encourage altruistic data sharing for the common good[66], while Personal Information Management Systems are frequently mentioned in data strategies as a technical instru-

[64] Arrow, in: *The Rate and Direction of Inventive Activity: Economic and Social Factors*, 1962, 609.

[65] See for a more in-depth economic analysis of open government data Haberer/Schnurr, *Open Government Data in Digital Markets: Effects on Innovation, Competition and Societal Benefits*, 2022.

[66] European Commission, Proposal for a Regulation of the European Parliament and of the Council on European data governance (Data Governance Act) – COM/2020/767 final, 2020, p. 8.

ment to facilitate privacy-compliant sharing of user data.[67] With respect to private-sector organizations and businesses, the Data Governance Act proposal is envisioned to facilitate inter-organizational data sharing by providing legal guidelines for data intermediaries.[68] Moreover, as part of the European data strategy, data infrastructure projects such as GAIA-X have been initiated in an effort to promote data exchanges, while also maintaining data sovereignty in the European Union.[69] Finally, even regulatory proposals aimed at curtailing the economic dominance of digital gatekeepers, such as the Digital Markets Act proposal[70], have emphasised data access remedies that would require dominant gatekeepers in specific markets to share their data resources with competitors.[71] For instance, this may include mandated access to search query data of large and dominant online search engines that are deemed gatekeepers.

From an economic welfare perspective, the goal of broad data sharing is supported by data being a non-rival and valuable good with production and distribution costs close to zero, which implies that broad data sharing can achieve large social gains.[72] However, purely voluntary and market-based data sharing is likely to fall short of this goal due to the special economic properties of data. In consequence, two fundamental economic challenges arise: (i) insufficient data access due to data agglomeration by a few dominant firms and (ii) insufficient data availability due to data fragmentation and a lack of data exchange. In the following, both these challenges are discussed in more detail with respect to the main economic trade-offs that policymakers must navigate when aiming for coherent data strategies and effective data policies. 40

I. Data Concentration and the Efficiency Trade-off of Data Access Remedies

Scale and scope advantages from data as well as data-driven network effects have raised significant concerns among scholars and policymakers about data-driven market power and data agglomeration by a few superstar firms.[73] At the policy level, these concerns have come to the forefront as a small number of digital platforms now dominates a large variety of digital markets at different layers of the Internet value chain and across the globe. Although business value creation from data is in principle replicable, especially due to the non-rivalry of data, additional factors may protect data-rich firms from imitation and promote sustained competitive advantages. Especially in the presence of significant data-driven network effects (see Section C.II.), data-driven market power, and ensuing data agglomeration can harm competition 41

[67] European Commission, *A European strategy for data – COM/2020/66 final*, 2020; The Federal Government of Germany, *Data Strategy of the Federal German Government*, 2021. See also §§ 25, 26 TTDSG.

[68] European Commission, Proposal for a Regulation of the European Parliament and of the Council on European data governance (Data Governance Act) – COM/2020/767 final, 2020, p. 8.

[69] Gaia-X European Association for Data and Cloud, What is Gaia-X, n.d.; European Commission, *A European strategy for data – COM/2020/66 final*, 2020.

[70] European Commission, Proposal for a Regulation of the European Parliament and of the Council on contestable and fair markets in the digital sector (Digital Markets Act) – COM/2020/842 final, 2020.

[71] See also Krämer/Schnurr, *Journal of Competition Law & Economics*, 18(2), 2022, 255.

[72] Jones/Tonetti, *American Economic Review*, *110*(9), 2020, 2819.

[73] See, among others, Fast/Schnurr/Wohlfarth, *Journal of Information Technology*, 2023, forthcoming; Krämer/Schnurr/Broughton Micova, *The role of data for digital markets contestability: case studies and data access remedies*, 2020.

and innovation in digital markets. These harms may then not only occur within isolated markets, but instead, data-driven market power may spread across markets due to the 'domino effect' and the expansion of digital ecosystems that integrate diverse services across markets.

42 In network industries, structural conditions conducive to the emergence of sustained market power have provided the economic justification for introducing ex-ante regulation to facilitate market entry and to preserve a level playing field for competition. Among other measures, these regulatory frameworks frequently include access remedies that aim to provide competitors of dominant firms with access to an upstream input good in order to stimulate competition in the downstream retail market. For example, the European regulatory framework for the telecommunications sector mandates that independent network operators can obtain access to regulated wholesale products, such as the physical cable on the 'last mile' to a household or the virtual connection to a household's bitstream. From an economic perspective, these access remedies have been justified by the rationale that access to the wholesale input good is essential for competing in the retail market, but competitors are unable to replicate this wholesale input good economically on their own.

43 A similar argument has been made with respect to data as an input resource.[74] However, the direct applicability of this argument seems to be more limited in the data context, as data rarely constitutes an essential input for providing a service or product in the sense that the service or product could otherwise not be provided at all.[75] Notwithstanding, even if data does not qualify as an essential input, it is likely to enhance the quality of services or products or to generate business value in other dimensions (see Section B. I.). In turn, this can provide a data-rich firm with a sustained competitive advantage, which, especially in combination with reinforcing network effects, could establish long-term data-driven market power and elicit economic harm by shielding dominant firms from competition.[76]

44 A complementary argument for data access remedies is rooted in the non-rival nature of data. As replicating and sharing of data resources does not impede the original data holder from accessing and using the data, data access remedies may be justified based on the relatively lower costs incurred by the regulated firm and the less severe intervention into the firm's business practices. In other words, static efficiency gains due to broader data availability and more intense competition can be achieved at lower overall costs than in the case of traditional rival goods.[77] Moreover, if data can be used for diverse purposes and business value creation, opening data access may stimulate new business activities and spur innovation.[78] Although this may not immediately constrain the market power of the respective dominant firm, it might still enable new firms to emerge and grow in market niches or new markets, where they could otherwise not compete with established firms that are able to leverage data resources from their core markets.[79] In the long run, data access remedies may thus support small and medium sized firms as well as start-up firms in growing a larger scale and gaining broader customer bases, such that they then can compete with data-

[74] See, for example, Graef/Prüfer, *Economisch Statistische Berichten, 103(4763)*, 2018, 298.

[75] Krämer/Schnurr/Broughton Micova, *The role of data for digital markets contestability: case studies and data access remedies*, 2020.

[76] *Ibid.*

[77] Jones/Tonetti, *American Economic Review, 110*(9), 2020, 2819.

[78] Haberer/Schnurr, *Open Government Data in Digital Markets: Effects on Innovation, Competition and Societal Benefits*, 2022; Wu/Hitt/Lou, *Management Science*, 66(5), 2020, 2017.

[79] Krämer/Schnurr, *Journal of Competition Law & Economics*, 18(2), 2022, 255.

rich and dominant firms on a more equal footing, which in turn could discipline the market power of these firms.[80]

However, opening a firm's data resources to other firms by imposing data access remedies involves a central economic trade-off as open access limits the exclusive use and thus the business value of the data for the regulated firm. In consequence, this can reduce the incentives of for firms to collect data of high quality in the first place and to invest in data-driven innovation that is subject to high risks.[81] Therefore, economic theory predicts that data access remedies entail significant negative long-term effects on dynamic efficiency (especially due to higher investments and more innovation), which must be weighed against short-term gains in static efficiency (especially due to more intense competition). 45

Although this open access trade-off also arises in other contexts and industries – for example, copyrights and patents offer innovators legal protection from imitation and competition – data access remedies involve additional considerations. On the one hand, the non-rivalry of data favors open access and resource duplication, as argued above. On the other hand, non-rivalry may also magnify the downsides from having to relinquish exclusive control of a data resource. This is especially the case if a firm's business value is derived from selling the data or the information itself or if the data is used by competitors as an input to create a close substitute to the regulated firm's goods. In these cases, the economic rent that can be generated from data diminishes drastically if data is non-exclusive.[82] In turn, this again reduces the economic incentives to collect and process this data in the first place. 46

Research on data intermediaries indicates that if a firm is unable to establish exclusive control over a data resource, competition will drive down the revenue that can be derived from this data to marginal costs.[83] In consequence, the data holder would be unable to make a profit and reduce or even stop investing in such data offers and the respective data sourcing and data processing. Competition is particularly intense for non-exclusive data, because if a data user (i.e. the potential buyer) has learned the information once, the same information (e.g. offered by a competitor) becomes worthless. Non-rivalry reinforces these competitive dynamics further, because data users may expect to obtain the same data at a possibly lower price from an alternative seller in the future.[84] In consequence, the original data producers, which in the case of user data are the consumers themselves, are also likely to receive a lower benefit for creating such data, which could result in a higher usage price for digital services, a lower service quality or a lower reward for their data.[85] This negative effect due to intense competition may be mitigated in use cases where data is processed and used by competitors to offer goods and services that are more differentiated, but the general implications and potential downsides of mandated data sharing still apply. 47

In order for data strategies and data policies to achieve economically desirable outcomes, they must navigate and balance this central efficiency trade-off of data access remedies. Due to the context-specificity of data, policies should ideally be tailored to the 48

---

[80] *Ibid.*

[81] Haberer/Schnurr, *Open Government Data in Digital Markets: Effects on Innovation, Competition and Societal Benefits*, 2022.

[82] Ichihashi, *The RAND Journal of Economics*, *52*(3), 2021, 515; Gu/Madio/Reggiani, *Oxford Economic Papers*, 74(3), 2022, 820.

[83] *Ibid.*

[84] Ichihashi, *The RAND Journal of Economics*, *52*(3), 2021, 515.

[85] Ichihashi, *The RAND Journal of Economics*, *52*(3), 2021, 515; Haberer/Krämer/Schnurr, *Do Consumers Benefit from Selling their Data? The Economic Effects of Personal Data Brokers in Digital Markets*, 2022.

respective specific conditions. So far, guiding empirical evidence on the implications of different policy designs for data access remains scarce and subject to ongoing research efforts. Notwithstanding, some general principles have been proposed in the economic literature based on theoretical considerations: For example, only raw user data that was created as a by-product of consumers' usage may be subject to access remedies, whereas inferred data that results from data processing should fall outside of the scope of such remedies to preserve the regulated firm's legitimate business interests and innovation incentives.[86] An alternative proposal are 'in-situ data rights': instead of raw data being transferred to external organizations, access seekers may 'bring' their algorithm to the regulated firm's infrastructure, where the data naturally resides and only the algorithm's output is made available to external firms.[87] In consequence, plain imitation and potential negative effects on dynamic efficiency may be mitigated. However, the technical feasibility of such approaches is still to be explored in large-scale practice.

49 Finally, in the context of user data, data access remedies must be implemented such that users' privacy is preserved. In consequence, data must be anonymised, which raises significant technical challenges in the context of fine-granular big data.[88] Moreover, anonymization will also lower the business value of the respective data sets and thus competitors, even with data access remedies, will remain at a competitive disadvantage relative to data-rich firms, unless the same anonymization is also enforced at these firms.[89] An alternative or complementary data access regime could be built on top of data portability rights for individual consumers. Here competitors may benefit from the advantage that consumers can give their consent for the sharing and processing of personally identifiable data, which likely yields a higher business value. However, questions then remain with respect to whether such an approach targeted at the individual consumer can provide competitors with sufficient data scale. Many consumers will be reluctant to voluntarily share their personal information with unknown or small firms, especially if portability incurs noticeable transaction costs or involves privacy risks. Therefore, a hybrid policy approach that combines mandated business-to-business data sharing and data portability rights for consumers may promise to balance the privacy and data scale trade-off.[90]

II. Data Fragmentation and Lack of Data Exchange

50 Whereas the first major challenge for data strategies and data policies is presented by data concentration at a few data-rich firms, the second challenge is rooted in the opposite phenomenon of data fragmentation and a lack of data exchange to merge dispersed data sources. Especially in markets that are traditionally characterised by many small and medium enterprises, digital transformation of firms' technologies and processes leads to data creation at many dispersed locations and at different organizations. Here, it is often the lack of organizational scale that prevents firms from exploiting the business and social value of the data.

51 Firstly, each firm in these markets may only have access to limited data sets. These limits may refer to the data volume, but also to the data variety. Especially in industrial

[86] See Krämer/Schnurr, *Journal of Competition Law & Economics*, 18(2), 2022, 255 for a more elaborate discussion.

[87] Van Alstyne/Petropoulos/Parker/Martens, *Communications of the ACM*, *64*(12), 2021, 34.

[88] See, for example, De Montjoye/Hidalgo/Verleysen/Blondel, *Scientific Reports*, *3*, 2013, Article 1376.

[89] Krämer/Schnurr, *Journal of Competition Law & Economics*, 18(2), 2022, 255.

[90] *Ibid.*

contexts, business value is frequently created along vertical supply chains. Hence, data is created and collected by different organizations at different stages of the production and distribution process. This is in stark contrast to the platform business model that dominates the internet economy and that favors data concentration at the intermediary. Thus, a specialised supplier in an industrial value chain may only have access to very homogeneous data derived from the goods it produces, distributes, or sells, whereas inference of valuable knowledge and new insights may require the combination and aggregate analysis of more diverse data (e.g. the combination of production data and end customer sales data).

Secondly, smaller firms often lack the scale and expertise to efficiently procure and develop the complementary inputs that are necessary to derive business value from data. For example, small and medium enterprises often find it economically challenging to establish the necessary information technology infrastructure, to recruit skilled human resources, and to develop the organizational skills required for the profitable processing and use of data. This is because they lack scale and scope advantages of large-scale firms, but also core competences and organizational expertise of firms that have emerged as 'digitally native' businesses. 52

Thirdly, the integration and combination of dispersed data in business-to-business relationships frequently require much higher relation-specific efforts and investments than in more standardised use cases of consumer user data (e.g. demographic information to support personalised coupons or targeted advertising). This is because the analysis and use of data hinges on a common understanding of the data format and data schemas as well as interoperable technical interfaces. However, these requirements are much more difficult to satisfy if data is collected across many firms and within distinct organizational boundaries. This is even more the case if firms collect and use data for highly specialised purposes and if the collected data is stored in data infrastructures that are not primarily designed to share this data with other businesses. 53

In consequence of the high specificity of data and data use in these contexts, data exchange and information sharing across organizations has mostly emerged on a bilateral basis between closely connected business partners. In particular, along vertical supply chains, firms often collaborate and integrate data resources with their respective input suppliers or output processors on adjacent stages of the supply chain. For example, this includes the design and adoption of electronic data interchange interfaces that facilitate forward and backward flow of information along the supply chain in order to improve efficiency of production and logistics of physical goods. 54

Limiting data sharing to one-on-one relationships enables firms to better manage the complexity and coordination costs of data integration. To some extent, bilateral data exchanges also mitigate potential public good dynamics and the associated negative consequences on data availability and data quality that are likely to arise in multilateral data sharing scenarios, where firms can benefit from other firms' data contributions without providing any (valuable) data themselves (cf Section B. III.). A mutual understanding of the business goals, reciprocity and repeated interactions are important factors in long-lasting bilateral relationships that constrain purely opportunistic behaviour of firms that may otherwise arise to the detriment of the other parties involved in the data exchange. 55

Despite these advantages of bilateral data exchanges, there are also significant drawbacks and shortcomings with respect to the overall economic value that can be achieved by such one-to-one interactions. Most importantly, bilateral data exchanges do not scale with a larger number of involved actors, as the number of relationships grows quadratically in the number of exchange partners. In consequence, establishing and 56 managing data exchanges with each individual counterpart would impose excessive coordination effort and transaction costs on firms, especially if data sets, data formats, and exchange interfaces do not follow a common standard. In addition, bilateral data exchanges are likely to favor established firms that can rely on their existing business network and long-lasting relationships with other organizations. However, innovation is often driven by entrepreneurs, market entrants, or market outsiders. In part, this is because these firms face lower opportunity costs when engaging in innovation and when experimenting with new business models, as they do not need to worry about self-cannibalization of existing revenues or the marginalization of existing business units and respective capabilities due the creative destruction of innovation. Yet, such entrepreneurs and market outsiders can typically not draw on established networks of business partners within these markets. Therefore, to promote data mobility beyond existing organizational relationships and to really generate broader benefits from data use, open data platforms and data markets that support multilateral data exchanges among a wide number of potential participants are envisioned.

57 However, such data platforms and data markets have so far only emerged to a limited extent and in highly specialised forms. Moreover, they are fragmented across geographies, industries, and data types.[91] This can be explained by the economic properties of data and the impediments that they present for data exchanges and data transactions.[92] Due to the context-dependent and highly heterogeneous business value of data, data procurement over such platforms frequently requires a specific evaluation of each data set before a transaction. This is further complicated by data being an experience good, such that it is difficult for data providers to assure potential data acquirers about the quality of the data. In particular, such quality assurances often require a subjective and individual value assessment that is difficult to proxy by objective quality criteria. In consequence, these properties present a significant challenge for scaling data transactions and efficient market mechanisms. But even if individual value assessments were feasible, the information paradox would indicate that data providers would only share limited quality information with potential acquirers in order to protect the economic value of the information in the given transaction context.

58 Furthermore, potential data providers may fear the loss of exclusive data control over their data, as acquirers can easily duplicate and resell the data, due to the non-rivalry property. As discussed before, the loss of exclusive control could significantly dissipate the economic value of a data set for the data holder, because intense competition is likely to diminish the economic rent from selling the data. In consequence, data holders may be hesitant to offer their data on multilateral data sharing platforms or on open data markets.

59 In some use cases, there may also exist uncertainty about the (legal) attribution of a particular data resource. For example, in the case of machine-generated data, sensors from different firms may create joint data sets that exhibit business value in their combined form, but it may remain unclear which firm is then allowed to monetize this data. In this vein, a lack of clearly defined property rights can impede data transactions even if such transactions could create mutual economic value.

60 Finally, offering data to an open and external audience can entail several risks for the data provider.[93] In particular, data security and privacy issues may arise if data is stored such that it can be made available for external parties. In addition, potential data acquirers may use the data in ways that endanger the safety or privacy of third

---

[91] De Reuver, *Governance of data platforms: Rethinking platform openness in the data economy*, 2021.
[92] *Cf* ibid.
[93] *Ibid.*

parties. For fine-grained behavioural data sets, these issues may arise even if the data provider anonymizes data before the data exchange, as identifiable information may become available only after the data is combined with additional data sets. Other data sets may inadvertently entail risks of disclosing confidential business information of a third party. Altogether, these risks further diminish the incentives of firms to make data available on open data platforms and thus impede the emergence of efficient data markets.

In this context, market-based institutions as well as policy measures to overcome these **61**
obstacles are still underexplored. Based on a systematic review of the literature, Abbas et al. conclude that more research is needed on the non-technological aspects of data platform adoption that go beyond the technical design of such platforms.[94] So far, policy proposals such as the Data Governance Act[95] in the European Union primarily focus on trust as a facilitator of data sharing, but largely neglect the economic incentives that are necessary to support sustainable data sharing business models. However, from an economic perspective, it is crucial that data policies aimed at increasing trust, privacy, and security do not raise market entry costs to a level where business activities become economically inviable. Therefore, business incentives and transactions costs must be carefully weighed against the benefits of trust-improving measures and regulatory rules aimed at more legal certainty.

To facilitate data exchanges on data platforms across geographic, industry and data- **62**
specific boundaries, interoperable standards that promote platform-to-platform openness represent a central policy issue that should be considered by data strategies.[96] Here, the general economic trade-off of standardization must be considered: On the one hand, standardization creates economic benefits by lowering transaction costs and reducing uncertainty for the involved economic actors. On the other hand, this comes at the costs of more static rules that constrain flexibility and specialization of businesses. In this context, policymakers may draw from a wide range of diverse standardization policies and institutions to balance this trade-off. To assess and anticipate outcomes of alternative policy approaches, important insights can be drawn from the rich economic literature on standardization that has emerged in the context of standardization efforts in other information technology domains and in related network industries.[97]

In order to design and implement effective policies, the continuous evaluation of **63**
enacted policies and learning from their actual consequences after implementation are important. For example, current policy initiatives on the re-use of public sector information reveal many of the hurdles that arise for open data policies.[98] In particular, open government data policies demonstrate the challenges in designing data access such that the contained information is indeed available, discoverable, accessible and of value for a general audience of potential data re-users. It is therefore vital that the success of policies should not be assessed exclusively on the basis of the data quantity that is made available but must also consider the data quality and actual data re-use as important

[94] Abbas/Agahari/van de Ven/Zuiderwijk/de Reuver, *Journal of Theoretical and Applied Electronic Commerce Research*, *16*(7), 2021, 3321.

[95] European Commission, Proposal for a Regulation of the European Parliament and of the Council on European data governance (Data Governance Act) – COM/2020/767 final, 2020, p. 8.

[96] See for a more in-depth analysis of data platform-to-platform openness Mosterd/Sobota/van de Kaa/Ding/de Reuver, *Technovation*, *108*, 2021, Article 102331.

[97] See for overviews Besen/Farrell, *Journal of Economic Perspectives*, *8*(2), 1994, 117; Farrell/Klemperer in: Armstrong/Porter (eds.), *Handbook of Industrial Organization*, Volume 3, 2007, 1967.

[98] Haberer/Schnurr, *Open Government Data in Digital Markets: Effects on Innovation, Competition and Societal Benefits*, 2022.

indicators of effective value-generating data policies.[99] So far, many open government data initiatives still fall short of achieving these goals, even though state actors themselves are in full control of the data resources. In the case of open data sharing policies targeted at private actors, the envisioned rules and institutions must additionally consider the economic incentives of the involved stakeholders and how they are shaped by the specific properties of data as discussed above. Here again, it is important to evaluate policies not only exclusively in terms of the available data quantity, but to consider data quality and data value which is best captured by actual re-use of the data.

64 Finally, the two presented challenges for data policies should not be considered in isolation. In fact, prospective or actual data concentration has important implications on data policies targeted at data fragmentation. In particular, if such policies are effective in making new data resources available on a non-discriminatory basis, it is likely that especially large and data-rich firms will benefit from these new data sources. Hence, the danger arises that such data policies aimed at open data sharing will further reinforce the competitive advantages of data-rich firms. In consequence, these policies could amplify data concentration and associated competition issues, despite opposite intentions.

65 With respect to these tensions and trade-offs, data strategies can play an important role if they initiate and integrate an explicit discussion on what should be the primary policy objective. Only if data strategies give clear guidance on the relative priorities of the different policy objectives, the outlined economic trade-offs can be navigated by coherent data policies. In this vein, both challenges highlighted in this discussion should be considered in combination from a strategic policy perspective, as they both reinforce each other, possibly in a positive as well as in a negative way.

E. Recommendations for Designing Effective Data Policies

66 In this chapter, fundamental principles and recent empirical evidence on the economics of data were reviewed. Across individual studies, there is now comprehensive evidence that big (user) data generates business value, although this value is highly diverse and context-dependent on the respective use case. It is important to note that this business value does not monotonically and mechanically grow along with the quantity of the available data. Instead, important moderating factors, which are mainly rooted in users' individual valuation for their own personal data, limit the business value that firms may derive from data collection and data use. Thereby, consumers' valuation for their data is found to be highly heterogeneous across individuals and cultures, but at the same time systematically affected by the same factors, such as individuals' intrinsic privacy preferences, the anticipated economic consequences of data use, and perceived information sensitivity. It is by now well-recognized that individuals' data valuation and privacy decisions are significantly influenced by behavioral effects and ensuing behavioral paradoxes. Such behavioral effects may undermine well-intended policies aimed at empowering consumers through improved transparency and enhanced control over their personal data. Behavioral aspects also play an important role with respect to scenarios where data is of large social value but provides low individual benefits and therefore data constitutes a public good. In this context, data altruism may serve as a promising approach to unlock the social value of data, which should therefore be supported by accompanying data policies.

[99] *Cf* also Gasser/Hennemann § 2.

Beyond moderating factors for business value creation and individuals' behavioral effects, the creation, use and exchange of data are significantly affected by the special properties of data as an economic good. Whereas non-rivalry of data implies that social welfare is maximized by broad data sharing and diverse data use, data-driven network effects favor data agglomeration and market concentration. Data's tendency to facilitate market concentration is reinforced by economies of scale and scope that arise from complementary inputs, which are needed to derive economic value from data. Moreover, the economic value of data is critically determined by its quality. However, data quality forms along several dimensions and its assessment is highly subjective as well as context-dependent. At the same time, quality is difficult to assess for entities without full access to the entire data set due to data being an experience good. In combination with the Arrow information paradox, these inherent evaluation difficulties complicate data transactions and thus impede the emergence of efficient data markets. 67

The special properties of data give rise to two fundamental economic challenges that policymakers must address when aiming to make data widely available for broad re-use. On the one hand, data-driven network effects as well as economies of scale and scope foster data concentration, especially in markets that are dominated by digital platform gatekeepers. Such intermediaries find themselves in an advantageous position to collect data of high quality on a large scale, which is difficult for other firms to replicate, despite the non-rivalry of data. On the other hand, data fragmentation is likely to occur in more traditional markets characterized by vertical supply chains of many small and medium firms. In these markets, data is frequently generated within distinct and highly specialized organizations. Moreover, data is regularly created as a by-product of business processes or the usage of physical goods, such as in the case of machine-generated data. This data may only entail economic value if isolated data sources are integrated into larger, combined data sets and if complementary inputs for data processing and data analysis are available. However, sharing and trading institutions that could facilitate the integration of dispersed data in these markets face significant challenges due to the complexity involved in the quality assessment of external data resources, data being an experience good and the implications of the Arrow information paradox. 68

Data policies may address data concentration by mandating data access remedies for data-rich and dominant firms in digital markets. This can enable more firms to access data inputs that would otherwise not be available at the same scale or quality. In consequence, potential competitors may improve the quality of their own services and compete on a more 'levelled' playing field with the data-rich incumbent. However, due to anonymization (which is often required with regard to data protection law) and technical requirements for implementing large-scale data transfers, competitors are likely to remain at some disadvantage relative to the incumbent in terms of data access. Notwithstanding, data access remedies can generate gains in static economic efficiency, which, however, may come at the expense of dynamic efficiency losses due to lower incentives for the access provider to invest in data collection and in data quality in the first place. This economic efficiency trade-off is therefore central for the design and the implications of data access policies. In contrast, data policies may also aim to facilitate data availability and data openness in order to address the second main challenge of mitigating data fragmentation. To this end, policies should consider standard setting and interoperability that can promote multilateral data sharing on open data platforms. However, data policies must also consider the necessary economic incentives for data holders in order to overcome the barriers to data sharing, which are rooted in the special characteristics of data as an economic good. 69

70 With respect to both of these economic challenges, data strategies can play an important role in providing guidance for data policies to effectively and coherently navigate the involved trade-offs. To this end, it is necessary that data strategies provide deliberate considerations and assessments of policy objectives and their relative priorities. Moreover, data strategies should anticipate the interdependencies and side-effects that arise from policies addressed at one particular economic challenge. In this context, ongoing research on specific data policies and data use cases should be integrated into the policymaking process to avoid unintended and adverse effects that may undermine the envisioned policy goals.[100] Finally, data strategies should develop procedures that ensure a continuous evaluation of enacted policies in order to learn from policy implementation and to monitor the actual consequences of policies on the economic use of data.[101]

Bibliography

71 Abbas/Agahari/van de Ven/Zuiderwijk/de Reuver, Business Data Sharing through Data Marketplaces: A Systematic Literature Review, 16(7) *Journal of Theoretical and Applied Electronic Commerce Research* 3321 (2021)

Acquisti/Brandimarte/Loewenstein, Privacy and human behavior in the age of information, 347 (6221) *Science* 509 (2015)

Arrow, Economic welfare and the allocation of resources for invention, *The Rate and Direction of Inventive Activity: Economic and Social Factors* 609, 1962

Benndorf/Normann, The Willingness to Sell Personal Data, *The Scandinavian Journal of Economics* 2018, 1260

Besen/Farrell, Choosing how to compete: Strategies and tactics in standardization, 8(2) *Journal of Economic Perspectives* 117 (1994)

Brandimarte/Acquisti/Loewenstein, Misplaced confidences: Privacy and the control paradox, 4(3) *Social Psychological and Personality Science* 340 (2013)

Brynjolfsson/McElheran, Data in action: data-driven decision making in US manufacturing, 2016, available at https://ssrn.com/abstract=2722502 (last accessed 14 December 2022)

Brynjolfsson/McElheran, The rapid adoption of data-driven decision-making, 106(5) *American Economic Review: Papers & Proceedings* 133 (2016)

Brynjolfsson/Jin/McElheran, The Power of Prediction: Predictive Analytics, Workplace Complements, and Business Performance, 2021, available at https://ssrn.com/abstract=3849716 (last accessed 14 December 2022)

Culnan/Armstrong, Information privacy concerns, procedural fairness, and impersonal trust: An empirical investigation, 10(1) *Organization Science* 104 (1999)

De Montjoye/Hidalgo/Verleysen/Blondel, Unique in the crowd: The privacy bounds of human mobility, 3 *Scientific Reports*, Article 1376 (2013)

[100] See Haberer/Krämer/Schnurr, *Do Consumers Benefit from Selling their Data? The Economic Effects of Personal Data Brokers in Digital Markets*, 2022, for an economic analysis of the effects of personal data brokers, which build on personal information management systems and data portability. The analysis shows analytically that such personal data brokers, which reward consumers for making their data available, may ultimately have adverse effects on consumer welfare. See also Haberer/Schnurr, *Open Government Data in Digital Markets: Effects on Innovation, Competition and Societal Benefits*, 2022, for an analysis of the economic effects of open government data on different policy objectives.

[101] *Cf* also in this regard Gasser/Hennemann § 2.

De Reuver, Governance of data platforms: Rethinking platform openness in the data economy, Presentation, Distinguished Keynote Lecture Series on Digital Platforms Ecosystems, 2021, available at https://www.digital.uni-passau.de/en/passaudpe/ (last accessed 14 December 2022)

Dinev/McConnell/Smith, Research commentary – informing privacy research through information systems, psychology, and behavioral economics: thinking outside the "APCO" box, 26(4) *Information Systems Research* 639 (2015)

European Commission, A European strategy for data – COM/2020/66 final, 2020, available at communication-european-strategy-data-19feb2020_en.pdf (europa.eu) (last accessed 14 December 2022)

European Commission, *Proposal for a Regulation of the European Parliament and of the Council on European data governance (Data Governance Act)* – COM/2020/767 final (2020)

European Commission, *Proposal for a Regulation of the European Parliament and of the Council on contestable and fair markets in the digital sector (Digital Markets Act)* – COM/2020/842 final (2020)

Fan/Geerts, *Foundations of Data Quality Management. Synthesis Lectures on Data Management*, 2012

Farrell/Klemperer, Coordination and lock-in: Competition with switching costs and network effects, in: Armstrong/Porter (eds.): 3 *Handbook of Industrial Organization* 1967 (2007)

Fast/Schnurr, The Value of Personal Data: An Experimental Analysis of Data Types and Personal Antecedents, in: *Proceedings of the 41st International Conference on Information Systems (ICIS 2020)*

Fast/Schnurr, Data Donations for Digital Contact-Tracing: Short- and Long-term Effects of Monetary Incentives, 2022, available at https://ssrn.com/abstract=3786245 (last accessed 14 December 2022)

Fast/Schnurr/Wohlfarth, Regulation of Data-driven Market Power in the Digital Economy: Business Value Creation and Competitive Advantages from Big Data, *Journal of Information Technology*, forthcoming 2023, preprint, available at https://ssrn.com/abstract=3759664 (last accessed 14 December 2022)

Frik/Gaudeul, A measure of the implicit value of privacy under risk, *Journal of Consumer Marketing* 457 (2020)

Frimpong/Helleringer, Strategies to increase downloads of COVID–19 exposure notification apps: A discrete choice experiment, 16(11) *PloS One*, Article e0258945 (2021)

Gaia-X European Association for Data and Cloud, What is Gaia-X, n.d., available at https://www.gaia-x.eu/what-is-gaia-x (last accessed 14 December 2022)

Gandomi/Haider, Beyond the hype. Big data concepts, methods, and analytics, 35(2) *International Journal of Information Management* 137 (2015)

Godel/Litchfield/Mantovani, The value of personal information: Evidence from empirical economic studies, 88 *Communications & Strategies* 41 (2021)

Graef/Prüfer, Mandated data sharing is a necessity in specific sectors, 103(4763) *Economisch Statistische Berichten* 298 (2018)

Gu/Madio/Reggiani, Data brokers co-opetition, 74(3) *Oxford Economic Papers*, 820 (2022)

Haberer/Krämer/Schnurr, Do consumers benefit from selling their data? The economic effects of personal data brokers in digital markets, 2022, available at https://ssrn.com/abstract=3141946 (last accessed 14 December 2022)

Haberer/Schnurr, Open Government Data in Digital Markets: Effects on Innovation, Competition and Societal Benefits, 2022, available at https://ssrn.com/abstract=3743648 (last accessed 14 December 2022)

Hagiu/Teh/Wright, Should platforms be allowed to sell on their own marketplaces?, *The RAND Journal of Economics*, 53(2) 297 (2022)

He/Kannan/Liu/McAfee/Qin/Rao, Scale Effects in Web Search, *13th International Conference on Web and Internet Economics*, Bangalore, India 294 (2017)

Hillebrand/Hornuf, The Social Dilemma of Big Data: Donating Personal Data to Promote Social Welfare, 2021, available at https://ssrn.com/abstract=3801476 (last accessed 14 December 2022)

Huberman/Adar/Fine, Valuating privacy, 3(5) *IEEE Security & Privacy* 22 (2005)

Ichihashi, Competing data intermediaries, 52(3) *The RAND Journal of Economics* 515 (2021)

Junqué de Fortuny/Martens/Provost, Predictive modeling with big data: is bigger really better?, 1(4) *Big Data* 215 (2013)

Johnson/Goldstein, Do defaults save lives?, 302 *Science* 1338 (2003)

Jones/Tonetti, Nonrivalry and the Economics of Data, 110(9) *American Economic Review* 2819 (2020)

Krämer, Personal data portability in the platform economy: Economic implications and policy recommendations, 17(2) *Journal of Competition Law & Economics* 263 (2021)

Krämer/Schnurr, Big data and digital markets contestability: Theory of harm and data access remedies, 18(2) *Journal of Competition Law & Economics*, 255 (2022)

Krämer/Schnurr/Broughton Micova, The role of data for digital markets contestability: case studies and data access remedies, 2020, available at https://cerre.eu/publications/data-digital-markets-contestability-case-studies-and-data-access-remedies/ (last accessed 14 December 2022)

Lambrecht/Tucker, Can big data protect a firm from competition? *Competition Policy International*, 2017, available at https://www.competitionpolicyinternational.com/wp-content/uploads/2017/01/CPI-Lambrecht-Tucker.pdf (last accessed 14 December 2022)

Lin, Valuing intrinsic and instrumental preferences for privacy, 41(4) *Marketing Science* 663 (2022)

Li/Sarathy/Xu, The role of affect and cognition on online consumers' decision to disclose personal information to unfamiliar online vendors, 51(3) *Decision Support Systems* 434 (2011)

Martens, An economic policy perspective on online platforms, 2016, available at https://ec.europa.eu/jrc/sites/default/files/JRC101501.pdf (last accessed 14 December 2022)

Martens/Provost/Clark/de Fortuny, Mining massive fine-grained behavior data to improve predictive analytics, 40(4) *MIS Quarterly 869 (*2016)

Milne/Pettinico/Hajjat/Markos, Information sensitivity typology: Mapping the degree and type of risk consumers perceive in personal data sharing, 51(1) *Journal of Consumer Affairs* 133 (2017)

Mosterd/Sobota/van de Kaa/Ding/de Reuver, Context dependent trade-offs around platform-to-platform openness: The case of the Internet of Things, 108 *Technovation*, Article 102331 (2021)

Mothersbaugh/Foxx/Beatty/Wang, Disclosure antecedents in an online service context: The role of sensitivity of information, 15(1) *Journal of Service Research* 76 (2012)

Munzert/Selb/Gohdes/Stoetzer/Lowe, Tracking and promoting the usage of a COVID-19 contact tracing app, 5(2) *Nature Human Behaviour* 247 (2021)

Müller/Fay/Vom Brocke, The effect of big data and analytics on firm performance: An econometric analysis considering industry characteristics, 35(2) *Journal of Management Information Systems 488* (2018)

Nohr, Management der Informationsqualität, in: Riekert/Michelson (eds.) *Informationswirtschaft – Innovation für die Neue Ökonomie* 57 (2001)

Norberg/Horne/Horne, The privacy paradox: Personal information disclosure intentions versus behaviors, 41(1) *Journal of Consumer Affairs* 100 (2007)

Orr, Data quality and systems theory, 41(2) *Communications of the ACM* 66 (1998)

Prince/Wallsten, How Much is Privacy Worth Around the World and Across Platforms?, 2021, available at https://ssrn.com/abstract=3528386 (last accessed 14 December 2022)

Prüfer/Schottmüller, Competing with big data, 69(4) *Journal of Industrial Economics* 967 (2021)

Riemer/Ciriello/Peter/Schlagwein, Digital contact-tracing adoption in the COVID-19 pandemic: IT governance for collective action at the societal level, 29(6) *European Journal of Information Systems* 731 (2020)

Schaefer/Sapi, Complementarities in Learning from Data: Insights from General Search, 2022, available at https://drive.google.com/file/d/1RRxhTW560PwtMGLEN-0wHikW7oVS9CEn/view (last accessed 14 December 2022)

Schepp/Wambach, On big data and its relevance for market power assessment, 7(2) *Journal of European Competition Law & Practice* 120 (2016)

Smith/Dinev/Xu, Information privacy research: An interdisciplinary review, 35(4) *MIS Quarterly* 989 (2011)

Tambe, Big data investment, skills, and firm value, 60(6) *Management Science* 1452 (2014)

The Federal Government of Germany, Data Strategy of the Federal German Government, 2021, available at https://www.bundesregierung.de/resource/blob/992814/1950610/fb03f669401c3953fef8245c3cc2a5bf/datenstrategie-der-bundesregierung-englisch-download-bpa-data.pdf (last accessed 14 December 2022)

Tucker, Social networks, personalized advertising, and privacy controls, 51(5) *Journal of Marketing Research* 546 (2014)

Urban/Hoofnagle, The privacy pragmatic as privacy vulnerable, in: *Symposium on Usable Privacy and Security (SOUPS 2014) Workshop on Privacy Personas and Segmentation (PPS)*, 2014, available at https://ssrn.com/abstract=2514381 (last accessed 14 December 2022)

Van Alstyne/Petropoulos/Parker/Martens, 'In situ' data rights, 64(12) *Communications of the ACM* 34 (2021)

Wagner/Wessels/Buxmann/Krasnova, Putting a price tag on personal information – A literature review, in: *Proceedings of the 51st Hawaii International Conference on System Sciences* (2018)

Wang/Strong, Beyond accuracy: What data quality means to data consumers, 12(4) *Journal of Management Information Systems* 5 (1996)

Wu/Hitt/Lou, Data analytics, innovation, and firm productivity, 66(5) *Management Science* 2017 (2020)

§ 4 EU AND GERMAN DATA STRATEGIES – ASPIRATION AND REALITY

Content

A. Introduction

1 This paper is the written version of the presentation given by the authors* at the conference 'Global Data Law I: Global Data Strategies' in Passau, Germany, on September 20, 2021. It gives an overview over relevant political initiatives and developments in the field of data policy on EU level and in Germany. The paper deals primarily with the 2020 EU Data Strategy and the 2021 German Data Strategy.

2 Data policy is, of course, a moving target and after our initial thoughts in September 2021, the EU has finished negotiations on the Data Governance Act, the Digital Services Act and the Digital Markets Act. And the European Commission has presented its proposal for the Data Act. Germany has since then received a new federal government, which has – with the coalition treaty – laid a foundation for their work in the next four years.

3 The authors both work for the German government and are insofar also responsible for data policy, but views presented here are entirely their own.

B. What is a (Political) Strategy?

4 The term 'strategy' is used differently in different contexts. It is used in particular in management theory, war language, chess and game theory. By strategy, therefore, one may understand

- the art and science of developing and deploying all the forces in such a way as to ensure the most profitable long-term survival possible,
- a defined plan with a precise procedure for the rapid and favourable achievement of a set goal, or
- a pragmatic, constantly changing, dynamic entity that must live and be lived and change as conditions change.

5 A political strategy of the executive, however, should rather modestly be understood as a longer term plan. It usually is a conglomeration of political objectives, as well as planned or existing policy measures and initiatives. Strategies may be updated and further developed and include – to say the least – a lot of political-executive prose.

6 Does a strategy have to be explicit? No, it does not. A political strategy may also include a hidden agenda. Does it have to be coherent? No, especially in political contexts it usually is the result of constant negotiations and compromises between many different actors and may include political package deals.

7 The ambition of the 2020 and 2021 EU and German data strategies is to provide a coherent, overarching framework. However, those strategies did not start with a blank sheet of paper. On the contrary, they had to encompass what was already there and build on the existing legal regime.

* Dr. Winfried Veil, Federal Ministry of the Interior, Building and Community, took part in negotiating the General Data Protection Regulation (EU) (GDPR). Franziska Weindauer, German Federal Chancellery, took part in writing the German Data Strategy.

C. EU Data Strategy

After the European Parliamentary elections in May 2019 the then new European Commission – led by President Ursula von der Leyen – was only sworn in on 13 January 2020. The EU Commission published their Working Programme on 29 January 2020. The EU Data Strategy was published only 3 weeks later, on 19 February 2020. It seems therefore that the data strategy was drafted in quite a hurry. With just 34 pages it is rather short. The public was invited to a public consultation (lasting until 31 May 2020) only after the strategy was published. A White Paper on Artificial Intelligence was published on the same day. 8

Politically, among the most discussed topics in the drafting process was how much to commit to a free flow of data worldwide and how much to follow the path of strengthening digital sovereignty, which Ursula von der Leyen had started to propagate (potentially including data localisation requirements). 9

I. Problems Addressed by the EU Data Strategy

The following problems for the EU data ecosystem were identified by the EU Commission: 10

- Availability of data: Especially more public sector data should be made available. B2B data sharing was – according to the strategy – not working properly. The reasons given were, among others, a lack of economic incentives, a lack of trust and a lack of legal certainty.
- Imbalances of market power, especially with regard to the so-called GAFA.
- Data standardisation, interoperability and data quality, which the EU Commission describes as insufficient.
- The European data infrastructure, which the EU Commission describes as not sufficient and not powerful enough.
- Data portability is described by the EU Commission as too difficult for individuals to use.
- The EU Commission complains about a skills shortage, a shortage in data experts and low data literacy.

II. Vision of the EU Data Strategy

The EU Commission aims at a single market for data. The potential of data shall be unlocked by its use and re-use. 11

To reach this aim the EU Commission unfolds a colourful bouquet of promises. It proposes: better access to data, responsible usage of data, high data quality, more data being stored and processed in the EU, investments in standards, investments in tools, investments in technologies, investments in competences (to improve data literacy), investments in infrastructure, improvements in data flows across borders within the EU, improvements in data flows across sectors (by horizontal regulation), respect for values, efficient enforcement (in the fields of data protection, consumer protection and competition law), fair, practical and clear rules, trustworthy data governance mechan- 12 isms, EU data pools to enable big data analytics and machine learning, cross-sectoral actions and sectoral data spaces. It's hard not to call this a buzzword bingo.

13 However, the EU Commission means business when it says it wants to release Europe's potential by finding a European way in balancing the flow and wide usage of data with at the same time preserving high privacy, security, safety and ethical standards.

III. Key Content of the EU Data Strategy

14 Therefore, the European Data Strategy is based on four pillars:
- Pillar 1: Governance
- Pillar 2: Enablers
- Pillar 3: Competences
- Pillar 4: Data Spaces

1. Pillar 1: Governance

15 In the first pillar, the EU Commission proposes a cross-sectoral governance framework for data access and use. The term 'governance' is used 23 times in the strategy. However, it is not completely clear what is meant by 'governance'. The meaning in the strategy seems to be regulation by law and regulation by sub-legislative measures (like standardisation, codes of conduct or certification). Data governance would then mean the legal framework that forms the basis for dealing with and managing data for all internal and external stakeholders of an organisation or the data economy on the whole.

16 The most important measures mentioned in this context are a Data Governance Act, a Data Act and an Implementing Act on high-value data sets. The proposed data governance shall include publicly-held data bases, data altruism, compulsory data access ('only where specific circumstances so dictate'), an Open Data Portal ('as open as possible, as closed as necessary'), interoperability and standardisation activites (below legislative level), the implementation of FAIR principles (findability, accessibility, interoperability, reusablitiy) and incentives for horizontal data sharing across sectors (B2G, B2B, adaptation of the Database Directive).

2. Pillar 2: Enablers

17 In the second pillar, the EU Commission announces investments and funding programmes, among others € 4–6 billion for a High Impact Project on European data spaces and federated cloud infrastructures. One goal is to support data-driven innovation, i.e. start-ups, scale-ups and disruptive new business models. The EU Commission expects to be able to stimulate the demand for products and services that rely on data as a factor of production. Memoranda of Understanding on a cloud federation with the Member States are announced. A cloud services marketplace is to be launched. And an EU (self-)regulatory cloud rulebook is to be created. Standard setting, tool development and best practices collection (e.g. on pseudonymisation) are further aspects mentioned.

18 Of course, things have moved on since the EU Commission announced its strategy. The EU Commission has e.g. since then set up the European Alliance for Industrial Data, Edge and Cloud (consisting of public and private actors), which is among others going to work on a cloud rulebook.

3. Pillar 3: Competences

The aim of the third pillar is to empower individuals with regard to handling their own data and to invest in digital skills and data literacy. 19

One of the key measures is to update the Digital Education Action Plan. The strategy assumes a current gap of one million digital specialists. The aim is for this gap to be halved in 2025. A dedicated capacity building scheme for SMEs is also mentioned. 20

Another important policy measure is to enhance the right to data portability for individuals. Data portability is enshrined in Art. 20 GDPR and gives the data subject the right to receive personal data from the controller and transmit them to another controller. For that to work, the data set has to be transmitted in a commonly used and machine-readable format. 21

The EU Commission admits that this instrument is not yet working as planned. According to the EU Commission, data subjects should be given more control over who can access and use machine-generated data, especially concerning those data the individuals themselves co-generate. The strategy also talks about 'personal data spaces' to re-balance power between providers and individuals. To get this going, stricter requirements on interfaces for real-time data access would be necessary. Machine-readable formats would have to be compulsory (e.g. for smart home apps and wearables). Providers of personal data spaces (so-called intermediaries as e.g. MyData and Digi.me) could function as neutral brokers. 22

4. Pillar 4: Data Spaces

In the fourth pillar the EU Commission identifies nine crucial economic sectors and domains of public interest where the use of data would have a systemic impact on the entire ecosystem, but also on citizens. The aim is to stipulate the use of data and the demand for services enriched with data. Those nine common European data spaces are: 23

a) Industrial Data Space

The Industrial Data Space[1] concerns manufacturing which is assumed to primarily comprise non-personal data. According to the EU Commission, data sharing in industries has the potential to power strong growth, help companies optimise existing processes, develop new products, and create new businesses. Accordingly, the update of the 2020 New Industrial Strategy explains that an industrial (manufacturing) data space will lead to more flexible and resilient supply chains. 24

b) Green Deal Data Space

The Green Deal Data Space[2] is to provide more accessible and exploitable environmental observation data in support of the European Green Deal priority actions on climate change, circular economy, zero pollution, biodiversity, deforestation and compliance assurance. 25

This involves the launch of a 'GreenData4All' initiative consisting of evaluating and possibly reviewing the Directive establishing an Infrastructure for Spatial Information in the EU (INSPIRE Directive 2007/2/EC), together with the Access to Environmental 26

[1] SWD(2022) 45 final, p. 12–13.
[2] SWD(2022) 45 final, p. 14–17.

Information Directive (Directive 2003/4/EC). The initiative would aim to modernise both directives to align them with the contemporary state of technology; promote active dissemination and sharing of government- and private-held public data in support of the environmental acquis and the European Green Deal objectives; and define and implement interoperable building stones for sharing public data in the Green Deal data space. In its work programme for 2022, adopted on 19 October 2021, the EU Commission announced that it would put forward, under the European Green Deal, a revision of both directives, following their evaluation in 2021.

27 It also involves the Destination Earth (DestinE) initiative and its development of digital earth twins. DestinE aims to develop – on a global scale – a highly accurate digital model of the earth to monitor and predict the interaction between natural phenomena and human activities.

c) Mobility Data Space

28 The overall goal of the Mobility Data Space[3] is – according to the EU Commission – to accelerate the digital transformation of the EU transport sector and to fully reap the benefits of data for the sector and for society at large. As stated in the Smart and Sustainable Mobility Strategy, digitisation and enhanced use of data in all modes of transport (passenger and freight) are said to be essential enablers for the transformation to a safer, more efficient, accessible and sustainable mobility. The mobility data space would facilitate access, pooling and sharing of data from existing and future transport and mobility databases.

d) Health Data Space

29 Setting up a Health Data Space[4] will be part of building an European health union, a process launched by the EU Commission on 11 November 2020 with a first set of proposals to reinforce preparedness and response during health crises. According to the EU Commission, the European health data space will promote safe exchange of patients' data (including when they travel abroad) and citizens' control over their health data; support research on treatments, medicines, medical devices and outcomes; encourage the access to and use of health data for research, policy-making and regulation, with a trusted governance framework and upholding data-protection rules; support digital health services; and clarify the safety and liability of artificial intelligence in health. A proposal (Regulation) to set up a Health Data Space (EHDS) has been put forward by the EU Commission on 3 May 2022.

e) Financial Data Space

30 The Financial Data Space[5] will have the task to develop innovation, market transparency, sustainable finance, access to finance data.

31 The Digital Finance Strategy[6] announced the creation of a European financial data space. Data is described as the core of financial services. Financial data are publicly and privately held personal and non-personal data. This includes publicly disclosed company information and business registry data, as well as data reported by financial institutions to supervisory authorities. Financial data also relates to data about individual savings, mortgages, consumer credit, investments, pensions and insurance. Furthermore, innova-

[3] SWD(2022) 45 final, p. 17–20.
[4] SWD(2022) 45 final, p. 20–23.
[5] SWD(2022) 45 final, p. 23–24.
[6] COM/2020/591 final.

tion in finance also increasingly relies on non-financial data. Therefore, to ensure interoperability, the European financial data space is to be developed in close connection with data spaces in other sectors.

The European financial data space includes three main components: First, digital access to publicly disclosed financial and sustainability related information. Second, easier reporting and sharing of supervisory data among EU and national supervisory authorities. Third, business-to-business and business-to-consumer data sharing and reuse in the EU financial sector (open finance). 32

f) Energy Data Space

The aim of the Energy Data Space[7] is to benefit the green and digital transitions. It shall help to further integrate renewables as a source of energy production, increase the energy system efficiency, and ensure a smooth and competitive transition towards the electrification of sectors such as heating and transport. 33

Steps to creating a common European energy data space are: Firstly, energy-sector legislation and cross-sectoral data space building blocks, such as those provided by the Data Governance Act. Secondly, various national and EU-wide initiatives, including EU Research and Innovation projects, explore the potential of data sharing among companies and develop new use-cases for the benefit of the energy transition. Thirdly, a data sharing infrastructure in the form of a set of agreements, protocols and a governance system that defines who shall or can share data, under what conditions and in what format, is announced. 34

g) Agriculture Data Space

The Agriculture Data Space[8] should facilitate trustworthy pooling and sharing of agricultural data between private stakeholders (e.g. farmers, machinery companies, data service providers), as well as with public authorities. Tailored use of data and data analytics in the field of agriculture should contribute to increased competitiveness and the sustainability performance of the sector, e.g. through increasing the effectiveness of precision farming applications, and thus to the ambitions laid out in the Common Agricultural Policy and the Farm-to-Fork-Strategy. Several actions are already in place for improving the discoverability of and accessibility to interoperable European agricultural data by re-using the European Spatial Data Infrastructure (INSPIRE Directive). 35

h) Data Spaces for Public Administration

Data spaces for public administration[9] contain transparency and accountability of public spending and spending quality, corruption, law enforcement needs, effective application of EU law, and innovative 'gov tech'. The data spaces for public administration include: 36

- the Public Administrations Legal Data Space,
- the Public Procurement Data Space (PPDS), and
- the Public administrations security data space for innovation.

The Public Administration Legal Data Space aims at providing easily accessible, reusable, interoperable data in the area of legislation and case-law across the EU. These 37

[7] SWD(2022) 45 final, p. 24–26.
[8] SWD(2022) 45 final, p. 26–28.
[9] SWD(2022) 45 final, p. 28–32.

data should then be used in decision-making, research and the development of innovative legal tools. The legal data space will support legal practitioners, public administrations and society in general as well as further uphold justice and the rule of law. The Publications Office of the European Union (OP) will have to consolidate a number of initiatives to lay the foundations of the legal data space.

38 Public procurement data is said to be essential to improve transparency and accountability of public spending, fighting corruption and improving spending quality.

39 The governance of the European security data space is announced to follow a hybrid model, namely a federation of national and local data spaces with central services at European level.

i) Skills Data Space

40 The Skills Data Space[10] aims at sharing and accessing skills data for various purposes, from analytical and statistical purposes to policy development or reuse in innovative applications, as well as at providing easy, cross-border access to key datasets. The European skills data space will – according to the Commission – also aim to reduce the skills mismatches between education and training systems on the one hand and labour market needs on the other. Besides improving skills intelligence, this data space should deliver services to its users, with recommendations of learning opportunities to support their upskilling efforts, tailored to the information on their skills profiles.

41 High-quality data on qualifications, learning opportunities, jobs and skills should – according to the EU Commission – feed the creation of this data space. Several Commission's initiatives, such as reference frameworks for qualifications and for digital skills and competence, the European skills classification (ESCO) and the Europass e-portfolio, increase transparency of information on people's skills, qualifications, and learning opportunities and deliver on the European Skills Agenda.

j) European Open Science Cloud

42 The European Open Science Cloud (EOSC) shall bring together institutional, national and European stakeholders to develop an inclusive research data and services ecosystem in Europe. As requested by the Council, the EOSC is already being implemented since 2018 as a trusted open data environment to allow reliable reuse of research data to European researchers, innovators, companies, and citizens.

k) Significance of Data Spaces

43 By promoting these data spaces, the EU Commission implicitly suggests that a 'one-size fits all' approach does not work in the data policy sphere. Although a horizontal legal regime will prevail (e.g. 'full respect' of the GDPR is emphasised) and build the legal basis for data access and use, sector-specific initiatives shall respond to the peculiarities of the different sectors. These sectorial measures could be additional legislative or investment initiatives. Large data pools with varying degrees of accessibility, technical tools, standards, mechanisms for ensuring interoperability and decentralised infrastructures are announced by the EU Commission. The degree of public interest is said to be diverse (higher: health; lower: manufacturing).

---

[10] SWD(2022) 45 final, p. 32–33.

A Commission Staff Working Document on Common European Data Spaces has been published on 23 February 2022.[11] In this, the EU Commission states the key features of a Data Space[12]: 44

- A secure and privacy-preserving infrastructure to pool, access, share, process and use data.
- A clear and practical structure for access to and use of data in a fair, transparent, proportionate and non-discriminatory manner and clear and trustworthy data governance mechanisms.
- European rules and values, in particular personal data protection, consumer protection legislation and competition law, are fully respected.
- Data holders will have the possibility, in the data space, to grant access to or to share certain personal or non-personal data under their control.
- Data that is made available against compensation, including remuneration, or for free.
- Participation of an open number of organisations/individuals.

While the 2020 EU Data Strategy had a non-exhaustive list of ten data spaces, the 45
2022 Staff Working Document adds two more data spaces: a data space for media and a data space for cultural heritage.

D. German Data Strategy

This section contains a brief rundown of the main elements of the German Data 46
Strategy, as well as the landscape of and political structures surrounding data policy in Germany.

I. German Data Policy Environment

Germany's data policy landscape is shaped on the one hand by laws that have been 47
passed on EU level and were henceforth implemented or immediately applicable in Germany. On the other hand, Germany has gone beyond that in some areas and created its own laws of relevance for the sphere of data policy, e.g. in the fields of data protection (esp. also on state level), open data, combating hate crime and criminally punishable fake news online, as well as competition law.

The political responsibilities for data policy are very much spread across different 48
governance levels and different actors on each level. On federal and state government level, several ministries each are responsible for general and sectoral aspects of data policy. When it comes to the supervisory authorities for data protection for example, there is at least one data protection authority in every state (17 in total), responsible for overseeing compliance with data protection laws in its state, as well as one federal data protection authority. This has not led to a particularly stringent line on data policy and enforcement of data laws.

Several advisory committee reports touching upon the issue of data policy preceded 49
the drafting process of the German data strategy, such as a report on competition law 4.0, a study on mobility data, a report on data ethics, as well as a report of an AI inquiry committee set up by the German Bundestag. Therefore, the drafting process of the German data strategy was quite firmly set in a multitude of different previous initiatives

[11] SWD(2022) 45 final.
[12] SWD(2022) 45 final, p. 2–3.

and laws. However, it was felt that Germany was not handling the digital transformation with regards to harnessing value from data for the good of the society and economy well enough and that not enough data were being used and shared. Therefore, the time for the government seemed right, encouraged also by the digital council advising the government on matters of digital policy, to come forward with the first comprehensive strategy on data policy in Germany.

II. German Data Strategy Process

50 The German Federal Chancellery took over responsibility for the drafting process and first cornerstones of the data strategy were published in November 2019. An expert hearing took place in January 2020, as well as a broad and open public consultation (online) for all interested citizens and stakeholders between February and April 2020. Over 1200 participants (half stemming from organisations, the other half participated in a private capacity) took part in the consultation process, the results of which fed into the drafting process.

51 The drafting process included intensive consultation and participation of all federal ministries, especially the Ministry of Economics, the Ministry of Research and Education, as well as the Ministry of the Interior. The strategy was published in January 2021 after having been endorsed by the federal cabinet.

III. Key Content of the German Data Strategy

52 The German Data Strategy is comprised of four chapters with around 230 policy measures being proposed in total. It is, compared to other data strategies around the globe, very broad in scope and in that similar to the EU's data strategy. It covers all aspects of data policy, ranging from infrastructure to skills, from governance framework for the use of data to the role of the federal government itself as a data user.

53 While one of the strategy's achievements was to put the topic of data policy firmly on the map of all federal ministries and to get an overview of what each and every player in government was doing in the field of data policy, the strategy in its annex provides an index of all data policy measures currently planned or employed by the federal government.

54 The strategy also pushed for a range of entirely new policy measures for which significant funds were provided. The government itself, when announcing the strategy stated that it wanted to induce a paradigm shift towards more extensive usage of data for the benefit of the economy, society, research, and government.

1. Pillar 1: Data Infrastructure

55 The goal of the first chapter of the data strategy is to strengthen and build a powerful and secure data infrastructure, as well as to influence and encourage (international) standard-setting in the field of data – both as a prerequisite for new generation data processing. The government concluded that the data infrastructure landscape in Germany was too fragmented and that measures should be taken to join forces and bring together existing initiatives. One of the key measures proposed was therefore to interlink the two projects GAIA-X (project to develop a federated and secure European data infrastructure) and NFDI (national research data infrastructure). Furthermore, the chapter includes initiatives in the field of High Performance and Quantum Computing as two parts in the data infrastructure puzzle, in which Germany wants to be successful.

2. Pillar 2: Use of Data

The second chapter addresses the governance framework for a functioning data ecosystem and the roles and functioning of a diverse set of players within the ecosystem. One of the key shortcomings of the governance frameworks in Germany according to the stakeholder consultation is lacking legal certainty when it comes to handling data, especially personal data. Therefore, proposed policy measures aim at increasing legal certainty by among others improving collaboration of supervisory authorities enforcing data protection laws. Other measures in this realm aim at strengthening research into data anonymization. When it comes to available players in the ecosystem, the German government concluded that trusted intermediaries could play a very valuable role to increase data sharing and therefore set up programmes to establish and pilot different forms of data intermediaries. Furthermore, different policy measures to set up sectoral data spaces in close cooperation with the EU level were included in the strategy. **56**

3. Pillar 3: Data Skills

The third chapter addresses the field of individual and collective skills of confidently handling data, strengthen data skills through including suitable programmes in school and university education, as well as vocational training, industry and civil society. It was concluded that Germany needs more skilled 'data workers' in all parts of society and economy to be able to set up an internationally competitive data ecosystem. Policy measures include studies on assessing the level of data literacy in society, strengthening data skills in all parts of the educational system (e.g. through dedicated PhD programmes) and establish data exchange structures for civil society. **57**

4. Pillar 4: Government as Trailblazer

The fourth chapter of the German Data Strategy recognizes the important role the government itself plays in the effort of creating a functioning and internationally competitive data ecosystem in the country. The goal of the strategy therefore is to establish the federal government as a pioneer of a new data culture. The government wants to actively work more with data, learn from data and make its decisions more evidence-based and transparent. Therefore, a new governance framework for open data was announced, the hiring of a chief data scientist, as well as the set-up of a data lab in each federal ministry, the establishment of more research data centers across the government and the establishment of an inter-ministerial working group on data policy. **58**

E. Aspiration and Reality: A Collection of Observations

In the following chapter, we assess whether from our point of view the strategies until now keep what they promise by looking at four specific examples. We add some observations about specifics and general characteristics of the EU's and Germany's data policy from a birds-eye-view. **59**

I. Lack of Strategy Did not Mean Lack of Legislation

60 First of all, it has to be acknowledged that the 2020 and 2021 data strategies do not start on a blank sheet of paper. On the contrary, both the EU and Germany have been very active in the area of data-related legislation over the past decades – before data strategies were formulated. In former times it just was not called 'data policy'.

61 In chronological order, the EU adopted the following legal acts, all of which are to a certain extent data-related:

- Data Protection Directive (1995)
- Data Bases Directive (1996)
- eCommerce Directive (2000)
- ePrivacy Directive (2002)
- PSI Directive (2003)
- Cookie Directive (2009)
- Review PSI Directive (2013)
- eIDAS Regulation (2014)
- General Data Protection Regulation and Directive (2016)
- NIS Directive (2016)
- Free Flow of Data Regulation (2018)
- Cybersecurity Act (2019)
- Digital Content Directive (2019)
- Open Data and PSI Directive (2019)
- P2B Regulation (2019)

62 These legal acts were accompanied by communications, strategies and white papers of the EU Commission:

- Comprehensive data protection approach (2010)
- Cybersecurity Strategy (2013)
- Towards a thriving data-driven economy (2014)
- Building a European Data Economy (2017)
- European Interoperability Framework (2017)
- Stronger protection, new opportunities (2018)
- Towards a common European data space (2018)
- Guidance on free flow of non-personal data (2019)
- Data protection rules as a trust-enabler (2019)
- White Paper on Artificial Intelligence (2020)
- A European strategy for data (2020)
- Data protection as a pillar (2020)
- Cyberstrategy for the Digital Decade (2020)
- The European way for the Digital Decade (2021)

63 When putting these initiatives in a rough timeline, you come to the following conclusions:

- Data protection since 1995: Data protection legislation in the EU exists since 1995 and got a well-known update in 2016.
- E-commerce since 2000: Legislation concerning buying or selling of products on online services and concerning platform activities on the Internet started 2000.
- E-privacy since 2002: The confidentiality of communications (secrecy of telecommunications), the processing of communications data and the storage and reading of information on terminal equipment (e.g. cookies) have been regulated since 2002.

- Data economy since 2014: Considering the EU as a data economy started with the use of the corresponding wording in 2014.
- Free Flow of Data since 2017: Lots of talk about (and respective legislation with regard to) the free flow of data started roughly in 2017.
- Data Space(s) since 2018: The idea of the EU as a large data space and the ideas of sectoral data spaces within the EU have been promoted by the EU since 2018.

In Germany since the 1970s and especially since the famous 1983 'Volkszählungsur- **64**
teil' (census ruling) data protection legislation took place on national, regional and local level. For a long time, Germany had a Federal Data Protection Act and Data Protection Acts on *Länder* level. Every law that regulates the actions of administrative authorities in Germany contains sector-specific data protection laws, which means that there are thousands of laws in Germany that contain data protection standards. A widening understanding of data use issues, not solely limited to the protection of personal data, has only come to play in recent years.

II. Recent Paradigm Shifts

A holistic view of data as a cross-sectional issue probably began with the career of the **65**
term 'data economy' approximately 2014/15. What you may observe since then are paradigm shifts. After the Snowden revelations, the emphasis in public debate was on data protection (although the data protection reform did not regulate intelligence activities). For a while, the idea of free flow of data was dominant (especially during the Estonian Presidency during which free flow (or movement) of data was promoted as 5th freedom besides freedom of persons, goods, services and capital. Meanwhile, the optimism regarding a worldwide free flow of data has given way on the one hand, to the idea of sectoral data spaces, which are in some cases sealed off. And on the other hand, increasing notions of data localisation requirements put in place for some kinds of data or data in general, closing off national information infrastructures.

In Germany, the data protection discourse has always been dominant. The fear of the **66**
'gläserne Mensch' (transparent human being), the surveillance state and the surveillance capitalism characterises the debate. In recent years, there has also been a discussion about data ownership.

Of course, the realisation that data are a valuable asset has only in recent years led to **67**
talk of a data economy and data policy – and fostered data strategies.

III. Comprehensive Legislation Announced after Publication of the Data Strategies

In the aftermath of the publication of the data strategies, comprehensive legislation **68**
has been proposed on EU level by the EU Commission (and partly is already about to be adopted) and is proposed by the new German government elected in December 2021.

The EU Commission proposed no fewer than seven legal acts, all of which contain **69**
data references or even exclusively data-related regulations. In chronological order, the EU Commission proposed:

- 25 November 2020: Data Governance Act (DGA) (enacted 30 May 2022)
- 15 December 2020: Digital Markets Act (DMA)
- 15 December 2020: Digital Services Act (DSA)

- 16 December 2020: NIS 2 Directive
- 21 April 2021: Artificial Intelligence Act (AIA)
- 3 June 2021: European Digital Identity Regulation
- 23 February 2022: Data Act
- 3 May 2022: Health Data Space Regulation

70 *Moritz Hennemann* called this a sweeping blow for regulating among others online services, the use of algorithms and algorithmic systems, market power, data access rights, and data usage rights (concerning personal and non-personal data) – hence the 'roaring 20s in digital policy'.

71 Germany obviously does not want to be left behind in the attempt at comprehensive regulation. On 21 September 2021, a new parliament was elected in Germany. Germany's data strategy was adopted only nine months before federal elections in the country. Every new government, of course, has the chance to review or change any political stance that was taken by the previous government. Therefore, it remains to be seen whether all policy measures announced in the data strategy by the previous government will be taken up by the current coalition government.

72 However, the coalition agreement contains the announcement of a lot of new legislative projects of relevance for data policy. The following laws were announced:

- *Nationales Datengesetz* (= Data Act)
- *Forschungsdatengesetz* (= Research Data Act)
- *Mobilitätsdatengesetz* (= Mobility Data Act)
- *Beschäftigtendatenschutzgesetz* (= Employment Data Protection Act)
- *Gesundheitsdatennutzungsgesetz* (= Health Data Use Act)
- *Registergesetz* (= Registry Act)
- *Bundestransparenzgesetz* (Transparency Act)

73 In addition, the coalition agreement contains the announcement that data infrastructures are to be built, the legal foundations for data trustee models and data hubs are to be laid, the EU data spaces are to be further developed, data access is to be improved, data donations are to be favoured, data standardisation is to be advanced, data licences are to be established, data quality is to be improved, databases are to be revised, data literacy is to be expanded, a data institute is to be founded, a legal right to open data is to be created and the Freedom of Information Acts are to be further developed into a uniform transparency law.

74 It is questionable whether and to what extent all these projects will still be within the framework of the old government's data strategy. The coalition agreement at least does not mention this data strategy. Until now, the government has regularly monitored the implementation progress of the data strategy, stating that in January 2022 around three-quarter of policy measures were in the process of being implemented, one-tenth already completed, while thirteen percent of all measures were still in the planning phase. However, the new government's plans were obviously not developed from the 'old' data strategy and new ideas were included, partly of course stemming from the fact that two previous opposition parties are now part of the government.

IV. Are the Promises Being Kept? – 4 Examples

75 The EU and the German Data Strategy make a lot of promises (see chapter II. and III.). It would be too early to say whether these goals can be achieved by the coming laws and policy measures, which have yet to be implemented. However, it is already possible to show examples of deficits in the comparison between aspirations and reality.

1. Example: Availability of Data

One aim of the EU Data Strategy is to increase the availability of data. One of the proposed means to reach this aim is data altruism enshrined in the Data Governance Act (DGA). Data altruism means 'the consent by data subjects to process personal data pertaining to them, or permissions of other data holders to allow the use of their non-personal data without seeking a reward, for purposes of general interest, such as scientific research purposes or improving public services' (Art. 2 (10) DGA). 76

If you want to promote data altruism, a reasonable solution would have been to make it easier for data subjects and other data holders to give away their data. You could, for example, have created an altruism exemption (which means excluding the processing of personal data for altruistic purposes from the scope of the GDPR). Altruistic controllers could have been given certain privileges over commercial controllers. Certain information, documentation and accountability obligations could have been waived in the case of processing for altruistic purposes. It could have been recognised that data processing serving the common good and data donations need more legal certainty and less prescriptive rules. 77

However, the numerous GDPR provisions concerning the processing of personal data remain untouched under the DGA. Instead, the DGA invents a rather bureaucratic 'framework for voluntary registration' of altruistic entities (Art. 1 (1) (c) DGA), which means that you have to be registered if you want to collect and process data for altruistic purposes. Thus, it becomes even more complicated to collect, store and analyse data for the common good. 78

Also, the other DGA provisions do not sound very inviting for data subjects, companies and authorities that are willing to share data. There are 'conditions for the re-use […] of data held by public sector bodies' (Art. 1 (1) (a) DGA). It must be underlined that these are additional conditions on top of the existing conditions resulting from the GDPR. And there is a 'notification and supervisory framework' for data intermediation services (Art. 1 (1) (b) DGA). This framework also extends the already numerous obligations of the GDPR. 79

It is very doubtful whether additional record-keeping obligations, an annual activity report, additional obligations to inform data subjects, as well as an upcoming rulebook, will support the availability of data. At the very least, these provisions cause a considerable compliance effort. Even if they also promote the trust of users, which obviously is the aim of most of the provisions, it is astonishing that the EU apparently no longer considers its 'gold standard' GDPR sufficient. 80

2. Example: Imbalances in Market Power

Another example of problems with the data ecosystem that the data strategy addresses is the imbalance in market power. This problem is tackled especially by the Digital Markets Act (DMA) and also by the Digital Services Act (DSA). 81

The DMA only places obligations on 'gatekeepers'. Gatekeepers are defined in Art. 3 (6) DMA. According to the Commission proposal, if you are a gatekeeper depends on inter alia 'entry barriers derived from network effects and data driven advantages, in particular in relation to the provider's access to and collection of personal and non-personal data or analytics capabilities' and on 'scale and scope effects the provider benefits from, including with regard to data'. 82

83 The idea is to tame players that create bottlenecks between businesses and consumers and have an entrenched position in digital markets. The thresholds set by the DMA are relatively high: Only those companies are gatekeepers in the sense of the DMA if they have an annual turnover of € 7.5 billion in the EU or a global market value of € 75 billion. Gatekeepers must also have at least 45 million monthly end users and 100,000 business users.

84 Finally, gatekeepers must control one or more 'core platform services', such as 'marketplaces and app stores, search engines, social networking, cloud services, advertising services, voice assistants and web browsers.' In the end, only Meta (Facebook), Apple, Alphabet (Google), Amazon, and a limited range of other companies will have to fulfil the DMA obligations.

85 Restrictions imposed on gatekeepers include limiting how data from different services may be combined, banning forced single sign-ons, and forbidding app stores from conditioning access on the use of the platform's own payment systems. Users shall be able to freely choose their browser or search engine, and force companies to make unsubscribing from their 'core platform services' as easy as subscribing was in the first place. To improve anti-monopoly enforcement, the DMA also requires gatekeepers to inform the EU Commission about their mergers and acquisitions.

86 The Digital Services Act also addresses the data market power problem. It provides specific rules for 'very large online platforms' (VLOPS) that are supposed to pose particular risks in the dissemination of illegal content and societal harms. Specific rules are foreseen for platforms reaching more than 10 % of 450 million consumers in the EU. Among them are provisions that oblige only very large platforms to provide the user with a choice not to have recommendations based on profiling and obligatory data sharing with authorities and researchers.

87 Whether the DMA and other legal acts will be able to reshape the power balances in the EU data ecosystem remains to be seen. Introducing a regulatory framework that prevents the misuse of market power and tries to come to a fairer distribution of market power can only be one side of the coin. If Europe does not manage to bring about large market players itself in the field of data driven businesses, the market power in data-driven markets will not be more equally distributed in future.

3. Example: Empowering Individuals

88 Another aim of the EU Data Strategy is to empower individuals. One of the instruments in which the EU has high hopes is to enable data portability:

- The basic portability right is enshrined in Art. 20 GDPR: It is the right of personal data.
- Another portability right is provided for in the proposal of the Digital Markets Act: It is a portability right of business users and end users against gatekeepers concerning data generated through the activity of the user. The right includes the provision of continuous and real-time access (Art. 6 (1) (h) DMA).
- The proposal of the Data Act realises that the possibilities for the portability of data generated by products connected to the Internet of Things are limited. Therefore, the Data Act intends to facilitate the portability of the user's data to third parties. According to the Explanatory Memorandum, it should 'allow for a competitive offer of aftermarket services, as well as broader data-based innovation and the development of products or services unrelated to those initially purchased or subscribed to by the user.' Open interoperability specifications and European

standards for interoperability shall enhance portability. Furthermore, easier cloud switching is tackled in one chapter of the Data Act.

4. Example: Empowering the Government

One key promise and aim of the German data strategy is to transform the government into a trailblazer for data culture. Coming from a point, where the government clearly has some catching up to do when it comes to mapping and mining, processing, and using its own or external data and to increase the level of data literacy and expertise of its employees, this seems to be a very ambitious goal. A German saying speaks of 'überholen ohne einzuholen' – overtaking without catching up. Whether the measures envisaged in the data strategies will be able to enable the government to do just that remains to be seen. 89

However, they seem to be a very good and also quite far-reaching start. The data strategy foresees and also finances the founding of data labs in and the hiring of a chief data scientist for each federal ministry. And indeed, there are a number of ministries, which have already appointed a chief data scientist. Furthermore, all ministries drafted concepts for their data labs and several have started hiring further staff and setting up the labs. The labs will likely serve a range of different purposes – from mapping, structuring and starting to make better use of one's own data, to providing analyses and data-based informational products to colleagues and leadership, to acquiring needed data sets from external actors and contributing to the increase of data literacy in organisations. 90

V. Comparison of EU and German Strategy

Though the EU and the German Data Strategy take a very broad approach to the topic of data policy and the scope of both strategies is similarly wide, there are several key differences. 91

The EU has a stronger focus on hard law and regulatory measures as seems only natural according to the intended role of competencies granted to the EU by the respective treaties. Correspondingly, there are far fewer and less impactful measures proposed for the field of data literacy. The field of transforming the EU's own administrative bodies in terms of data usage and skills is left out entirely. Overall, the strategy focuses on far fewer but larger-scale policy measures. 92

The German data strategy is far less ambitious on the regulatory side and places a strong emphasis on finding a common language and government stance on data policy. It is even broader in scope, placing a focus also on the transformation of government structures. The number of policy measures included in the strategy far outstrips the number of policy measures in the EU data strategy. The measures itself however tend to be much smaller in scale with the strategy serving as kind of an index of policy measures in the field of German federal data policy. 93

VI. Regulatory Ideas Not Included

It is interesting to also note, which regulatory ideas were not included in the strategies: 94

- Although both fundamental criticism and criticism on detailed issues of data protection laws have been formulated, the data protection laws in place have been left

entirely untouched, both on EU, as well as German level. The same (almost) goes for the way they are enforced.
- Although proposed both on EU (under Commissioner Oettinger) as well as on national level, ideas for introducing data property and data producer rights were not included in the data strategies.
- The same goes for ideas similar to the 'data-for-all-law' once suggested by the German Social Democratic Party (SPD).
- The basic idea of sharing or using 'data for public good' is also not very pronounced in the strategies.
- Both strategies do not make a considerable effort to improve legal certainty of data anonymisation and pseudonymisation, which could provide a significant lever to increase data sharing.
- Finally, both strategies do not place much emphasis on technological developments with regard to the processing of data (decentralised data processing, edge computing, etc.) or ways to be able to improve the re-usability of personal data other than anonymisation, such as creating synthetic data sets.

VII. A New Regulatory Approach?

95 A pretty obvious contrast to the 'one size fits all' approach of the GDPR is that most of the new initiatives concentrate on sector-specific provisions. On the hand, the proposed data spaces are clearly sector-specific. On the other hand, provisions that are made only for a certain group of actors (like very large online platforms, gatekeepers, data intermediaries or altruistic organisations) show that rules that apply indiscriminately to all controllers are not sufficient. Many of the new proposals, such as the DSA, DMA, AIA and DGA contain graduated duty models according to the type of activity, the size, and the importance of companies or organisations, to the risk associated with employing or providing a specific type of service, and to the concrete role of the actor.

96 The DSA provides specific rules and obligations for e.g. providers of very large online platforms and differentiates between different types of services provided (e.g. caching, hosting, mere conduits). The latter differentiation however already in principle originates from previous legislation. The DMA introduces obligations and restrictions gatekeepers have to comply with if they meet the quantitative and qualitative criteria of gatekeepers and operate a core platform service. The AIA classifies algorithmic systems and applications into different risk categories, ranging from providing an unacceptable risk to a very low or minimal risk. The DGA provides rules and obligations for data intermediaries and data altruistic organisations, addressing two very specific types of data intermediary actors according to their field of operation.

VIII. Relationship to the GDPR

97 Another observation is that all legal acts within the scope of the EU Data Strategy claim that the GDPR remains untouched:
- The Free Flow of Data Directive says that it does not affect and shall not prejudice the GDPR.
- The Open Data and Public Sector Information Directive says that it does not affect the GDPR and is without prejudice to the GDPR, that data processing is permissible

only if it meets the principles of the GDPR and that it has to be performed in accordance with the GDPR.
- The proposal of the Data Governance Act says that it is without prejudice to the GDPR and that data processing has to be in accordance with the GDPR and to rely on grounds provided in the GDPR.
- The proposal of the Digital Services Act says that it is without prejudice to the GDPR, that the protection of individuals is solely governed by the GDPR and that data processing has to be in compliance with the GDPR and within the limits laid down by the GDPR.
- The proposal of the Digital Markets Acts says that it is without prejudice to the GDPR, that it is in full respect of the GDPR and in line with the GDPR, that data may be processed to the extent allowed under the GDPR, that data processing is subject to compliance with and has to be in compliance with the GDPR.
- The proposal of the Artificial Intelligence Act says that it is without prejudice to and complements the GDPR, that it is in line with the GDPR and that it continues to comply with all requirements resulting from the GDPR.
- Finally, the proposal of the Data Act says that the GDPR shall apply to personal data processed in connection with the rights and obligations laid down in the Data Act, that it shall not affect the applicability of the GDPR and that the Data Act shall complement the right of data portability under Art. 20 of the GDPR.

The prayerful repetition of the phrase 'without prejudice' suggests that the GDPR is **98** practically invincible. However, this should not obscure the fact that this wording does not resolve any conflict of norms that arises when the legal act in question meets a substantive provision within the scope of application of the GDPR. And this is presumably precisely the case with numerous provisions of the aforementioned legal acts, because they contain provisions on processing personal data, for example on
- data localisation (FFD),
- the re-use of data (OD-PSI and DGA),
- data trusts and data altruism (DGA),
- data power and data portability (DMA),
- profiling and advertising (DSA),
- data collection and data management (AIA), and
- B2B, B2C and B2G data sharing (DA).

And, indeed, provisions for purpose limitation, erasure of personal data and provi- **99** ders of data sharing services simply cannot be 'without prejudice' to the GDPR because they are provisions in the heart of data protection law.

F. Conclusion

The EU Data Strategy and the German Data Strategy are both set in a complex and **100** vast landscape of pre-existing legislation and initiatives. These also had pursued strategic goals. However, there had not been an explicit strategy in which these goals were embedded. The data reference had not been seen as a cross-cutting commonality of regulations and measures in earlier times. And the legal regime created by former laws and other measures had not been called data governance.

Generally, both strategies announce in very lyrical and flowery words 'what a wonder- **101** ful world' will and can be created if all foreseen policy measures are implemented.

However, there remains considerable doubt as to whether the policy measures envisaged are indeed well suited to solve the problems explicitly addressed by the strategies.

102 Of course, reality is far more complex and the foreseen measures cannot and will not solve many of the problems currently apparent in the German and European data ecosystems. Some corresponding doubts and examples have been addressed by this paper.

103 The strategies are in many ways too contradictory and hardly make conflicts of goals clear. They give the impression that conflicting goals, which are actually mutually exclusive, can be achieved. The strategies do not have the courage to admit that sometimes one goal (e.g. an individual right) has to be restricted in favour of another goal (e.g. a public interest). Therefore, the strategies hardly make a preliminary decision with regard to the trade-offs that then become necessary later.

104 Unrelated from individual issues addressed by the policy measures, it remains to be seen whether also the more far-reaching and overarching goals of the strategies, i.e. to create a globally competitive European data ecosystem, can be achieved.

105 Nevertheless, both strategies are neither failed attempts nor unnecessary. They are trendsetters by propagating new paradigms such as data access or data spaces. Putting Germany and the EU on the global map with regards to data policy, formulating a shared goal as a government, alerting all stakeholders with regard to the ambition and direction of each governments data policy are other apparent achievements. However, we believe that policy makers in the EU and Germany urgently need to honestly assess whether their policy efforts are having the intended effects or whether some of them are not even achieving the opposite of what is desired. In our opinion, the strategies contain some blind spots in this regard.

106 At the moment, it looks like the EU will become world champion in regulating digital technologies, but not in their application.

Bibliography

107 European Commission, Commission Staff Working Document on Common European Data Spaces (EU), 23 February 2022, SWD(2022) 45 final, available at https://digital-strategy.ec.europa.eu/en/library/staff-working-document-data-spaces (last accessed 15 December 2022)

European Commission, Communication from the Commission to the European Parliament, the Council, the European Economic and Social Committee and the Committee of the Regions on a Digital Finance Strategy for the EU, 24 September 2020, COM/2020/591 final, available at https://eur-lex.europa.eu/legal-content/EN/TXT/PDF/?uri=CELEX:52020DC0591&from=EN (last accessed 15 December 2022)

§ 5 US DATA STRATEGY

Content

A. Introduction

There is no single 'US Data Strategy'. Strategy stands for 'a careful plan or method for achieving a particular goal usually over a long period of time'.[1] There is neither a careful plan nor is there a particular goal pertaining to data governance. Trying to identify such would amount to a futile endeavor. There are too many stakeholders with competing and, at times, incompatible visions for the digital society. This healthy pluralism of competing ideas or dragging lack of coordination – depending on the perspective – should not come as a surprise. Despite the largely national or global nature of questions to be addressed, policy responses remain divided along several lines. 1

The first divider separates the federal government and the states. The second line runs between different sectors of the economy, some of which have been regulated while others have largely evaded regulatory oversight. The third impediment to a unified strategy stems from the involvement of countless institutions taking different perspectives on the digital economy and society. In this chapter, I will thus focus on discrete elements and initiatives that have the potential to shape policy for the digital society in the years to come, instead of trying to detect traces of a data strategy that do not exist. Before diving into the details of these discrete elements, let us consider the Federal Data Strategy.[2] After all, the label comes close to providing what I claim does not exist. 2

B. Federal Data Strategy

The Federal Data Strategy 'encompasses a 10-year vision for how the Federal Government will accelerate the use of data to deliver on mission, serve the public, and 3

[1] Merriam-Webster, strategy.
[2] Federal Data Strategy, https://strategy.data.gov/ (last accessed 16 December 2022).

steward resources while protecting security, privacy, and confidentiality'.[3] It only covers the usage of data by the federal government, including its agencies, as a basis for evidence-based governance. The Federal Data Strategy Framework includes ten principles on 'Ethical Governance', 'Conscious Design', and 'Learning Culture' and forty practices guiding the practical implementation of the principles.[4] The Federal Data Strategy aims to 'fully leverage the value of federal data for mission, service, and the public good by guiding the Federal Government in practicing ethical governance, conscious design, and a learning culture'.[5] As part of the Federal Data Strategy the federal government develops an annual action plan, detailing the action taken by its agencies in furtherance of the Strategy's mission.[6] Despite its relevance within the federal bureaucracy, the Federal Data Strategy does not address regulatory questions or guide policy making. And it certainly does not provide the type of careful plan for a particular regulatory goal pertaining to data in general that this chapter set out to explore. After all the entire private sector and State-level public institutions remain unaddressed.

C. US Data Policies

4 In the following sections, I will focus on three main areas of policy and policy making. First, let us turn to the field of privacy and data protection.[7] Second, consider the impact of investments as a regulatory tool and specifically investments in broadband infrastructure.[8] Third and finally, I will lay out some of the approaches for a new industrial policy, which has primarily evolved in response to concerns about concentration in the platform economy.[9]

I. Privacy

5 Let us start with privacy and data protection. To provide some general background information, the United States has yet to implement a universal federal privacy or data protection framework. An equivalent to the EU's General Data Protection Regulation does not exist. Instead, federal privacy and data protection regulation only covers specific sectors.[10]

---

[3] *Ibid.*

[4] President's Management Agenda, FDS Framework, Mission, Principles, Practices, and Actions.

[5] Federal Data Strategy, https://strategy.data.gov/ (last accessed 16 December 2022).

[6] *Cf* Federal Data Strategy 2021 Action Plan.

[7] *Cf* Kelly, *Verge* (20 May 2021).

[8] *Cf* White House, President Biden's Bipartisan Infrastructure Law.

[9] For concerns about concentration in the (digital) economy see Council of Economic Advisers, *Benefits of Competition and Indicators of Market Power* 4–7 (May 2016); Cohen, *Between Truth And Power: The Legal Constructions Of Informational Capitalism*, 2019, pp. 16, 207; Philippon, *The Great Reversal: How America Gave Up on Free Markets*, 2019; Autor et al., *The Quarterly Journal of Economics* 2020, 645 (183); *ibid.* at 663–65; Bamberger/Lobel, *Berkeley Tech. L.J.*, 2017, 1051 (1067–71); Furman/Orszag in: Martin Guzman (ed.), *Toward a Just Society: Joseph Stiglitz and Twenty-First Century Economics*, 2018, 19, 33–38 ; Gutiérrez/Philippon, *NBER Working Paper* (July 2017); Khan, *Colum. L. Rev.*, 2019, 973; Jarsulic,*The Antitrust Bulletin*, 2019, 514; Kurz, *On the Formation of Capital and Wealth: IT, Monopoly Power and Rising Inequality*, No. ID 3014361 (June 2017) (linking technological progress, market power, and inequality); Hovenkamp/Scott Morton, *University of Pennsylvania Law Review*, 2021, 1843 (1852–53).

[10] Grimmelmann, *Internet Law: Cases and Problems*, 11th ed., 2021, p. 321.

6 For the health care sector, for example, there is the Health Insurance Portability and Accountability Act (HIPPA). This framework was originally passed in 1996, signed into law by President Bill Clinton, and implemented by the George W. Bush Administration.[11] It consists of several elements.[12] Some provisions address aspects of access, portability, and renewability, others the safeguarding of data and the protection of patient rights. One of the main motivating factors in passing HIPPA was to create a competitive market for health data and to open up the previously closed enterprise systems. Over time, Congress passed reforms to the framework; interoperability requirements were added.

7 Beyond that, there are the Family Educational Rights and Privacy Act (FERPA) and the Protection of Pupil Rights Amendment (PPRA), for example. Both leverage conditions on federal funding[13] to establish minimum protections for educational data and student's privacy rights. Across these various sectors, US privacy protection takes a highly individualized approach.[14]

1. Privacy – Federal Initiatives

8 In the wake of several major data scandals over the past five years,[15] initiatives for federal privacy legislation to protect citizens online have gained steam. After decades of debate, a federal privacy framework finally 'seemed possible' in 2021.[16] In the first eight months of the 117th Congress alone, 24 unique privacy bills have been introduced in the House and Senate.[17] Their focus varies and reaches from public health, emergency measures geared to countering the pandemic, to the opposite, namely prohibitions of vaccine passports.

9 Some of these initiatives have received more buy-in than others. Establishing fiduciary duties for data processors, as Jack Balkin suggests,[18] has found several supporters, for example.[19] Other proposals almost amount to legislative trolling, when sold as data privacy protection and stand little chance proceeding. In that category fall the House and Senate versions of a bill for a Protecting Investors' Personally Identifiable Information Act.[20] These bills would 'prohibit the Securities and Exchange Commission from requiring that personally identifiable information be collected under consolidated audit trail reporting requirements, and for other purposes'.[21] Finally, a few bills are very narrowly tailored around specific issues such as health data, the protection of children, cybersecurity, or data in relation to transportation and travel.

10 In the second half of 2021, the prospects of comprehensive federal privacy regulation dramatically changed. With the legislative agenda of the President in peril, Congressional attention focused entirely on forging deals that could rescue the Build Back Better agenda[22] and protect voting rights.[23] As a result, none of the privacy bills can be

[11] Winn, *Rutgers L.J.*, 2002, 617, (639–641).
[12] *Ibid.* at 641 52.
[13] Conditioning federal funding opens up a way for the federal government to exert power where it lacks the power to regulate activities directly or where political obstacles stand in the way of ordinary regulation.
[14] Solove, *Geo. Wash. L. Rev.*, 2021, pp. 1, 46; Viljoen, *Yale L.J.*, 2021, 573.
[15] *Cf*, for example, Confessore, *N.Y. Times* (4 April 2018).
[16] Kelly, *Verge* (20 May 2021); Rich, *Brookings* (14 January 2021); Levine, *Politico* (1 June 2021).
[17] Fazlioglu, *iaap* (24 August 2021).
[18] Balkin, *UC Davis Law Review*, 2016, 1185; Balkin, *Colum. L. Rev.*, 2018, 2011. See also Richards/Hartzog, *Stan. Tech. L. Rev.*, 2016, 431.
[19] Data Care Act of 2021, S.919, 117th Cong. (2021).
[20] Protecting Investors' Personally Identifiable Information Act, Sec. 1209, 117th Cong. (2021).
[21] *Ibid.* Sec. 1209.
[22] White House, The build back better framework.
[23] Brannon, *ACLU* (2021).

expected to see the date of light anytime soon. The 2022 midterm campaign did certainly not ease bipartisan progress on legislation in the area. And as the implementation of privacy frameworks at the state level progresses, the preemption of fragmented state-level regulation as motivation for federal legislation becomes obsolete.

11 The best hope for meaningful general purpose federal privacy protection now lies with the Federal Trade Commission (FTC). The Commission's new chair, Lina Khan, has made privacy protection online a priority. First in October and then, more concretely, in December of 2021, Chair Khan indicated that the FTC should engage in rulemaking for federal privacy protections under its regulatory authority.[24]

2. Privacy – States

12 Legislative progress looks different at a state level. Five states, California, Colorado, Connecticut, Virginia and Utah have already passed comprehensive privacy legislation,[25] with several other states considering such.[26] California has led the charge. The Golden State first passed the California Consumer Privacy Act (CCPA) and followed up with the California Privacy Rights Act (CPRA), which expanded users' rights and established the California Privacy Protection Agency.[27] The CCPA was passed in 2018 and became effective as of 2020; the CPRA was passed through a ballot initiative[28] in 2020 and will come in effect in 2023. The framework emphasizes consumer protection to maneuver around jurisdictional limitations and potential federal preemption. Like the GDPR, the new Californian regime relies on users' rights to protect their personal information. These include the right of users to know about the personal information a business collects about them and how it is used and shared, to delete personal information collected from them (with some exceptions), to opt out of the sale of their personal information, and to non-discrimination for exercising their CCPA rights. Also in line with the GDPR, the new framework does not question or challenge the currently dominant business models online. Other than the GDPR, however, it does not require justification for data processing comparable to Art. 6(1) GDPR.

13 In Colorado, the Colorado Privacy Act creates a set of consumer rights and defines data controllers and processors, concepts that the GDPR relies on as well.[29] Virginia also relies on a conceptualization as consumer protection legislation with its Consumer Data Protection Act. Virginia's approach includes notions of proportionality in the form size thresholds. It exclusively applies to the private sector and will enter into force in 2023. Other states have pursued more limited approaches, such as data broker registration mandates or specific requirements for certain types of services.[30] The themes covered in the new frameworks and bills overlap significantly, but not entirely.[31] The emerging landscape will be fragmented, but most likely based on similar concepts. Especially for small, but growing companies that fragmentation can create additional barriers, while adding comparatively little extra burden for incumbent platforms.

---

[24] Khan, *Statement of Chair Lina M. Khan Regarding the Report to Congress on Privacy and Security* (October 2021); Brody, *Protocol.*

[25] Desai, *iaap* (27 January 2023).

[26] *Ibid.* n 25.

[27] Determann, *ZD* 69 (2021).

[28] A ballot initiative is a type of referendum in the State of California.

[29] National Conference of State Legislatures, *ncsl.org* (2022).

[30] *Ibid.*

[31] *Ibid.*

II. Investments & Infrastructure

14 Regulating through investments has become a signature strategy of the Biden Administration – an administration tightly constrained by the narrowest possible majority in Congress even while it held both chambers of Congress before the 2022 midterm elections. Democratic lawmakers and the administration seemed convinced that the only way they could successfully implement policy was through a comprehensive spending bill. Relying on spending opens a legislative process called reconciliation that is not subject to the filibuster, a procedural hurdle to passing ordinary legislation in the Senate which requires 60 votes to overcome. In other words, regulating through spending requires less votes than regulating through passing ordinary substantive regulation.

15 The first part of the Biden Administration's signature proposals, the Infrastructure Investment and Jobs Act (IIJA), which received some bipartisan support in the Senate, includes '$65 billion to help ensure that every American has access to reliable high-speed internet through a historic investment in broadband infrastructure deployment'.[32] While some of the other line items, such as investments in charging networks for electric vehicles and power infrastructure might indirectly impact the digital economy, none of them specifically address data related issues.

16 The United States Innovation and Competition Act of 2021,[33] a bipartisan project to bolster investments in technologies deemed critical to ensuring competitiveness with China, passed as well. The act provides significant investments in the development of artificial intelligence and quantum network infrastructure, to name just two areas.[34] Much of that may translate into innovation in the data economy, just as spending on fundamental research and defense in the second half of the 20th century has created the foundation for the internet as we know it today.[35] That said, the amount committed to that research can be considered early seed funding at most.

III. Industrial Organisation & Competition Policy

17 The third element with the potential to reshape the data economy is industrial organization, mainly in the form of competition policy and antitrust enforcement. Its impact will likely be felt in many dimensions from data protection to inequality. One might – with good reason – doubt whether competition policy is suited to advance goals relating to sufficient privacy protection, equity and inclusion, and hate speech. Considering the political economy of the moment, however, industrial policy and, specifically, competition policy appears as the most promising vehicle for reform.

18 Standing antitrust doctrine, as applied by the courts, is still shaped by the contributions of the 'Chicago School,' a deregulatory project dedicated to scaling back enforcement actions.[36] Merger control became laxer and checks on unilateral conduct almost dormant. The case against Microsoft, which was eventually settled, had remained the sole significant enforcement action against Big Tech, before the recent antitrust awakening.[37]

[32] White House, President Biden's Bipartisan Infrastructure Law.

[33] United States Innovation and Competition Act of 2021, S.1260, 117th Cong. (2021).

[34] *Ibid.*

[35] Mazzucato, *The Entrepreneurial State: Debunking Public vs. Private Sector Myths*, 2015.

[36] *Cf* Hovenkamp/Scott Morton, *U. Pa. L. Rev.*, 2021, 1843 (1852–53); Posner, *U. Pa. L. Rev.*, 1979, 925.

[37] *Cf* United States v. Microsoft Corp., 253 F.3d 34 (2nd Cir. 2001).

19 The high levels of concentration in the digital economy trace back to the Clinton Administration's Framework for Global Economic commerce.[38] This Framework marked the first and last comprehensive and influential policy agenda for the digital economy of the United States. The Framework built on the idea of self-correcting markets and did not address the potential for emerging market power on the internet.[39] Other than envisaged, markets did not self-correct and competition turned out to be further than one click away.

20 The Biden Administration is the first to fundamentally pivot away from decades of antitrust restraint. This pivot manifests in personnel choices for key positions in the White House, at the FTC, and the Department of Justice and in the policy priorities of the first year. More specifically, consider the various law suits against Big Tech companies. As it relates to Meta, the FTC focuses on past mergers and history of acquiring competitors.[40] As it relates to Google, the Department of Justice addresses exclusive agreements with smart phone manufacturers and, as of recently its advertisement business.[41] More generally, several options to address market power in the digital economy are on the table, which I will summarize in the following sections.[42]

1. Policy Options

21 First, there are horizontal break-ups, structural remedies inspired by the historic example of *Standard Oil*.[43] Applied to today's digital platforms, that type of remedy would split up a company like Facebook into smaller entities that could again compete. Horizontal break-ups could undo former mergers, for example by spinning off Instagram and WhatsApp from the rest of Facebook or follow an entirely different logic of disaggregation.[44] Horizontal break-ups would bring immediate relief, but some worry that, without additional regulation, the market could tip once again in favor of one of the spin offs.[45]

22 Second, courts or legislators could separate the vertically integrated platforms' functions.[46] Amazon could no longer compete with merchants on its platform, by selling private label goods, and the app stores would be prevented from featuring their own applications. Meta could be split into marketplace, messaging, dating, advertisement brokerage, and Facebook Blue, for instance. That would mitigate many of the current conflicts of interests of integrated platforms.[47] The remedy could be combined with horizontal break-ups or regulation.

23 Third, platforms could become subject to interoperability mandates, requiring that they exchange information with competitors beyond their boundaries through applica-

[38] *Cf* Clinton/Gore, *The White House* (1 July 1997); Guggenberger, *Allocating Network Effects* (on file with author 2023).

[39] Guggenberger, *supra* n 38. Kades/Scott Morton, *Interoperability as a Competition Remedy for Digital Networks*, 2020.

[40] First Amended Complaint, FTC v. Facebook, No. 1:20-cv-03590, Doc. 75-1 (D.D.C. Aug. 19, 2021).

[41] Amended Complaint, United States v. Google, LLC, No. 1:20-cv-03010, Doc. 94 (D. D.C. Jan. 15, 2021).

[42] H. Subcomm. on Antitrust, Com. and Admin. L. of the H. Comm. on the Judiciary.

[43] *Cf* Standard Oil Co. v. United States, 1910 221 U.S. 1.

[44] Guggenberger, *Stan. Tech. L. Rev.*, 2021, 237 (327–29).

[45] Fukuyama et al., Report of the Working Group on Platform Scale (2020), https://cyber.fsi.stanford.edu/publication/report-working-group-platform-scale (last accessed 29 March 2023).

[46] *Cf* Khan, *Colum. L. Rev.*, 2019, 973.

[47] *Ibid.*

tion program interfaces (APIs).[48] Interoperability mandates help to overcome market entry barriers online. Instead of first having to create a large network to be attractive to customers, start-ups could benefit from the value of connection with existing networks.

Fourth, scholars and policy makers have discussed several variations of access rights for users and competitors. These approaches include the antitrust-based essential facilities doctrine, public utility regulation, common carriage frameworks, and consumer protection approaches.[49] All of them limit the business discretion of the digital platforms. They root in notions of power asymmetries and reliance. While they raise costs for the incumbent in what amounts to the equivalent of progressive taxation, they do not immediately restructure the market.[50] The very approaches and especially the antitrust essential facilities doctrine that have been treated with disdain for the past 30 years, are now making a comeback.[51] In fact, the essential facilities doctrine has lately received bipartisan endorsements.[52] 24

2. Competition Politics

Some of these four policy options described above have been included in recent bills in Congress and state legislatures.[53] Bipartisan alliances have solidified over the issue of competition policy reform. Even the most far-reaching proposals, like the Ending Monopoly Act have received Democratic and Republican buy in – a development all but unthinkable only three years ago. The 2020 House Majority Staff Report significantly contributed to the current momentum, as did the hearings held in the House under the leadership of Representative David Cicilline, during which the public witnessed CEOs under pressure to explain their business practices.[54] Another contributing factor lies in political shifts within the political parties. Consider the Republican Party. First, there are unproven allegations of anti-conservative bias and disagreement with alleged political stands taken by technology companies. Second, the wealth creation by digital platforms has been highly concentrated in a few hubs; large swaths of the country did not benefit from the boom. And third, a large portion of the traditional business community finds itself shut out by digital platforms, splitting the business community.[55] Within the Democratic Party, progressives, concerned with concentrations of power and inequality, have gained momentum with the rise of figures like Senators Bernie Sanders and Elizabeth Warren. 25

The likely biggest contribution to the shifts in antitrust enforcement and appetite for competition policy reform, however, came from the technology companies themselves. 26

---

[48] Guggenberger, *supra* n 44, at 317–22.

[49] *Cf* Abrahamson,*Yale L.J.*, 2014, 867; Guggenberger, *supra* n 44; Guggenberger, *Yale J.L. & Tech.*, 2021, 301; Rahman, *Cardozo L. Rev.*, 2018, 1621; Rahman, *Geo. L. Tech. Rev.*, 2018, 234; Volokh, *J. Free Speech L.*, 2021, 377.

[50] Guggenberger, *supra* n 49, at 354–59.

[51] *Ibid.* at 304; Guggenberger, *Wirtschaft und Wettbewerb*, 2020, 633; Wood, *Loyola University Chicago Law* Journal, 2019, 1 (15–16).

[52] Buck, The Third Way 12–13 (2020); H. Subcomm. on Antitrust, Com. and Admin. L. of the H. Comm. on the Judiciary, *supra* n 42, at 397–98.

[53] American Choice and Innovation Online Act, H.R.3816, 117th Cong. (2021); Augmenting Compatibility and Competition by Enabling Service Switching Act of 2021 (ACCESS Act of 2021), H.R.3849, 117th Cong. (2021); Platform Competition and Opportunity Act of 2021, H.R.3826, 117th Cong. (2021); Ending Platform Monopolies Act, H.R.3825, 117th Cong. (2021); Merger Filing Fee Modernization Act of 2021, S. 228, 117th Cong. (2021); Augmenting Compatibility and Competition by Enabling Service Switching Act of 2019 (ACCESS Act of 2019), S.2658, 116th Cong. (2019). See also Press Release, *U.S. House Judiciary Committee*; Nylen, *Politico* (3 March 2021).

[54] *Cf* H. Subcomm. on Antitrust, Com. and Admin. L. of the H. Comm. on the Judiciary, *supra* n 42.

[55] Guggenberger, *supra* n 49, at 305.

Scandal after scandal supplied critics with a never-ending stream of arguments for reform. Despite this historic opening for change, however, implementing real reform policies will remain an uphill battle. The emerging alliances are fragile and Big Tech invests enormously in lobbying power. At the end of the day, state legislatures might be the first to pass meaningful reforms. Several bills are already underway, with several states focusing on the app stores.[56]

D. Conclusion

27 There is no comprehensive US data strategy and there will likely not emerge one anytime soon. Different, at times antagonistic, actors will continue to define distinct elements which provide the framework for the digital society. A revamped industrial policy with stricter enforcement actions wields the most potential for change.

Bibliography

28 Abrahamson, Essential Data, 124 *Yale L.J.* 867 (2014)

Amended Complaint, United States v. Google, LLC, No. 1:20-cv-03010, Doc. 94 (D. D.C. 15 January 2021)

American Choice and Innovation Online Act, H.R.3816, 117th Cong. (2021)

Augmenting Compatibility and Competition by Enabling Service Switching Act of 2021 (ACCESS Act of 2021), H.R.3849, 117th Cong. (2021)

Augmenting Compatibility and Competition by Enabling Service Switching Act of 2019 (ACCESS Act of 2019), S.2658, 116th Cong. (2019)

Autor/Dorn/Katz/Patterson/Van Reenen, The Fall of the Labor Share and the Rise of Superstar Firms, 135 *The Quarterly Journal Of Economics* 645 (2020) *[cited as Autor et al.]*

Balkin, Free Speech is a Triangle, 118 *Colum. L. Rev.* 2011 (2018)

Balkin, Information Fiduciaries and the First Amendment, 49 *UC Davis Law Review* 1185 (2016)

Bamberger/Lobel, Platform Market Power, 32 *Berkeley Tech. L.J.* 1051 (2017)

Brannon, Here's Ahat You Need to Know About the White House's Plan to Promote Voting Access, *ACLU* (2021), available at https://www.aclu.org/news/voting-rights/heres-what-you-need-to-know-about-the-white-houses-plan-to-promote-voting-access (last accessed 16 December 2022)

Brody, Khan Wants the FTC to Look at Rules on Privacy and AI Discrimination, *Protocol*, available at https://www.protocol.com/bulletins/khan-privacy-rules (last accessed 16 December 2022)

Buck, The Third Way 12–13 (2020); available at https://buck.house.gov/sites/evo-subsites/buck-evo.house.gov/files/wysiwyg-uploaded/Buck%20Report.pdf (last accessed 16 December 2022)

Clinton/Gore, The Framework for Global Electronic Commerce, *The White House* (1 July 1997), available at https://clintonwhitehouse4.archives.gov/WH/New/Commerce/ (last accessed 16 December 2022)

Cohen, *Between Truth And Power: The Legal Constructions Of Informational Capitalism*, 2019

[56] Nylen, *Politico* (3 March 2021), available at https://www.politico.com/news/2021/03/03/apple-google-app-store-fights-move-to-the-states-473388 (last accessed 16 December 2022).

Confessore, Cambridge Analytica and Facebook: The Scandal and the Fallout So Far, *N.Y. Times* (4 April 2018), available at https://www.nytimes.com/2018/04/04/us/politics/cambridge-analytica-scandal-fallout.html (last accessed 16 December 2022)

Council of Economic Advisers, Benefits of Competition and Indicators of Market Power 4–7 (2016), available at https://obamawhitehouse.archives.gov/sites/default/files/page/files/20160414_cea_competition_issue_brief.pdf (last accessed on 16 December 2022)

Data Care Act of 2021, S.919, 117th Cong. (2021)

Desai, US State Privacy Legislation Tracker, *IAAP* (27 January 2023), available at https://iapp.org/resources/article/us-state-privacy-legislation-tracker/ (last accessed 27 January 2023)

Determann, Kaliforniens erste Datenschutzbehörde – dank Volksentscheid, *ZD* 2021, 69

Ending Platform Monopolies Act, H.R.3825, 117th Cong. (2021)

Fazlioglu, Privacy Bills in the 117th Congress, *IAAP* (24 August 2021), available at https://iapp.org/news/a/privacy-bills-in-the-117th-congress/ (last accessed 16 December 2022)

Federal Data Strategy 2021 Action Plan, available at https://strategy.data.gov/assets/docs/2021-Federal-Data-Strategy-Action-Plan.pdf (last accessed 16 December 2022)

Federal Data Strategy, https://strategy.data.gov/ (last accessed 16 December 2022)

First Amended Complaint, FTC v. Facebook, No. 1:20-cv-03590, Doc. 75-1 (D.D.C. Aug. 19, 2021)

Fukuyama/Richman/Goel/Schaake/Katz/Melamed, Report of the Working Group on Platform Scale, *Stanford Cyber Policy Center* (2020), available at https://cyber.fsi.stanford.edu/publication/report-working-group-platform-scale (last accessed 16 December 2022) *[cited as Fukuyama et al.]*

Furman/Orszag, A Firm-Level Perspective on the Role of Rents in the Rise in Inequality, in: Martin Guzman (ed.), *Toward A Just Society: Joseph Stiglitz And Twenty-First Century Economics*, 2018

Grimmelmann, *Internet Law: Cases And Problems*, 11th ed., 2021

Guggenberger, Essential Platforms, 24 *Stan. Tech. L. Rev.* 237 (2021)

Guggenberger, Good Times for Antitrust in the U.S., 70 *Wirtschaft Und Wettbewerb* 633 (2020)

Guggenberger, Allocating Network Effects (on file with author 2023)

Guggenberger, The Essential Facilities Doctrine in the Digital Economy: Dispelling Persistent Myths, 23 *Yale J.L. & Tech.* 301 (2021)

Gutiérrez/Philippon, Declining Competition and Investment in the U.S., *NBER Working Paper* (July 2017)

House Subcommittee on Antitrust, Commercial and Administrative Law of the Committee on the Judiciary, Investigation of Competition in Digital Markets: Majority Staff Report and Recommendations (October 2020) *[cited as H. Subcomm. on Antritrust, Com. and Admin. L. of the H. Comm. on the Judiciary]*

Hovenkamp/Scott Morton, Framing the Chicago School of Antitrust Analysis, 168 *University of Pennsylvania Law Review* 1843 (2021)

Jarsulic, Antitrust Enforcement for the 21st Century, 64 *The Antitrust Bulletin* 514 (2019)

Kades/Scott Morton, Interoperability as a Competition Remedy for Digital Networks, *Washington Center for Equitable Growth* (September 2020), available at https://equitablegrowth.org/wp-content/uploads/2020/09/092320-WP-Interoperability-as-a-competition-remedy-for-digital-networks-Kades-and-Scott-Morton.pdf (last accessed 16 December 2022)

Kelly, Senators Roll out Bipartisan Data Privacy Bill, *Verge* (20 May 2021), available at https://www.theverge.com/2021/5/20/22444515/amy-klobuchar-data-privacy-protection-facebook-state-laws (last accessed 16 December 2022)

Khan, *Statement of Chair Lina M. Khan Regarding the Report to Congress on Privacy and Security* (October 2021) available at https://www.ftc.gov/system/files/documents/public_statements/

1597024/statement_of_chair_lina_m_khan_regarding_the_report_to_congress_on_privacy_and_-security_-_final.pdf (last accessed 16 December 2022)

Khan, The Separation of Platforms and Commerce, 119 *Colum. L. Rev.* 973 (2019)

Kurz, *On the Formation of Capital and Wealth: IT, Monopoly Power and Rising Inequality* (June 2017), available at https://papers.ssrn.com/sol3/papers.cfm?abstract_id=3014361 (last accessed 16 December 2022)

Levine, A U.S. Privacy Law Seemed Possible this Congress. Now, Prospects Are Fading Fast, *Politico* (1 June 2021), available at https://www.politico.com/news/2021/06/01/washington-plan-protect-american-data-silicon-valley-491405 (last accessed 16 December 2022)

Mazzucato, *The Entrepreneurial State: Debunking Public Vs. Private Sector Myths*, revised ed., 2015

Merger Filing Fee Modernization Act of 2021, S.228, 117th Cong. (2021)

Merriam-Webster, strategy, https://www.merriam-webster.com/dictionary/strategy (last accessed 16 December 2022)

National Conference Of State Legislatures, State Laws Related to Digital Privacy, *ncsl.org* (2022), available at https://www.ncsl.org/research/telecommunications-and-information-technology/state-laws-related-to-internet-privacy.aspx (last accessed 16 December 2022)

Nylen, Apple, Google App Store Fights Move to the States, *Politico* (3 March 2021), available at https://www.politico.com/news/2021/03/03/apple-google-app-store-fights-move-to-the-states-473388 (last accessed 16 December 2022)

Philippon, *The Great Reversal: How America Gave Up On Free Markets*, 2019

Platform Competition and Opportunity Act of 2021, H.R.3826, 117th Cong. (2021)

Posner, The Chicago School of Antitrust Analysis, 127 *U. Pa. L. Rev.* 925 (1979)

President's Management Agenda, FDS Framework, Mission, Principles, Practices, and Actions, available at https://strategy.data.gov/assets/docs/2020-federal-data-strategy-framework.pdf (last accessed 16 December 2022)

Press Releases, House Lawmakers Release Anti-Monopoly Agenda for "A Stronger Online Economy: Opportunity, Innovation, Choice," *U.S. House Judiciary Committee*, available at https://judiciary.house.gov/news/documentsingle.aspx?DocumentID=4591 (last accessed 16 December 2022)

Protecting Investors' Personally Identifiable Information Act, S.1209, 117th Cong. (2021)

Rahman, The New Utilities: Private Power, Social Infrastructure, and the Revival of the Public Utility Concept, 39 *Cardozo L. Rev.* 1621 (2018)

Rahman, Regulating Informational Infrastructure: Internet Platforms as the New Public Utilities, 2 *Geo. L. Tech. Rev.* 234 (2018)

Rich, After 20 Years of Debate, It's Time for Congress to Finally Pass a Baseline Privacy Law, *Brookings* (14 January 2021), available at https://www.brookings.edu/blog/techtank/2021/01/14/after-20-years-of-debate-its-time-for-congress-to-finally-pass-a-baseline-privacy-law/ (last accessed 16 December 2022)

Richards/Hartzog, Taking Trust Seriously in Privacy Law, 19 *Stan. Tech. L. Rev.* 431 (2016)

Solove, The Myth of the Privacy Paradox, 89 *Geo. Wash. L. Rev.* 1, 46 (2021)

Standard Oil Co. v. United States, 1910 221 U.S. 1.

United States Innovation and Competition Act of 2021, S.1260, 117th Cong. (2021)

United States v. Microsoft Corp., 253 F.3d 34 (2nd Cir. 2001)

Viljoen, Democratic Data: A Relational Theory For Data Governance, 131 *Yale L.J.* 573 (2021)

Volokh, Treating Social Media Platforms Like Common Carriers?, 1 *J. Free Speech L.* 377 (2021)

White House, *President Biden's Bipartisan Infrastructure Law*, https://www.whitehouse.gov/bipartisan-infrastructure-law/ (last accessed 16 December 2022)

White House, *The build back better framework*, https://www.whitehouse.gov/build-back-better/ (last accessed 16 December 2022)

Winn, Confidentiality in Cyberspace: The HIPAA Privacy Rules and the Common Law, 33 *Rutgers L.J.* 617 (2002)

Wood, The Old New (Or is It the New Old) Antitrust: "I'm Not Dead Yet!!", 51 *Loyola University Chicago Law Journal* 1 (2019)

§ 6 ASSESSING GHANA'S DATA PROTECTION FRAMEWORK WITHIN THE CONTEXT OF AFRICA'S DATA GOVERNANCE STRATEGY: TRENDS, DIRECTION AND PROSPECTS

Content

1 This article examines legislative instruments and policy documents relevant to the development of data protection law in Africa, within African regional communities and in Ghana. In doing so, it assesses the factors influencing the development of national and international legislation on data protection. The article then describes numerous laws in Ghana, amongst them the Data Protection Act 2012, and analyses their relevance and influence on the protection of personal data in the Ghanaian regulatory environment. It thereafter takes a look at numerous Ghanaian government policy documents to ascertain the relevant strategic interests concerning data protection in Ghana. Building on the various laws and policy documents, the article then establishes five key aspects of the Ghanaian data protection strategy.

A. Introduction

2 In the past decade, digitalisation and the developments in digital technology have led to a mounting global drive towards the adoption of more robust laws and mechanisms on personal data protection. Until recently, African countries lagged behind in the conversation on data protection awareness in comparison with their European and other counterparts. However, technological advancement, inter- and intracontinental trade resulted into adoption of varied data (protection) laws and policies by African countries. African regional bodies such as the East African Community (EAC), the Economic Community of West African States (ECOWAS), and the Southern African Development Community (SADC) have provided some instructive guidance on the direction, scope, and focus of data protection and regulatory regimes in many individual African countries, including Ghana.

3 It is noted, however, that the EU General Data Protection Regulation (GDPR)[1] has also exerted a strong influence on African countries 'interest and motivation for establishing stronger data regulation regimes to support the free flow and exchange of data between Africa and the EU.[2] *Daigle* noted a close alignment between newly enacted as well as updated data protection laws in Africa. He gives an example of such laws to include the 2019 Data Protection Regulation in Nigeria, Mauritius Data Protection Act of 2017 which repealed and replaced the 2004 Data Protection Act and Benin Data Protection Law of 2009 to have been specifically fashioned to align closely with the standards of the GDPR.[3]

4 In the last decade, over half of the countries in Africa, including Ghana, have progressively established and finetuned domestic legislation and regulatory structures on data protection. This article begins with a broad overview of the scope and impact of Africa's Data Protection plan for the protection of personal data as outlined in the

[1] Regulation (EU) 2016/679 of the European Parliament and of the Council of 27 April 2016 on the protection of natural persons with regard to the processing of personal data and on the free movement of such data, and repealing Directive 95/46/EC (General Data Protection Regulation) [2016] OJ L 119/1.

[2] Daigle, *Journal of International Commerce and Economics,* 2021; Collaboration on International ICT Policy in East and Southern Africa (CIPESA), *Challenges and Prospects of the General Data Protection Regulation (GDPR) in Africa*, 2018; Boshe/Hennemann/von Meding, *Global Privacy Law Review*, 2022, 56.

[3] Daigle, *Journal of International Commerce and Economics,* 2021, 8.

Malabo Convention, the African Union Digital Transformation Strategy for Africa, the African Union Data Policy Framework, relevant guidelines, and other sub-regional instruments. The article focuses on Ghana as one of the architects of domestic data protection law in the sub-Saharan region and evaluates its legislative and policy framework on data protection, looking at the scope, relevance, and overall enforceability. Building on these insights, the article assesses Ghana's data protection strategy.

B. Regional African Initiatives on Data Protection

Data in Africa as on any other continent is invaluable. Data is required for many purposes, and at the top of the pyramid is economic growth.[4] The AU acknowledges that data is utilised daily in every sector of the economy, at the micro level for supporting small-scale farmers level up on productivity,[5] and at the macro level for the running of essential supplies like water and electricity.[6] The adoption of digital technology and digitalisation has been on the increase in most African countries within the last decade.[7] African countries face unique and formidable challenges posed by digitalisation and the digital economy. These include the heightened need to ensure the integrity of personal data and data storage systems in the face of increased cyber-attacks and privacy infringements, the need to design, adapt, enact, and update laws appropriate for the digital economy, and the need to manage the impact of digitalisation on the labour market, in view of the proportionately huge and growing youth populations.[8] **5**

All this notwithstanding, Africa stands to reap significant benefits from digitalisation and the digital economy, including the progressive formalisation of the characteristically large informal sectors of many African countries, integration of African firms into global markets, improvement of the quality of life of consumers, and the enhanced capacity of governments to provided efficient public services.[9] In addition, African countries are moving towards a greater integration of trade policies through the African Continental Free Trade Agreement (AfCFTA), which, alongside trade, implies an increase in cross-border data transfers. In light of these developments, the benefits of digitalisation, however, can only be guaranteed and actualised with the enactment of a strong and appropriate data protection legislation and the adoption of efficient enforcement mechanisms. **6**

I. The Digital Transformation Strategy for Africa

The African Union had already adopted a strategy to support digital development, the Digital Transformation Strategy for Africa (2020–2030).[10] The Strategy is a recognition of the efforts of the African Union to accelerate digital transformation. The preamble to the Strategy emphasises that digital transformation is a driving force for innovative, inclusive, **7**

---

[4] African Union, *African Union leading on Data Economy in Africa ... for Africa*, 2022.
[5] *Ibid.*
[6] *Ibid.*
[7] Songwe, *The Role of Digitalization in the Decade of Action for Africa*, 2020.
[8] Ademuyiwa/Adeniran, *CIGI Paper*, 2016.
[9] *Ibid* p. 2.
[10] African Union, *The Digital Transformation Strategy for Africa (2020–2030)*, 2020; see also Boshe/Hennemann/von Meding, *Global Privacy Law Review* 2022, 56.

and sustainable growth.[11] The Strategy notes the contributions to job creation and poverty reduction that can be harnessed from digitisation, all packaged towards the achievement of Agenda 2063 and the Sustainable Development Goals. Essentially, the Strategy looks to combine digital resources to transform Africa's digital economy.[12]

8 The Strategy recognises vulnerability of personal data in the digital economy and express the need for its protection. In its vision of creating Africa digital single market by 2030,[13] the Strategy identifies proper policies and regulations as important enablers towards the single market.[14] Specifically, the Strategy emphasises the need for a strong 'collaboration between African Institutions and regulators in charge of digitalization and the protection of personal data'.[15] Eventually, the Strategy calls for policy coherence[16] and the creation of a rust framework to facilitate cross-border data flow.[17]

9 In the enclave of data protection under the general digitalisation theme, the Strategy's specific objectives directly addressing the matter are:

- 'Entry into force of the African Union convention on Cyber Security and Personal Data Protection by 2020[18] and for all Members States to adopt a complete set of legislation covering e-Transactions, Personal Data Protection and Privacy, Cybercrime and Consumer Protection',[19]
- to 'promote open standards and interoperability for cross-border trust framework, personal data protection and privacy',[20] and
- to 'create awareness and counterbalance issues of Cyber Security and Personal Data Protection and Privacy.[21]

10 Other objectives relevant for data protection include the aim to improve internet infrastructure,[22] to improve the knowledge base and provide education in digital matters throughout Africa[23] as well as a specific aim to ensure that '99.9 % of people in Africa (…) have a digital legal identity (…) by 2030'.[24]

11 The Strategy recommends a framework on Data Policy and management for Africa to transform the African Society.[25] It echoes the development and adoption of national cybersecurity strategies, and legal and regulatory frameworks for personal data protection and privacy, cybersecurity standards, and cybercrime.[26]

II. The Malabo Convention

12 Data security was one of the primary factors influencing the AU's decision to prioritise data protection.[27] The first strategy was to invent model legislation for the

[11] *Supra* n 10.
[12] *Ibid.*
[13] *Supra* n 2.
[14] *Supra* n 5.
[15] *Supra* n 9.
[16] *Supra* ns 2, 9.
[17] *Supra* n 3.
[18] This goal was not met; *infra* section B. II.
[19] *Supra* n 10.
[20] *Supra* n 3.
[21] *Ibid.*
[22] *Supra* n 2.
[23] *Supra* n 3.
[24] *Supra* n 3.
[25] *Infra* n 47; *infra* section B. VII. on the African Union Data Policy Framework.
[26] *Infra* n 46.
[27] In the preamble to the Malabo Convention, the African Union states that there is an urgent need to address the dangers and risk derived from the use of electronic data and individual records.

protection of personal data. In 2014, the AU adopted the 'Convention on Cyber Security and Data Protection (the 'Malabo Convention').[28] The Convention provides a blueprint for the establishment of data protection frameworks by AU member states. This blueprint is aimed at combating cybercrime and to effectively regulate the processing of personal data.[29]

The drafting of the Malabo Convention started in 2011 with an objective of establishing a 'credible framework of cybersecurity in Africa through the organization of electronic transactions, protection of personal data, promotion of cyber security, e-governance and the combating of cybercrime'.[30] However, a lack of stakeholder consultation in its development led to a three-year delay in its adoption.[31] The Malabo Convention was eventually adopted on 27 June 2014 in Malabo, Equatorial Guinea, at the 23rd Ordinary Session of the Assembly. The Convention provides that entry into force will be thirty days after the fifteenth ratification or accession to the treaty after it has been deposited.[32] 13

By September 2022, at least 34 out of the 55 African countries had adopted laws and regulations governing data protection,[33] and yet only 14 countries had ratified the Malabo Convention.[34] It would seem therefore, that although most African States may be implementing the requirements of the Malabo Convention, a good majority of them do not see a need to ratify it. The prevailing situation evokes the suspicion that African countries may not be purposefully modelling their legislative efforts on the Malabo Convention, but are rather drawing inspiration from some other sources.[35] 14

The Malabo Convention addresses three critical aspects of the digital economy: (i) electronic transactions; (ii) personal data protection and (iii) cyber security and cybercrime, making it the most comprehensive international law instrument on data protection in Africa. The scope of 'data protection' is comprehensively defined in the Malabo Convention to cover the processing of personal data by any entity, natural or artificial, any automated or non-automated process, any processing undertaken in the territory of a State Party, and data processing relating to public security subject to other national laws.[36] The Convention prescribes preliminary personal data processing formalities subject to recognised exceptions.[37] 15

State parties are obligated to ensure, not only that their national legislation reflect the standards of the Convention, but also that the national Data Protection Authority to oversee the processing of personal data is consistent with the provisions of the Convention.[38] A general prohibition is placed on the processing of sensitive data such as information about one's sex life or genetic information, subject to specified exceptions in the law. A data subject (individual who submits or consents to data collection 16

---

[28] African Union, *Convention on Cyber Security and Personal Data Protection*, 2014, available at https://au.int/en/treaties/african-union-convention-cyber-security-and-personal-data-protection (last accessed 16 December 2022).

[29] Turanskyi, *SAIIA Policy Insights* 2020.

[30] NATO Cooperative Cyber Defence Centre of Excellence, *African Union*.

[31] NATO Cooperative Cyber Defence Centre of Excellence, *African Union Adopts Conventions on Cyber Security*.

[32] Malabo Convention, article 36.

[33] See the list at Hennemann/Lienemann/Spirkl, *University of Passau IRDG Research Paper Series* 2022.

[34] African Union, *Malabo Convention Status List*, 2022, available at (https://au.int/sites/default/files/treaties/29560-sl-AFRICAN_UNION_CONVENTION_ON_CYBER_SECURITY_AND_PERSONAL_DATA_PROTECTION.pdf (last accessed 16 December 2022).

[35] Daniel, *Data protection laws in Africa: What you need to know*, 2021.

[36] Malabo Convention, article 9(1).

[37] *Ibid* articles 10(1)(a), (b) and (c).

[38] *Ibid* article 12(1).

or processing) is clothed with the right to information,[39] right to access,[40] right to object,[41] and the right to rectification and erasure[42] as against the data controller or processor (a person processing personal). In turn, data controllers bear the core obligations of confidentiality,[43] security,[44] storage,[45] and sustainability.[46]

17 The Malabo Convention is premised on six (6) basic principles on the processing of personal data, which are required to be enacted in country-specific legislation and enforced by the national Data Protection Authority. These principles are: (i) consent and legitimacy of personal data processing; (ii) lawfulness and fairness of personal data processing; (iii) purpose, relevance, and storage of processed personal data; (iv) accuracy of personal data; (v) transparency of personal processing data; and (vi) confidentiality and security of personal processing data.[47] These principles are to be applied in conjunction with legal enforcement mechanisms such as criminalising of cyber offences,[48] as well as legal measures that guarantee the rights of individuals under the national constitutions and the African Charter, including but not limited to, the freedom of expression and the right to privacy.[49]

18 In enforcing data protection law, Data Protection Authorities are mandated to impose sanctions where applicable and work with other stakeholder groups. Their main responsibility is to maximise trust amongst the citizenry.

III. The African Continental Free Trade Agreement Protocol on Trade in Services

19 The AfCFTA aims at accelerating growth of intra-Africa trade.[50] It has, as an annex, a Protocol on Trade in Services (the 'Protocol') which ultimately seeks to create a liberalised market for trade in services.[51] The Protocol addresses data sharing eventualities in relation to confidential and commercially prejudicial information. Accordingly, where the disclosure of confidential information and data will impede law enforcement or be contrary to the public interest, then state parties are not obliged to disclose confidential information. Furthermore, any information which will be prejudicial to legitimate commercial interests, public or private, need not be disclosed.[52] The Protocol iterates the central message for data protection in the Malabo Convention, which is that State Parties shall adopt necessary measures to secure compliance with laws for the privacy of individuals in relation to the processing and dissemination of personal data and the protection of confidentiality of individual records and accounts.[53]

---

[39] *Ibid* article 16.
[40] *Ibid* article 17.
[41] *Ibid* article 18.
[42] *Ibid* article 19.
[43] *Ibid* article 20.
[44] *Ibid* article 21.
[45] *Ibid* article 22.
[46] *Ibid* article 23.
[47] *Ibid* article 13.
[48] *Ibid* Chapter 25 concerning National Legislation.
[49] *Ibid* article 25.
[50] African Union, *Agreement Establishing the African Continental Free Trade Area*, 2018, available at https://au.int/en/treaties/agreement-establishing-african-continental-free-trade-area (last accessed 16 December 2022).
[51] bilaterals.org, *Trade in services in the AfCFTA*, 2019.
[52] Protocol on Trade in Services, article 6; *supra* n 50.
[53] *Ibid* article 15(c)(iii).

IV. The Declaration of Principles on Freedom of Expression and Access to Information in Africa

The Declaration is based on the African Charter on Human and Peoples' rights (African Charter), particularly the normative content of the right to receive and disseminate information. The Declaration advances the cause of the right to privacy in relation to the handling of personal data which is not recognised in the African Charter.[54] It secures the right to privacy and protection of personal data,[55] prohibits indiscriminate use and storage of personal data,[56] and establishes guidelines for the processing of data in situations involving surveillance for criminal justice enforcement.[57] The Declaration entreats States to adopt laws for the protection of personal information of individuals in accordance with international human rights laws and standards.[58] 20

V. Personal Data Protection Guidelines for Africa

The African Union Commission, pursuant to its mandate under the Malabo Convention to develop guidelines for personal data protection, jointly developed the Personal Data Protection Guidelines for Africa (the 'Guidelines') with the Internet Society in 2018.[59] The Guidelines provides guidance on how to help individuals take a more active part in the protection of their personal data, while recognising the essence of positive action by other stakeholders.[60] 21

The Guidelines emphasise on the need of all stakeholders to participate in the protection of personal data.[61] Stakeholders mentioned include governments and policy-makers, Data Protection Authorities, data controllers, civil society organisations and citizens. According to the Guidelines, the role of governments and policymakers amongst others, is 'to empower the digital citizen, and ensure the online environment is trusted, safe, and beneficial to all stakeholders' and to 'increase their understanding of the benefits and hazards of the data-driven economy'.[62] 22

VI. The African Union Data Policy Framework

The African Union Data Policy Framework,[63] based on the broader objectives of and called for in the AU Digital Transformation Strategy for Africa,[64] provides for a comprehensive and in-depth set of policy recommendations for African governments 23

[54] Ilori, *Data protection in Africa and the COVID-19 pandemic: Old problems, new challenges and multistakeholder solutions | African Declaration on Internet Rights and Freedoms*, 2020.
[55] Declaration of Principles on Freedom of Expression and Access to Information in Africa, principle 40(1).
[56] *Ibid* principle 41(1).
[57] *Ibid* principle 41(2).
[58] *Ibid* principle 42.
[59] Internet Society, *Personal Data Protection Guidelines for Africa – Internet Society*, 2018.
[60] *Ibid.*
[61] *Supra* n 4.
[62] *Ibid.*
[63] African Union, *AU Data Policy Framework,* 2022, available at https://au.int/en/documents/20220728/au-data-policy-framework (last accessed 16 December 2022).
[64] *Supra* section B. I.

in order to allow for the development of a data-driven economy in Africa,[65] with regulation of matters of data protection central to the framework. At its core, it contains a set of recommendations for AU member states, some of which restate goals previously contained in the Digital Transformation Strategy, such as the adoption of the Malabo convention 'as soon as possible' and the improvement of ICT infrastructure.[66]

24 Other key goals are to 'establish or maintain independent, well-resourced and effective Data Protection Authorities'[67] and strengthen their cooperation in Africa, and 'develop national legislations on personal data protection and adequate regulations, particularly around data governance and digital platforms'.[68]

25 A novelty is the stronger focus on competition law instruments, as these are often intertwined with questions of data protection, such as the goal to 'promote data portability'[69] and 'transversal data policy'.[70] Overall, one may notice that the Data Policy Framework, to no surprise in its position as a product of the AU, which is also pursuing the goal of creating a digital single market within the AfCTFA,[71] devotes much of its attention to questions relevant for cross-border trade, illustrated by the prominently located recommendations to 'enable data to flow on the continent', as well as by separate AU institutional objectives to facilitate data flows between member states and across borders.

C. Sub-Regional African Initiatives on Data Protection

26 Notable in the African context is the existence of the various Regional Economic Communities (RECs), of which there are many and which correspond with different geographic regions of the continent. They complement the African Union, with the Abuja Treaty establishing the AU explicitly promoting cooperation within the RECs.[72] Thus, many international legal instruments are implemented on REC level. Prior to adopting the Malabo Convention, a number of legal frameworks and model laws were promulgated at the sub-regional level to assist and guide African countries in drafting national laws and regulations on personal data protection. These are discussed briefly in this section.

I. The EAC Legal Framework for Cyberlaw

27 The East African Community ('EAC') was the first African sub-regional body to provide for a legal framework aimed to harmonise data protection and cyber security. In 2008, the EAC adopted the *draft EAC Legal Framework for Cyber Laws, 2008/2011* (The Framework). The Framework consists of a set of recommendations to guide Member States in reforming their national laws, with the objective of harmonising laws

---

[65] *Supra* n 63 VI.
[66] *Ibid* IX.
[67] *Ibid.*
[68] *Ibid* VIII.
[69] *Ibid.*
[70] *Ibid* VII.
[71] *Supra* section B. III.
[72] African Union, *Treaty Establishing the African Economic Community,* 1991, available at https://au.int/en/treaties/treaty-establishing-african-economic-community (last accessed 16 December 2022), article 28.

among member states to reflect international best practice.[73] Much like the Malabo Convention, the EAC touches on electronic transactions, cybercrime and data protection.

28 The Framework recommends a sectoral regulatory approach to address specific uses and abuses of personal data.[74] This regulatory proposal is based on the idea that an entity responsible for processing data must comply with principles of good practice such as transparency and accountability; fair and lawful processing; processing limitations; data accuracy and data security. It also addresses the obligation to supply the individual with a copy of any personal data being held and processed and to provide an opportunity for incorrect data to be amended.[75] The reason for proposing sectoral regulatory approach as opposed to a comprehensive regulatory approach is a perceived lack of economic capacity of member states to establish an enforcement authority – a Data Protection Authority – as required in comprehensive data protection frameworks.[76]

II. The ECOWAS Supplementary Act on Data Protection

29 The Supplementary Act A/SA.1/01/10 on Personal Data Protection adopted by ECOWAS in 2010[77] is specially accorded recognition as the first binding sub-regional data protection law in Africa.[78] The Supplementary Act, which has been said to be strongly influenced by the EU Data Protection Directive,[79] mandates Member States of the economic community to 'establish a legal framework for the protection of privacy of data relating to the collection, processing, transmission, storage and use of personal data without prejudice to the general interest of the State'.[80] It provides the guidelines and principles for data protection and sets a high threshold for the protection of special categories of data, some of which are data relating to offences, sentences or security measures, biometric data and genetic data and data relating to health research.[81]

30 The significance of the Supplementary Act is highlighted in Article 48, which makes the Act an integral party of the ECOWAS treaty, meaning that breaches of the Act or non-compliance by Member States can be enforced by the ECOWAS Court of Justice.[82] The Supplementary Act states the basic principles of data processing to include consent and legitimacy, legality and fairness, purpose, relevance and preservation, accuracy, transparency, confidentiality, and choice of data processor.[83] The Act states the rights of data subjects are to include the right to information, right of access, right to object and right to rectification and destruction, and stipulates the obligations of data controllers to include confidentiality, security, durability and preservation.[84] The Act requires every

[73] East African Community, *Draft Legal Framework for Cyberlaws*, 2008, available at http://repository.eac.int:8080/bitstream/handle/11671/1815/EAC%20Framework%20for%20Cyberlaws.pdf (last accessed 16 December 2022).

[74] *Ibid* 2.5 (Data Protection and Privacy).

[75] *Ibid.*

[76] *Supra* n 18.

[77] Economic Community of West African States, *Supplementary Act A/SA.1/01/10 on Personal Data Protection Within ECOWAS*, 2010, available at https://ictpolicyafrica.org/es/document/z69cbq7b51? (last accessed 16 December 2022).

[78] Adopted in Abuja, Nigeria on 16 February 2010; see Makulilo, *Computer Law & Security Review* 2015, 78, 82.

[79] *Greenleaf, Privacy Laws & Business International Report* 2012, 7.

[80] ECOWAS Supplementary Act, article 2.

[81] ECOWAS Supplementary Act, article 12.

[82] *Supra* n 78 Makulilo, 83.

[83] ECOWAS Supplementary Act, chapter V.

[84] ECOWAS Supplementary Act, articles 38–41, 42–45.

ECOWAS member to establish an independent data protection agency which will have the authority to determine complaints, issue codes of conduct, and impose administrative and financial sanctions.[85]

III. The SADC Model Law on Data Protection

31 The Southern African Development Community (SADC) adopted the SADC Data Protection Model Law in 2013.[86] The purpose of the Model Law is to guide Member States in the drafting of data protection legislation to address violations of data likely to arise from the collection, processing, transmission, storage and use of personal data. The SADC Model Law stipulates the obligations imposed on data controllers to include the provision of information prior to processing, confidentiality, security, notification of processing to the data protection authority and accountability. The rights of data subjects are outlined in Part VII of the Model Law to include the right of access, rectification, deletion, temporary limitation of access, right of objection, and representation of data subjects who are underage.[87] The Model law makes room for the establishment of a Data Protection Authority[88] and mandates it to ensure data protection.[89] Data Protection Authorities should have powers to mete out punitive sanctions for a breach of data protection rules.[90]

IV. The ECCAS Model Law/CEMAC Directive

32 The data governance strategy of Central Africa is relatively less developed. In 2013, The Economic Community of Central African States (ECCAS) and the Economic and Monetary Community of Central Africa (CEMAC[91]) adopted a framework for data protection. ECCAS adopted it as a Model Law, CEMAC as a draft Directive.[92] The Framework addresses electronic transactions, data protection, and cybercrime. This Framework has a similar structure and content as the SADC Model Law. This is to be expected as the SADC, ECCAS and CEMAC Frameworks were drafted within the same project that was initiated in order to support harmonisation of ICT policies and laws in Sub-Saharan Africa.[93]

D. Assessing the African Data Protection Landscape

33 When examining the various regional and sub-regional legal instruments concerning data protection, the multiplicity of various initiatives and frameworks immediately takes

[85] ECOWAS Supplementary Act, chapter IV.

[86] Southern African Development Community, *Data Protection: Southern African Development Community (SADC) Model Law*, 2013, available at https://www.itu.int/en/ITU-D/Projects/ITU-EC-ACP/HIPSSA/Documents/FINAL%20DOCUMENTS/FINAL%20DOCS%20ENGLISH/sadc_model_law_data_protection.pdf (last accessed 16 December 2022).

[87] SADC *Data Protection Model Law*, part V and VI.

[88] *Ibid*, part III.

[89] *Ibid*, article 4.

[90] *Ibid*, article 9.

[91] Abbreviated from French *Communauté Économique et Monétaire de l'Afrique Centrale.*

[92] Greenleaf/Georges, *Privacy Laws & Business International Report* 2014, 19.

[93] The Model Laws were drafted under the Harmonization of Information and Communication Technology Policies in Sub-Saharan Africa (HIPSSA). See Boshe/Hennemann/von Meding, *Global Privacy Law Review* 2022, 56; Greenleaf/Cottier, *University of New South Wales Law Research Series* 2020, 23.

one's attention, all designed to guide African countries in the development of proper legal and regulatory frameworks for the protection of personal data but also as means of enhancing their participation in the digital economy to reap the benefits thereof.

Commenting on the multiplicity of initiatives on data protection, *Makulilo* observes that even though they appear to espouse and formulate similar basic principles to guide the development of data protection laws in African countries, many of them are in the form of a soft law and do not have any mechanisms to compel Member States to transpose the ideals into their domestic laws.[94] He observes that this had led to a situation where African countries have felt more obliged to align their laws to the EU Data Protection Directive[95] and the GDPR than the various initiatives discussed.[96] **34**

Harmonisation of data protection policies at the regional and sub-regional levels in Africa has also been stifled by the absence of supranational enforcement bodies where issues of interpretation of national laws could be referred to.[97] As a result, the Malabo Convention, in Article 34, only provides for state parties to settle disputes arising from the Convention by mediation and reconciliation. Consequently, member states see little deterrence in non-compliance with the Convention. **35**

In stark contrast, the situation is drastically different in the context of the GDPR. Within the EU, the GDPR as a regulation[98] is a mandatory law which holds precedence over member state law.[99] In addition, the GDPR contains several mechanisms to enforce non-compliance by Member States and non-members even beyond EU. For example, although African countries are not bound by the GDPR, the extraterritorial nature of Article 3 of the GDPR reinforces data protection rights of EU residents beyond EU borders. Accordingly, any data processing activities taking place in any African country involving offering goods and services or monitoring behaviour of EU residents falls within the GDPR regulatory framework. Under certain circumstances, data controllers in Africa would be required to appoint a representative in the EU who shall be answerable to all processing activities involving EU residents in those specified contexts.[100] Offences and penalties prescribed in the GDPR would then apply accordingly. Furthermore, the mechanisms for the transfer of personal data of EU data subjects to countries outside of the EU in Chapter V of the GDPR, especially the adequacy decision mechanism, include significant incentives for countries to adopt data protection legislation similar to or compatible with the GDPR.[101] **36**

These effects of the GDPR have been cited as reasons for African countries to feel obligated to enact laws like the GDPR,[102] favouring it over regional and sub-regional models, and could be one of the reasons why, despite the growing number of data protection laws in Africa, the Malabo Convention has yet to enter into force.[103] **37**

---

[94] *Supra* n 78, Makulilo, 87.

[95] Directive 95/46/EC of the European Parliament and of the Council of 24 October 1995 on the protection of individuals with regard to the processing of personal data and on the free movement of such data [1995] OJ L 281/31.

[96] *Supra* n 78, Makulilo, 87.

[97] *Supra* n 88 *et seq*.

[98] Consolidated Version of the Treaty on the Functioning of the European Union [2008] OJ C 326/47, article 288.

[99] For more detail on the concept, see Avbelj, *European Law Journal* 2011, 744.

[100] GDPR, article 27.

[101] GDPR, article 45; see further Hennemann, *Wettbewerb der Datenschutzrechtsordnungen*, 2020, 883–890.

[102] *Supra* n 78, Makulilo; n 2, Daigle; also, in the cases of Bloggers Association of *Kenya (Bake) v. Attorney General & 3 others* [2018] eKLR in para 11; and *Anne Waiguru v. Google Inc & 2 others* [2014] eKLR 11.

[103] *Supra* section 2.2.

E. Ghana's Legislative Framework on Data Protection

38 Ghana, as member of the African Union and ECOWAS, has ratified the Malabo Convention and is bound by the Supplementary Act on Data Protection. Beyond Africa, Ghana is an observer to the Council of Europe's Convention 108. On the national level, Ghana currently has a significant amount of legislation explicitly dedicated to or related to data protection and privacy. This section will therefore give an overview of the relevant laws for data protection in Ghana, starting with constitutional law and the centrepiece of Ghana's data protection framework, the Data Protection Act, before addressing other relevant legislation.

I. Constitutional Law

39 The 1992 Constitution of Ghana[104] contains no explicit right to data protection. The word 'data' is found three times, twice in relation to the Statistical Service Board of Ghana[105] and once concerning an obligation a relevant commission to make available certain data with traditional authorities.[106] It does, however, contain protections of privacy, stating that '[n]o person shall be subjected to interference with the privacy of his home, property, correspondence or communication' save for exceptions in accordance to law and subject to certain interests.[107] Another mention of privacy exists concerning the possibility to hold non-public trials for individuals in certain cases.[108] A somewhat related concept, the Constitution considers individuals' reputation a basis for the possibility of restricting freedom and independence of the media by law,[109] thereby possibly protecting the privacy of those subject to press reporting.

II. Data Protection Act 2012

40 The Data Protection Act 2012 (DPA)[110] is the centrepiece of Ghanaian data protection legislation. One of the earlier African data protection laws,[111] it precedes the EU GDPR, which other African countries have modelled their laws on,[112] and contains several special, if not necessarily unique, features.[113]

41 The DPA, a comprehensive data protection framework, contains at its core eight principles for the processing of personal data, which are accountability, lawfulness of processing, specification of purpose, compatibility of further processing with purpose of

[104] Constitute Project, *Ghana 1992 Constitution (rev. 1996)*, 1996, available at https://www.constituteproject.org/constitution/Ghana_1996?lang=en (last accessed 16 December 2022).

[105] Constitution of Ghana, article 182.

[106] *Ibid*, article 267 (7).

[107] *Ibid*, article 18 (2).

[108] *Ibid*, article 19 (15) (b).

[109] *Ibid*, article 164.

[110] Data Protection Commission Ghana, *Downloads – Data Protection Act, 2019*, available at https://www.dataprotection.org.gh/resources/downloads/data-protection-act (last accessed 16 December 2022).

[111] *Supra* n 93, overview at Greenleaf/Cottier, 3.

[112] Daigle calls it a 'more flexible framework', *supra* n 2 Daigle, 10.

[113] For a comprehensive analysis of the DPA in the context of individuals' data disclosure, see Hoffmann, *University of Passau IRDG Research Paper Series* 2022.

collection, quality of information, openness, data security safeguards and data subject participation.[114] The concept of minimality, arguably a principle as well, is contained in a separate section.[115] It contains a general requirement to obtain either prior consent of the data subject or conform with other legal preconditions to process personal data.[116] Stricter requirements are set forth concerning the processing of particularly sensitive personal data, called 'special personal data' in the DPA's terminology.[117] Further, the DPA creates certain data subject rights, such as a right to access and information, and to prevent processing in certain situations.[118] It further creates obligations to notify the regulator and the affected subjects of security compromises, internationally often called 'leak' or 'breach'.[119] It also establishes the Data Protection Commission (the Commission) as a regulator and empowers it to act upon violations of the law.[120] Regarding these aspects, the DPA is similar to other international data protection frameworks.

The DPA, however, also contains several notable aspects and some divergence from 42
internationally common modes of regulation. The international applicability is broad and could possibly be considered 'extraterritorial', applying also to controllers who process personal data 'originat[ing] partly or wholly from [Ghana]'.[121] While this is in line with other international regulation, another notable provision requires that 'a controller or processor shall in respect of foreign data subjects ensure that personal data is processed in compliance with data protection legislation of the foreign jurisdiction of that subject where personal data originating from that jurisdiction is sent to this country for processing',[122] a nod to outsourcing that raises interesting questions, such as whether court disputes in Ghana might proceed on the basis of foreign laws.

Notable in the African context is the applicability of the DPA towards public 43
authorities,[123] with every government department required to designate a data supervisor.[124] However, despite being applicable to the public sector in principle, the DPA individually carves out many different public functions from its scope, the broadest exclusion being for vaguely defined 'purposes of public order, public safety, public morality, national security or public interest', with the Act largely leaving this decision up to the Ministry of Communications,[125] other exclusions being for 'regulatory activity' in certain sectors,[126] for the 'combat effectiveness of the Armed Forces'[127] or even for marks in academic examinations,[128] *inter alia*.

Another rule that distinguishes Ghana from many other countries' data protection 44
rulebooks is the requirement of controllers to register with a Data Protection Register.[129] The fees associated with registration are a main source of financing for the Commis-

[114] The Ghanaian Data Protection Commission has compiled corresponding sections of the DPA relating to the individual principles, see Data Protection Commission Ghana, *Data Protection Principles*, 2022, available at https://www.dataprotection.org.gh/index.php/data-protection/data-protection-principles (last accessed 16 December 2022).

[115] DPA, section 17.

[116] DPA, section 20.

[117] DPA, section 37.

[118] DPA, sections 32–35, 39–42.

[119] DPA, section 31.

[120] DPA, sections 44, 75–81.

[121] DPA, section 45 (c).

[122] DPA, section 18 (2).

[123] DPA, section 91; see also *supra* n 2, Daigle, 10.

[124] DPA, section 91 (3).

[125] DPA, section 60 (1).

[126] DPA, section 63.

[127] DPA, section 69.

[128] DPA, section 72.

[129] DPA, sections 46–59.

sion,[130] and much enforcement is currently focused on the registration requirement.[131]

45 Other features are potentially problematic: an example of this is the broad and unspecific 'general penalty' for noncompliance with the DPA, which allows for imprisonment of up to 10 years.

46 The other is the question of independence (or lack thereof) of the Commission. While independence of data protection watchdogs is internationally considered to be of great importance, the DPA makes no mention of the word 'independence' whatsoever. Rather on the contrary, the president can at all times revoke membership of the members of the board,[132] and important questions are to be decided not by the Commission, but the Minister of Communications: *Inter* alia, the Minister may give directives relating to policy,[133] prescribe situations where individuals' rights concerning automated-decision taking are not applicable,[134] designate acts to be assessed as processing by the Commission and thereafter reviewed,[135] and is broadly empowered to create more detailed regulations on certain matters,[136] thus allowing for a great amount of control of the Commission by the Minister. In this regard, the DPA is in direct conflict with the Malabo Convention, which requires the 'national protection authority (…) be an independent administrative authority'[137], and the ECOWAS Supplementary Act.[138]

III. Protection Against Unfair Competition Act 2000

47 Unlike many other countries, Ghana has no comprehensive competition law framework.[139] However, the Protection Against Unfair Competition Act 2000[140] contains protections of 'secret information', which could be relevant concerning individuals' or companies' data, albeit restricted to information that is not generally known, has commercial value related to its secrecy, and has been 'subject to reasonable steps (…) to keep it secret'.[141]

IV. Electronic Communications Act 2008 and Accompanying Regulations

48 The Electronic Communications Act 2008 (ECA), amended in 2009, and the accompanying Electronic Communications Regulations from 2011 (EC Regulations),[142] while

[130] International Association of Privacy Professionals, *LinkedIn Live: Privacy Around the Globe: Ghana – Interview with Patricia Adusei-Poku*, 2021 minute 25 onwards.

[131] Safo, *Register with Data Protection Commission or face prosecution – Adusei-Poku*, 2022.

[132] DPA, section 5 (5).

[133] DPA, section 10.

[134] DPA, section 41 (4) (e).

[135] DPA, section 57.

[136] DPA, section 94.

[137] Malabo Convention, Art. 11 1. b).

[138] Babalola, *International Data Priacy Law* 2022, 44, 46.

[139] Koomson, *MIPLC Master Thesis Series*, 2019/20.

[140] WIPO IP Portal, *Ghana – Protection Against Unfair Competition Act, 2000 [Act 589]*, 2020, available at https://wipolex.wipo.int/en/text/157035 (last accessed 16 December 2022).

[141] *Ibid*, section 5 (3).

[142] All available at National Communications Authority, *Legal Instruments*, available at https://nca.org.gh/regulatory-framework/ (last accessed 16 December 2022).

largely dealing with questions related to the relevant infrastructure, provide for some sectoral rules concerning informational privacy.

The ECA[143] provides that the National Communications Authority[144] shall prepare a consumer code, including, *inter alia*, rules for the protection of consumer information.[145] It also creates criminal offences relating to the interception of communications with a fine or penalty of imprisonment of up to five years.[146] However, it also provides for broad obligations to intercept communications by providers responsible in the same section,[147] for relatively vague causes such as to 'protect the network or service from harm'[148] and to 'protect users'[149]. The same goes for the obligation to intercept communications on behalf of public authorities, such as by court order.[150] Especially problematic from a privacy rights perspective, the ECA gives the president broad authority to 'intercept communications, provide any user information or otherwise in aid of law enforcement or national security'.[151] **49**

The EC Regulations create 'General Principles' concerning electronic communications, amongst which are the 'security of public communications networks and services'[152], 'privacy and secrecy in electronic communications'[153], but also, mirroring the strong public authority rights in the ECA, the 'priority of national security and defence'[154]. It further creates criminal offences concerning the privacy and secrecy of transmitted messages and data, partly in parallel to the ECA offences and also punishable by fine or imprisonment of up to 5 years.[155] **50**

V. National Identity Register Act 2008 and Accompanying Regulations

The National Identity Register Act 2008[156] and the accompanying regulations[157] provide for the creation of a centralised national identity register, conceived as a database containing information about Ghanaian citizens and permanent foreign residents.[158] **51**

[143] The Electronic Communications (Amendment) Act 2009 is not relevant to data protection or privacy.

[144] Established by the National Communications Authority Act 2008, available at n 142.

[145] Electronic Communications Act 2008, section 28 (1) (c). Curiously, however, such a code is not listed on the NCA website. See National Communications Authority, *Legal Instruments – Guidelines, Codes & Others*, available at https://nca.org.gh/regulatory-framework/#guide (last accessed 16 December 2022).

[146] Electronic Communications Act 2008, section 73 (1) (f)-(i).

[147] *Ibid*, section 73 (4).

[148] *Ibid*, section 73 (4) (a) (iv).

[149] *Ibid*, section 73 (4) (a) (v).

[150] *Ibid*, section 73 (4 (b).

[151] *Ibid*, section 100; see also *ibid*, section 73 (4) (c).

[152] Electronic Communications Regulations 2011, section 1 (d).

[153] *Ibid*, section 1 (e).

[154] *Ibid*, section 1 (g).

[155] *Ibid*, section 6.

[156] Laws of Ghana, *National Identity Register Act, 2008 [Act 750]*, available at http://elibrary.jsg.gov.gh/fg/laws%20of%20ghana/2%20REP/NATIONAL%20IDENTITY%20REGISTER%20ACT,%202008%20ACT%20750.htm (last accessed 16 December 2022); amended by National Identification Authority, *National Identity Register (Amendment) Act, 2017 [Act 950]:* available at https://nia.gov.gh/wp-content/uploads/2021/05/act_950.pdf (last accessed 16 December 2022).

[157] E.g. the National Identity Register Regulations 2012, available at National Identification Authority, *National Identity Register Regulations, 2012 [L. 2111]*, availabe at https://nia.gov.gh/wp-content/uploads/2021/05/registration_act.pdf (last accessed 16 December 2022).

[158] National Identity Register Act 2008, section 4 (1).

52 Centrally and on the surface level, the National Identity Register legislation serves the purpose of establishing a system of national identity cards (Ghana cards).[159] Despite being initiated as early as 1973,[160] registration of citizens stalled, and, after initiating a new policy directive,[161] a new phase of mass registration began in (2017).[162] Up until June 2021, about 15 million Ghanaians were registered,[163] meeting the National Identification Authority's goal of 80 % of the population aged 15 and above.[164]

53 The National Identity Register, in the form envisioned by in the 2008 Act, contained only elementary information concerning citizens, such as their full name, sex, date of birth, marital status, level of education, and biometric information such as a fingerprint and photograph.[165] With the 2017 Amendment Act, this was greatly expanded, adding 20 new categories of information that is to be collected.[166]

54 Besides allowing for a trustworthy identity card system, the National Identity Register tries to make use of modern technology for identification verification. To support such (biometric) identity verification processes, the Act allows select government institutions and private third parties (currently consisting of banking and telecommunications service providers)[167] direct access to the National Identity Register, called 'user agencies'.[168] Coincidentally, a new government requirement to provide proof of identity to open mobile money accounts[169] (and to obtain SIM cards[170]) led to a significant increase in applications for Ghana Cards and thus to registration with the National Identity Register.[171]

55 Besides the establishment of national ID cards and improvement of capabilities of identity verification, the National Identity Register aims to improve governance by more efficiently integrating with other state institutions, such as the Ministry of Health and the Ghana Revenue authority, responsible for taxation.[172] While not explicitly mentioned, the National Identity Register seems to be used for at least some degree of data analysis, with statistics named as a case.[173] Furthermore, the National Identification Authority website names the 'obtaining beneficial insights' as a goal in management of the database.[174]

56 The National Identity Register Act also provides some insight to the use in its provisions on protection of personal information, allowing for the passing on of personal information contained in the register for purposes of national security, enforcement of criminal law, health insurance and immigration without the consent of the individual.[175]

---

[159] National Identification Authority, *The GhanaCard*, 2022, available at https://nia.gov.gh/the-ghana-card-introduction/ (last accessed 16 December 2022).

[160] National Identification Authority, *Our History*.

[161] See also Attafuah, *Profile of Ghana's National Identification System (NIS)*.

[162] National Identification Authority, *Synopsis of the National Identification System Project*).

[163] National Identification Authority, *Press Briefing by NIA on the National Identification System Project*, 2021.

[164] BusinessGhana, *NIA achieves over 80 percent registration target*, 2021.

[165] National Identity Register Act 2008, section 4 (2) and (3).

[166] National Identity Register (Amendment) Act 2017, section 1, amending section 4 (2) of the National Identity Register Act 2008.

[167] *Supra* n 163, National Identification Authority, 8–13.

[168] National Identity Register Act, sections 53–61.

[169] Mobile Money plays a significant role in the Ghanaian economy, see Collins, *African Business*, 2021.

[170] Boshe/Hennemann/von Meding, *Global Privacy Law Review* 2022, 56.

[171] Macdonald, *BiometricUpdatecom*, 2022.

[172] *Supra* n 163, National Identification Authority.

[173] *Supra* n 11.

[174] National Identification Authority, *National Database Management*.

[175] National Identity Register Act 2008, section 49.

While such a register may be greatly beneficial for purposes of improving state governance, such centralised accumulation of personal data of individuals carries significant risks for individuals' privacy. Additionally, making connection of biometric identification to access SIM cards and mobile money reduces the possibilities for privacy preservation of individuals. The National Identity Register Act addresses this by providing for certain rules concerning data protection matters, which focus on what kinds of information can be disclosed about individuals with or without consent,[176] that employees or contracted personnel keep confidentiality,[177] and establishing rights of individuals similar to those provided for in data protection legislation, such as a right to access[178] and right to correction.[179] It also establishes more detailed rules on data protection concerning user agencies.[180] What is notable in this context is that while the rules concern unauthorised access by employees or third parties, no specific rules cover possible abuses of the register by government offices for prosecution or national security. 57

VI. Right to Information Act 2019

In a significant step towards government transparency, the Right to Information Act[181] was passed in 2019,[182] following several court disputes highlighting the fact that the constitutional obligation to provide for such a right to information[183] had not previously been implemented. It provides that all information held by public institutions be in principle made transparent and establishes an individual right to information.[184] Restricting this general rule then are a large number of categories of exempt information, which include categories such as unpublished presidential and cabinet documents,[185] information concerning law enforcement and public safety,[186] but also economic information[187] and tax information.[188] In the context of data protection, the Act states that '[i]nformation, the disclosure of which is unreasonable concerning the personal affairs of an individual (…) is exempt from disclosure',[189] thereafter listing more specific cases in which disclosure is unreasonable[190] or reasonable.[191] 58

While the stated aim of the Act is the fostering of a 'culture of transparency and accountability in public affairs', the introduction of such a right to information offers 59

[176] *Ibid*, sections 48 *et seq*.
[177] *Ibid*, section 50.
[178] *Ibid*, section 51.
[179] *Ibid*, section 52.
[180] *Ibid*, sections 53 *et seq*.
[181] African Platform on Access to Information, *Right to Information Act 2019 [Act 989]*, available at https://www.africanplatform.org/fileadmin/user_upload/Ghana-RTI-Act-__1_.pdf (last accessed 16 December 2022).
[182] Media Foundation for West Africa, *Essentials of the Right to Information Law (989): A Guide Book – Ghana*.
[183] Constitution of Ghana, article 21 (1) (f).
[184] Right to Information Act 2019, section 1 (1).
[185] *Ibid*, sections 5 and 6.
[186] *Ibid*, section 7.
[187] *Ibid*, sections 10 and 11.
[188] *Ibid*, section 12.
[189] *Ibid*, section 16 (1).
[190] *Ibid*, section 16 (2).
[191] *Ibid*, section 16 (3).

significant possibilities concerning the availability of publicly held data, thus offering a counterpoint to data protection legislation. Another indirect effect of such a right to information lies in the necessity of implementation: in order to effectively comply, government institutions need to more professionally manage their data and information, which could lead to more effective data governance.[192]

VII. Security and Intelligence Agencies Act 2020 and National Signals Bureau Act 2020

60 The Security and Intelligence Agencies Act 2020[193] empowers the internal[194] and external intelligence agencies of Ghana to collect and monitor information related to its activities,[195] which centrally includes the combatting of threats to national security and the assistance of law enforcement concerning what the Act calls 'serious offences',[196] which include terrorism and other serious crimes.[197] With regard to such monitoring, the Act allows for interception of communications or the seizure of other information upon a warrant,[198] the procedural requirements for which are put forth.[199] A judicial complaint mechanism is provided for in form of the Complaints tribunal,[200] but hearings can be held in a non-public manner.[201]

61 As a consequence, the relevant agencies, particularly the National Intelligence Bureau, have, at least potentially, access to a great amount of personal data. Despite this, the Security and Intelligence Agencies Act itself does not mention matters of data protection, and the DPA[202] contains an exclusion for matters of national security and prevention, detection and prosecution of crime,[203] leading to the conclusion that the intelligence agencies can act without regard for data protection concerns.

62 The National Signals Bureau Act 2020 is almost identical to the Security and Intelligence Agencies Act in its scope and wording and allows for the same mechanisms of obtaining warrants for the collection of information and the interception of communications. However, the focus of the relevant government actor, the National Signals Bureau, lies in the digital realm. As such, similar tension exists concerning the privacy of individuals affected.[204]

---

[192] See the analysis by Issah Armstrong, *LinkedIn*, 2020.

[193] Judicial Service of Ghana, *Security and Intelligence Agencies Act 2020 [Act 1030]*, available at http://elibrary.jsg.gov.gh/fg/laws%20of%20ghana/2%20REP/Security%20and%20Intelligence%20Agencies%20Act,2020%20Act%201030.pdf (last accessed 16 December 2022).

[194] The National Intelligence Bureau and the Research Department, see Security and Intelligence Agencies Act 2020, section 12.

[195] *Ibid*, section 14 (1) (b) and (2) (b).

[196] *Ibid*, section 14 (1) (c) and (g).

[197] *Ibid*, section 49.

[198] *Ibid*, section 36.

[199] *Ibid*, section 34 and 35.

[200] *Ibid*, sections 26–33.

[201] *Ibid*, section 29 (1).

[202] *Supra* section E. V.

[203] Data Protection Act 2012, sections 60 and 61.

[204] See the analysis by Owusu-Darko, *The National Signals Bureau Bill and the constitutional right to be left alone*, 2020.

VIII. Cybersecurity Act 2020

The Cybersecurity Act 2020[205] covers a range of issues concerning different kinds of threats from the digital sphere. To this extent, it creates the Cyber Security Authority,[206] responsible for a variety of tasks in regulation of cybersecurity matters,[207] such as responding to threats and the formulation of guidelines and standards[208]), allows for the designation of certain computer systems as 'critical information infrastructure'[209] subject to stricter oversight,[210] mandates security incident reporting[211] and establishes an emergency response team,[212] and creates a licensing scheme for 'cybersecurity services'.[213] Additionally, it creates criminal provisions concerning online sexual exploitation and harassment, particularly in the case of children as victims.[214] 63

Contrary to the omission in the aforementioned Acts, the Cybersecurity Act 2020[215] explicitly states that it shall be 'read together with' the DPA.[216] Other than this, the Act itself is largely silent on matters of data protection and privacy, with some exceptions: The naming of a representative of the Commission as part of the Joint Cybersecurity Committee,[217] which could improve awareness of data protection matters within the agency, requiring clarification on protection of the privacy of those not party to the investigation in the application for[218] and as a precondition for the granting of[219] warrants for the interception of traffic and content data for surveillance purposes.[220] The required cybersecurity incident reporting[221] can also improve the protection of personal data in leak situations and is parallel to the reporting duties under the DPA.[222] Further reference to privacy can be found in the criminal prohibition of non-consensual sharing of intimate images,[223] which requires there to have been a 'reasonable expectation of privacy', a phrase known from US legal doctrine.[224] 64

Despite such provisions aiming at the protection of individuals' privacy, the Cybersecurity Act creates strong obligations for companies facilitating surveillance measures and empowers government agents[225] to intercept certain types of data. Service providers are required to retain all subscriber information for a period of six years, and traffic data 65

[205] Cyber Security Authority, *Cybersecurity Act 2020 [Act 1038]*, available at https://www.csa.gov.gh/resources/cybersecurity_Act_2020(Act_1038).pdf (last accessed 16 December 2022).
[206] *Ibid*, section 2 (1).
[207] *Ibid*, sections 3 *et seq*.
[208] *Ibid*, section 59.
[209] *Ibid*, section 35.
[210] *Ibid*, sections 38 and 39.
[211] *Ibid*, section 39 (1) (a), sections 47 and 48.
[212] *Ibid*, section 41. See also sections 45 and 46.
[213] *Ibid*, sections 49–56.
[214] *Ibid*, sections 62–68.
[215] Centre for Strategic and Defence Studies Africa, *Cybersecurity Act 2020 (Act 1038)*, available at https://csdsafrica.org/wp-content/uploads/2021/08/Cybersecurity-Act-2020-Act-1038.pdf (last accessed 16 December 2022).
[216] *Ibid*, section 1 (2) (j).
[217] *Ibid*, section 13 (2) (d).
[218] *Ibid*, sections 71 (3) (e) and 73 (3) (e).
[219] *Ibid*, sections 72 (1) (c) and 74 (1) (c).
[220] The protection of the privacy of the suspect is, in contrast, not explicitly mentioned.
[221] *Ibid*, sections 47 *et seq*.
[222] *Supra* section E. V. on the DPA; DPA, section 31.
[223] Cybersecurity Act 2020, section 67.
[224] See i.e. Winn, *Mcgeorge Law Review* 2009, 1.
[225] Named 'investigative officer', definition in Cybersecurity Act 2020, section 97.

as well as 'relevant' content data for twelve months.[226] Law enforcement personnel may then apply for warrants for the interception of such data.[227]

66 Perhaps more problematic for privacy, the Act allows for the ordering of service providers to build interception capabilities into their technology,[228] allowing for law enforcement access in a manner incompatible with encryption of communications. Furthermore, the licensing requirement for the provision of cybersecurity services[229] could be read as to include provision of encryption services, which could in turn lead to a *de facto* government permission requirement for any kind of encryption – countering generally accepted measures for the protection individuals' personal data.[230] The Cybersecurity Act thus contains both provisions furthering individuals' privacy and those possibly infringing on it. While the DPA is explicitly quoted, the DPA contains exclusions for such matters of security[231] and is thus not applicable to the acts of surveillance mentioned in the Cybersecurity Act. This does not mean, however, that the judiciary will not factor in questions of privacy, i.e. stemming from the Constitution,[232] as part of the decision-making process for the granting of a warrant.

IX. Conclusion

67 Apart from the Acts explicitly discussed, there exist numerous legal provisions relevant for the question of protection of individuals' personal data and privacy which are scattered between different pieces of legislation. These include, *inter alia*, the Children's Act 1998,[233] which states that 'a child's right to privacy shall be respected throughout the proceedings at a family tribunal',[234] the Credit Reporting Act 2007[235] which obliges credit bureaus and data providers to maintain confidentiality of information as well as privacy and secrecy of communication,[236] the Payment Systems and Services Act 2019,[237] a sectoral regulation, which requires the covered financial services providers to protect customers' privacy in the provision of services[238] (section 44 (d)), and the Anti-Money Laundering Act 2020,[239] which requires identification of individuals for the purpose of preventing money laundering.[240]

---

[226] *Ibid*, section 77.

[227] *Ibid*, sections 69–75.

[228] *Ibid*, section 76.

[229] *Ibid*, section 49 (1).

[230] Freedom House, *Ghana: Freedom on the Net 2021 Country Report|Freedom House*, 2022.

[231] See previous section.

[232] *Supra* section E. I.

[233] International Labour Organization, *The Children's Act 1998 [Act 560]*, available at https://www.ilo.org/dyn/natlex/docs/ELECTRONIC/56216/101251/F514833765/GHA56216.pdf (last accessed 16 December 2022).

[234] *Ibid*, section 38 (3).

[235] Ghana Business Regulatory Reforms Portal, *Credit Reporting Act 2007 [Act 726]*, available at https://bcp.gov.gh/acc/registry/docs/Credit%20Reporting%20Act,%202007%20(Act%20726)%20.pdf (last accessed 16 December 2022).

[236] *Ibid*, section 34 (b) and (f).

[237] Bank of Ghana, *Payment Systems and Services Act 2019 [Act 987]*, available at https://www.bog.gov.gh/wp-content/uploads/2019/08/Payment-Systems-and-Services-Act-2019-Act-987-.pdf (last accessed 16 December 2022).

[238] *Ibid*, section 44 (d).

[239] Financial Intelligence Centre, *Anti-Money Laundering Act 2020 [Act 1044]*, availabe at https://fic.gov.gh/AML%20ACT%202020%20(ACT%201044).pdf (last accessed 16 December 2022).

[240] *Ibid*, section 30.

Altogether, the state of the Ghanaian legal framework shows the inherent difficulty in balancing data protection and the government's interest in utilising information about individuals for the purpose of governance and particularly, law enforcement. However, it is notable that the more recent trend in legislation skews towards enabling surveillance, seen particularly in the Security and Intelligence Agencies Act 2020, National Signals Bureau Act 2020 and the Cybersecurity Act 2020.[241] In relation to data protection, this is made possible by the exclusion from the applicability of the DPA of matters of criminal law enforcement and public security. Taken as a whole, the Ghanaian data protection framework focuses on violations of privacy by private actors rather than such that may originate from government institutions. **68**

F. Ghana's Policy Framework on Data Protection

Following the discussion of Ghana's legislative framework on data protection, this section will examine Ghanaian government policy concerning data protection. To do this, multiple official policy documents will be examined for their relevance in matters of data protection. **69**

I. The ICT4AD Strategy

In June 2003, the Government of Ghana launched 'The Ghana ICT for Accelerated Development (ICT4AD) Policy'[242] to establish a road map for addressing Ghana's developmental challenges[243] through information and communications technology.[244] In this policy document, the Government posited that laws were to be enacted in relation to data protection and security. To this end, the policy carves out 14 priority areas to facilitate the process of transforming Ghana.[245] Of these priority areas, all have some form of connection to data processing. In the context of greater development of ICT systems and the accompanying risks, enforcement of data protection was explicitly addressed under the 12th priority area of the ICT4AD, which is 'Legal, Regulatory, and Institutional Framework Provisions',[246] as well as in the 14th priority area, called 'Facilitating National Security and Law and Order'. **70**

Within the section on the 12th priority area, the policy statement emphasises that 'the Government is (…) committed to the enactment of the necessary cyber laws and legislative provisions to govern and regulate cyber-related activities within the country', of which 'data protection and security, freedom of access to information' as well as 'computer and cyber crime' are considered part,[247] later stating that 'development, deployment and exploitation of ICTs' should be subject to protection by provisions on 'community and individual interests, including privacy and data protection issues'.[248] **71**

---

[241] *Supra* sections E. VII. and E. VIII.

[242] Republic of Ghana, *The Ghana ICT for Accelerated Development (ICT4AD) Policy:* available at https://nita.gov.gh/theevooc/2017/12/Ghana-ICT4AD-Policy.pdf (last accessed 16 December 2022).

[243] See terminology in preamble, *supra* n 6.

[244] *Supra* n 7.

[245] *Supra* n 9.

[246] *Ibid.*

[247] *Supra* n 70.

[248] *Supra* n 71.

72 In the 14th priority area, the policy objectives include the enactment of necessary cyber-laws as well as those relating to data protection.[249] Grouping data protection with matters of national security as well as law and order, the statement here said that policy directives should be implemented to 'address security issues relating to privacy, data and consumer protection'.[250] The priority area, however, does not go into greater detail, explicitly listing mostly policy goals related to making use of information technology to aid security forces, including the police and military.[251]

73 The ICT4AD strategy's timeline extends up to 2022.[252] The named successor to the policy is to be the Digital Economy Policy,[253] which is supposed to enhance the digitalisation process of the Ghanaian economy. The government is currently in the final stages of formulating the policy.[254]

II. Ghana National Cyber Security Policy & Strategy

74 In 2015, the Ministry of Communications published the Ghana National Cyber Security Policy & Strategy.[255] It addresses the problem of prevalent cybercrime in Ghana, particularly in the form of fraud, where it noted the problems in prosecution such as lack of knowledge and training in how to pursue perpetrators, as well as legal gaps.[256]

75 Further, it references pillar 14 of the ICT4AD strategy and notes there that the DPA 'ensures protection of private data of government, citizens and businesses in Ghana', but says that legislation is insufficient.[257] Rather than concern itself with violations of data protection and privacy, it aims to enhance law enforcement agency capability.[258] Prominent is also the aim to establish the necessary institutional and technology infrastructure for governance.[259] Altogether, one can see that the goals addressed here largely mirror the content of the Cybersecurity Act.[260]

III. National Financial Inclusion and Development Strategy

76 More recently, the National Financial Inclusion and Development Strategy (NFIDS)[261] was launched, as part of three policy initiatives[262] targeting digital development in the

---

[249] *Supra* n 76.
[250] *Ibid.*
[251] *Supra* n 77.
[252] *Supra* n 84.
[253] See on the background GP Business Consulting, *Ghana's Digitization Drive: Report*, 2021, 3; see also Presidency of the Republic of Ghana Communications Bureau, *Time for a Digital Roadmap For Ghana – VP Bawumia*, 2019.
[254] European Commission, *Joint Programming Ghana 2021–2027*, available at https://international-partnerships.ec.europa.eu/system/files/2022-01/mip-2021-c2021-9368-ghana-annex_en.pdf (last accessed 16 December 2022).
[255] Ministry of Communications, *Ghana National Cyber Security Policy and Strategy*, 2015 available at https://www.itu.int/en/ITU-D/Cybersecurity/Documents/Country_Profiles/National-Cyber-Security-Policy-Strategy-Revised_23_07_15.pdf (last accessed 16 December 2022).
[256] *Supra* n 10.
[257] *Supra* n 17.
[258] *Supra* n 24.
[259] *Supra* n 35.
[260] *Supra* Section E. VIII. and the comments on the Act's relationship to matters of data protection there.
[261] Ministry of Finance, *National Financial Inclusion and Development Strategy (NFIDS): 2018–2023*, 2018, available at https://mofep.gov.gh/sites/default/files/acts/NFIDs_Report.pdf (last accessed 16 December 2022).
[262] The other two, the Digital Financial Services Policy and the Digital Payments Roadmap, will be discussed in the following sections.

sphere of financial services.[263] The NFIDS addresses the inclusion of the part of the population previously without access to formal financial services, which it seeks to improve via digital technology.[264] To do so, it sets policy goals to be achieved within the time period from 2018–2023. In doing so, it addresses multiple questions highly relevant for data protection policy.

As such, it notes the importance of the 'increasingly electronic nature of the payment systems'[265] and says that 'increased capacity is needed to (…) improve the oversight of an increasingly complex and data-intensive marketplace'.[266] Additionally, it states that 'government and regulators should encourage the use of big data and alternative data to boost the effectiveness of credit reporting',[267] not without risk from the point of view of data protection. It further notes that fintech should be leveraged to achieve the goal of financial inclusion, and explicitly lauded a mobile network operator for using payment data 'to develop scores and offer mobile money-based loans'.[268] Despite noting the data protection provisions in the Credit Reporting Act 2007,[269] the NFIDS does not discuss in any detail the potential issues with data protection related to the promoted measures, implying a comparatively unconcerned approach to data protection in the context of this strategy. 77

IV. The Digital Financial Services Policy

Complementing the NFIDs, the Ministry of Finance developed the Digital Financial Services Policy,[270] which explicitly lists a number of policy objectives to be achieved to promote the development of digital finance[271] and addresses the period from 2020 to 2023. Through these objectives, the policy gives a great deal of insight into the Ghanaian government's goals concerning data protection matters in the context of digital payments. 78

One objective relevant for questions of data protection policy named is the introduction of 'a data-sharing regulation between data controllers (banks, mobile network operators (MNOs), electronic money issuers (EMIs), social media platforms) and other appropriately regulated DFS[272] stakeholders'[273] (no. 2.6). In more detail, the policy sets out that 'mandating some sort of data-sharing or data portability would equilibrate the market' and thus 'the Government of Ghana would support the introduction of a limited data-sharing regulation between data controllers (…) and other appropriately regulated DFS stakeholders, such as FinTechs, based on the provision of explicit user consent and the acceptance of strong customer security requirements'.[274] The recommendation of establishing standards for an API[275] further suggests that such a right would also be exercised in a digital manner.[276] In essence, the policy recommends 79

---

[263] Better Than Cash Alliance, *Ghana Launches New Policies to Speed Up Financial Inclusion and Digital Payments to Transform the Economy*, 2020.

[264] *Supra* n 261 Ministry of Finance V.

[265] *Ibid* xiv.

[266] *Ibid.*

[267] *Ibid.*

[268] *Supra* n 33.

[269] *Supra* n 43.

[270] Ministry of Finance, *Digital Financial Services Policy*, 2020, available at https://mofep.gov.gh/sites/default/files/acts/Ghana_DFS_Policy.pdf (last accessed 16 December 2022).

[271] *Ibid* 3.

[272] Digital Financial Services.

[273] *Supra* n 270, Ministry of Finance, 10.

[274] *Supra* n 31.

[275] *Ibid.*

[276] *Ibid.*

introducing a data portability mechanism, a hybrid legal instrument between data protection and competition law that has made its way into numerous jurisdictions worldwide.[277]

80 Objective 2.7 reads 'introduce a national competition law and authority',[278] which is remarkable insofar as there is currently no comprehensive competition law framework in Ghana,[279] leaving the government with limited tools to address matters of anti-competitive behaviours, which are often linked to issues of data protection, as can be seen in the many discussions over the handling of data by the so-called 'big tech' companies.[280] On this matter, the policy details that 'in the long term a national competition law should be passed, and a national authority be created', which could transform the regulatory landscape in Ghana, also for data protection.[281]

81 Explicitly addressing data protection enforcement, objective 3.3 is to 'increase the technical capacity of the Data Protection Commission in regard to DFS data, facilitate its cooperation with financial supervisors and evaluate the need for additional measures with regard to alternative DFS data'.[282] The report notes that the Data Protection Commission 'has only been recently established and thus is still focused on institution building, having just started the registration process for data controllers',[283] and that '[u]ntil the registration process has been completed, the DPC is not in a position to take any action to enforce the law'.[284] It notes that data are at the core of business models in fintech, with high risks to data privacy and security to customers, concluding that the regulatory capacity of the Commission needs to be increased and cooperation with other regulators improved.[285]

V. The Digital Payments Roadmap

82 The Digital Payments Roadmap[286] is another policy document which deals with the digitalisation of finance via mobile banking and is focused on the 'benefits of a shift from cash to digital payments by developing a national inclusive digital payments ecosystem'.[287] It emerged from a partnership between the Ghanaian Ministry of Finance and the Better than Cash Alliance at the UN[288] alongside multiple other Ghanaian and international contributors.[289]

83 It deals with a range of issues aiming at improving the regulatory ecosystem for the use of digital payments in Ghana, one of these being the state of data protection, particularly in the financial services industry. In general, it does not significantly diverge

[277] See for example Engels, *Internet Policy Review* 2016, 5(2); See also the comprehensive overview in n 33 Hennemann/Lienemann/Spirkl.

[278] *Supra* n 270, Ministry of Finance, 10.

[279] See also on the Protection Against Unfair Competition Act Section E. III.

[280] See, for example, Kerber, *Journal of Intellecutal Property Law & Practice* 2016, 856; see also, with regard to the Bundeskartellamt's enforcement against Facebook, Buiten, *Journal of Antitrust Enforcement* 2021, 270.

[281] *Supra* n 270 Ministry of Finance, 32.

[282] *Supra* n 10.

[283] *Supra* n 34.

[284] *Supra* n 35.

[285] *Ibid.*

[286] Ministry of Finance, *Toward a Cash-Lite Ghana – Building an Inclusive Digital Payments Ecosystem: Digital Payments Roadmap*, available at https://mofep.gov.gh/sites/default/files/acts/Ghana_Cashlite_Roadmap.pdf (last accessed 16 December 2022).

[287] *Supra* n 6.

[288] Better Than Cash Alliance, *About the Better Than Cash Alliance.*

[289] *Supra* n 286, Ministry of Finance, 2.

from the stated aims of the Digital Financial Services Policy and the National Financial Inclusion and Development Policy. Relating to data protection, the Roadmap recommends, *inter alia*, to 'institute a data governance policy framework to enhance provisions of the Data Protection Act',[290] followed by more detailed goals, notably to 'issue guidelines on data management, data sharing, and data protection', to 'build structures to enforce data-privacy laws', to 'introduce consent-based data-sharing regulation between data controllers and other appropriately regulated DFS stakeholders', and to empower consumers in relation to their 'own transactional data', calling them the 'real owners of data'.[291] A further stated goal is to 'increase the technical capacity and skill levels of the Data Protection Commission with regard to management of DFS[292] data and enforcement of data protection laws'.[293]

VI. National Medium-Term Development Policy Framework 2022–2025

As part of the long-term national development policy framework, which sets goals for **84**
national development until the year 2057, there exist multiple Medium-Term National Development Policy Frameworks (MTNDPF), covering shorter periods. The Ghanaian National Medium-Term National Development Policy Framework 2022–2025, in the responsibility of the Government of Ghana's National Development Planning Commission, thus comprehensively states multiple regulatory goals for the next years.[294] While it concerns itself with a multitude of issues, it references the development of data protection shortly, under point 9.1.11., which states the policy objective to '[e]nhance the implementation of the Data Protection Act, 2012 (Act 843)'[295] as a sub-goal to the enhance ICT in Ghana, in response to the stated key issue of 'weak online data protection'.

Further relevant is the goal to 'enhance Ghana's soft infrastructure through a national **85**
data centre that centralizes all digital information, data storage, management and protection', which echoes the development so far with the National Identity Register, but more broadly refers to better governance of publicly held data.[296]

VII. Development Cooperation Frameworks

Data protection as an issue may also be found in policy documents from interna- **86**
tional development cooperation frameworks, specifically concerning credit assistance of 200 million USD by the World Bank for a Ghana Digital Acceleration Project,[297] and 'Team Europe'[298], which will contribute funding of 203 million EUR for the first half of the 'Joint Programming in Ghana for 2021–2027'.[299]

---

[290] *Supra* n 25.

[291] *Ibid.*

[292] Digital Financial Services.

[293] *Supra* n 286, Ministry of Finance, 27.

[294] National Development Planning Commission, *National Medium-Term Development Policy Framework: 2022-2025, 2021*, available at https://ndpc.gov.gh/media/MTNDPF_2022-2025_Dec-2021.pdf (last accessed 16 December 2022).

[295] *Supra* n 52, appendix I.

[296] *Supra* n 113, appendix I.

[297] News Ghana, *$200M Approved By WB For Ghana's Digital Transformation Agenda*, 2022.

[298] More precisely the 'EU, the Czech Republic, Denmark, France, Hungary, the Netherlands, Spain and Switzerland, in cooperation with the European Investment Bank', *supra* n 254 European Commission, 1.

[299] European Union, *Ghana | Team Europe Initiative and Joint Programming tracker*, 2016, available at https://europa.eu/capacity4dev/tei-jp-tracker/ghana?tab=jpt (last accessed 16 December 2022).

87 The Ghana Digital Acceleration Project aims to 'expand access to broadband, enhance the efficiency and experience of selected digital public services, and strengthen the digital innovation ecosystem'.[300] Within this project, Subcomponent 1.3 is named 'Safeguards for Cybersecurity and Data Protection', allocated a budget of 12 million USD.[301] The aim of this subcomponent[302] is to improve enforcement of the Cybersecurity Act[303] and the Data Protection Act.[304] Particular focus lies on assessing regulatory challenges as well as improving the regulatory capabilities of the relevant authorities such as the Data Protection Commission, but also on strengthening public awareness of matters of cybersecurity and data protection.[305] Similarly, the Joint Programming aims to leverage digital transformation for developmental progress and states that the 'future EU-Ghana partnership should aim at supporting [the] digital transformation agenda'.[306] Regarding data protection, it also focuses on capacity building, stating that the 'EU will also support the Data Protection Commission to protect personal data (…)'.[307]

VIII. Conclusion

88 Viewed together, the policy documents allow for the piecing together of a clearer picture of stated aims by the Ghanaian government concerning data protection. Some conclusions that may be drawn from the examined documents are the following:

- Earlier policy goals, at least those concerning the implementation of legislation, have largely been met, particularly since the enactment of the Cybersecurity Act. Enforcement is now key.
- It is widely seen as necessary to strengthen the institutional capability of the Data Protection Commission in order to allow for improvement in enforcement of data protection legislation. While most promises to improve the regulatory capability concerning data protection stay comparatively vague, the fact that the World Bank and EU developmental cooperation initiatives explicitly aim to finance such an expansion indicate that tangible process may be made in the near future.
- The very strong development of digital payments necessitates particular focus on sectoral issues in this regard, as the sensitivity of payment data and inherent dangers require attention concerning data protection.
- While the legal framework is largely already developed, some very innovative instruments for Ghana are mentioned, such as the introduction of a competition law framework and regulator, and data portability rights in the realm of digital payments.

G. Assessing Ghana's Data Protection Strategy

89 As set out in the article thus far, there exists a significant amount of legislation and policy on the African, sub-regional and national level that are relevant for the question

[300] The World Bank, *Project Appraisal Document on a Proposed Credit in the Amount of US$200 Million to the Republic of Ghana for a Ghana Digital Acceleration Project*, 2022, 10.

[301] *Supra* n 11.

[302] *Supra* n 16.

[303] *Supra* section E. VIII.

[304] *Supra* section E. II.

[305] *Supra* n 300, The World Bank, 16–17.

[306] *Supra* n 254, European Commission, 1.

[307] *Ibid* 7.

of protection of personal data. On the basis of the demonstration of the different relevant instruments in the Ghanaian and broader African context, this section will identify five key policy goals of Ghanaian strategy regarding data protection.

I. International Convergence

The first identified policy goal is the Ghanaian commitment to international approaches concerning data protection, apparent on the global, African, sub-regional and national level. **90**

Within Africa, Ghana is part of the minority of countries that have signed and ratified the African Union's Malabo Convention.[308] It is, via ECOWAS, bound by the organisation's Supplementary Act.[309] It has, with the 2012 Data Protection Act,[310] enacted a comprehensive law on data protection and has established a dedicated supervisory authority, the Data Protection Commission. In doing so, Ghana has demonstrated a significant degree of commitment to African regional and continental legislation. **91**

However, when looking more closely at the Malabo Convention and the ECOWAS Supplementary Act, significant incompatibilities with the Ghanaian DPA emerge, notably regarding the independence of the Ghanaian Data Protection Commission.[311] This situation calls into question whether Ghanaian policy is actually interested in implementing international agreements or is committed primarily to outward appearances. It remains to be seen whether future developments move towards actual compliance with specifically the Malabo Convention and the Supplementary Act. **92**

Looking further abroad, Ghana is, as one of two countries in Africa,[312] an observer to the council of Europe's Convention 108.[313] While the Data Protection Act, as many laws concerning data protection worldwide, echoes European-style data protection legislation, the 'Brussels Effect' as well as the international effects of the GDPR specifically[314] have so far not extended to a revision of the DPA after the passing of the GDPR.[315] Additionally, the requirements for obtaining an adequacy decision are perceived as currently unattainable by the Data Protection Commission, weakening the pull to converge with the GDPR.[316] On the other hand, the explicit requirement in the Data Protection Act for controllers to respect other countries regulations on the matter demonstrates that Ghanaian legislation on data protection is, to a significant degree, internationally minded.[317] **93**

II. Economic Development

Ghanaian policy is, secondly, deeply influenced by the desire to harness technological innovations for economic development. This can be seen in the focus on the creation of **94**

[308] African Union, *African Union Convention on Cyber Security and Personal Data Protection*, 2014, available at https://au.int/en/treaties/african-union-convention-cyber-security-and-personal-data-protection (last accessed 16 December 2022).

[309] *Supra* section C. II.

[310] *Supra* section E. II.

[311] *Ibid.*

[312] And beside three other countries who have ratified the Convention.

[313] Council of Europe, *Convention 108 and Protocols – Parties*, available at https://www.coe.int/en/web/data-protection/convention108/parties (last accessed 16 December 2022).

[314] *Supra* section D.

[315] Bradford, *The Brussels effect: How the European Union rules the world*, 2021.

[316] *Supra* n 130, International Association of Privacy Professionals.

[317] *Supra* section E. II.

internet infrastructure in multiple policy frameworks, especially the ICT4AD strategy,[318] but also in the stated goals of allowing for a greater share of the population to benefit from digital innovations such as mobile payments.[319]

95 Regarding data, specific reference is made to the economic value of personal data for certain business cases, especially in the area of financial technology.[320] Data-oriented business models are challenged by implementation of data protection regulation – the Ghanaian policy on data protection will thus be constrained by a desire not to impede favourable economic results, implying that Ghanaian strategy on data protection will focus partially on avoiding regulation seen as too strict.

III. Improving Governability

96 Third, several indicators point toward Ghanaian interest in utilising personal data to improve governability of the country. Standing out in particular in this regard is the national identity register, which collects incredible amounts of personal data, aiming to assess the entire population in a multitude of categories for identification.[321] As can be seen from the developments regarding the register as well as the relevant policy documents, there is significant potential for the use of this register to provide a variety of government services, collect taxes and thus improve the overall effectiveness of government.

97 This focus on allowing for effective public-sector action can also be seen in the Data Protection Act, which carves out many essential functions of the government from the scope of the Act entirely.[322] This shows that compliance with data protection legislation is seen as a significant burden for the respective government institutions, and thus, shows the focus on sustaining governability. However, this regulatory strategy could prove unsustainable in the long run due to lack of pressure to professionalise attitudes towards data governance.

98 Furthermore, the lack of independence of the Data Protection Commission[323] provided in the DPA implies that government is unwilling to give the reigns out of its hands with regard to data protection, again showing a focus on governability that leads to less interference with government but can have adverse effects on the effectiveness of regulatory action.

99 Governability may further improve, despite not necessarily being the intended goal, through the Right to Information Act[324]: Where government institutions have to be prepared for individuals requesting information, structures must be put in place to allow for effective organisation and dissemination of the relevant data, personal or otherwise.

IV. Law Enforcement

100 Perhaps most worryingly from the perspective of data protection, there are clearly emerging trends that indicate strong interest in utilising the capabilities of modern technology for the purpose of strengthening (criminal) law enforcement, in line with the

[318] *Supra* section F. I.
[319] Prominently in the National Financial Inclusion and Development Strategy, *supra* section F. III.
[320] *Ibid.*
[321] *Supra* section E. V.
[322] *Supra* section E. II.
[323] *Ibid.*
[324] *Supra* section E. VI.

strategic goals voiced in the ICT4AD strategy.[325] These developments are, at least partially, motivated by the need to response to risks associated with digitalisation, as can be seen in the Ghana National Cyber Security Policy & Strategy.[326]

This can be seen most centrally in the Security and Intelligence Agencies Act as well as in the Cybersecurity Act, which gives the relevant law enforcement authorities broad powers to intercept digital communications for law enforcement purposes,[327] which are likely not subject to scrutiny under the DPA due to the exclusions for such matters put forth there.[328] Furthermore, the national identity register also provides for many opportunities for law enforcement agencies, particularly after the 2017 amendment which greatly increased the number of categories for which the register contains information on individuals.[329] **101**

This allows for the perspective that the Ghanaian government is keen on utilising the possibilities that exist with regard to digital technologies to allow for surveillance and more effective criminal law enforcement. However, this strategy carries significant risk to individuals' privacy and for personal data protection. In spite of this, there currently seems to be little awareness concerning such risks when they emerge from government rather than from businesses or individuals, which is a strategic challenge for the development of data protection in Ghana. **102**

V. Building Regulatory Capacity

Concerning the effectivity of data protection regulation, the central strategic goal must be seen in the creation and improvement of existing regulatory capacity. While the legislative framework now comprehensively addresses issues relevant to the topic, there is a significant divide between the law in the books and the law in action, leading to a significant degree of non-compliance with legislation, particularly the DPA.[330] **103**

The Data Protection Commission is significantly understaffed and under-resourced, and can thus not effectively pursue its goals.[331] This is compounded by the fact that enforcement of the DPA is often onerous for the Commission, as there exist no administrative sanctions, but it must pursue criminal penalties in court.[332] To improve this issue, the Data Protection Commission is currently in talks with the Attorney-General's Department for the creation of a fast-track court for the Commission to hasten prosecutions of non-compliant institutions and companies.[333] **104**

Several policy documents include references to improving the Commission's position regarding enforcement, among these the Digital Financial Services Policy[334]and the Digital Payments Roadmap.[335] Furthermore, the development cooperation frameworks include funding at least partially reserved for strengthening enforcement of data protection matters, which implies that regulatory capacity may be improved in the near future. **105**

---

[325] *Supra* section F. I.
[326] *Supra* section F. II.
[327] *Supra* sections E. VII. and E. VIII., respectively.
[328] *Supra* section E. II.
[329] *Supra* section E. V.
[330] *Supra* n 113, Hoffmann, 2.
[331] *Supra* section F. IV.
[332] *Supra* section E. II.
[333] *Supra* n 130, International Association of Privacy Professionals, minute 49 onwards.
[334] *Supra* section F. IV.
[335] *Supra* section F. V.

106 In the long run, the developments regarding competition enforcement hinted at in the Digital Financial Services Policy could significantly change the broader regulatory environment in Ghana, particularly regarding digital business, where issues of competition law and data protection often overlap.

H. Conclusion

107 A great number of international legal instruments, policy suggestions, national and international interests play a role in the still-emerging data protection framework in both Ghana and within the African continent. This article has reviewed the scope and impact of legislation and policy documents within the African Union, Regional Economic Communities and Ghana and sought to illustrate the Ghanaian strategy against the backdrop of its international commitments.

108 The Ghanaian case shows the many, often contrasting and conflicting, strategic goals, practical hurdles and (international) constraints to be overcome in order to properly implement data protection legislation. The balancing of different policy considerations and ensuring effective institution-building is a challenging task, and the development of the discipline of data protection far from final.

109 Domestically, the most significant immediate challenge for data protection is the question of enforcement. The current situation is insufficient to relevantly enforce compliance with the DPA, with the Data Protection Commission understaffed and facing many headwinds. The developments in the near future will determine whether data protection law will be significantly more than mere 'law in the books'.

110 Taking a broader international view, the competition between the legal systems of data protection[336] has not yet been decided, whether in the African (AU) or Ghanaian regulatory ecosystem. It is in this context that the EU's standards for adequacy decisions are at the risk of failing at their intended function in swaying countries toward a GDPR-style model of regulation due to the (perceived or actual) high barriers to their acquisition.[337] Within Africa, many are wary of the danger in the emerging trend of implementation of data localisation requirements for intracontinental trade and, thus, economic development.[338] Further influence (and challenges in implementation) may arise from other international data protection laws, particularly in case the United States implement a federal law on data protection and data privacy.

111 It is clear that Africa will only partake in the benefits of data collection and sharing if effective attempts are made to implement cross-sectional, integrated and far-reaching legal, institutional and policy measures that can maintain a balance in the data economy. In this regard, the need for effective laws on personal data protection is paramount. While Ghana has made significant achievements in the design and enforcement of its data protection laws, it can further strengthen its data protection laws and institutions and enhance the efficiency of its regulatory agency to coordinate data governance strategies and enforce data protection laws. Ultimately, there is the need

---

[336] *Supra* n 101, Hennemann.

[337] There is currently no country in Africa that has obtained an adequacy decision. European Commission, *Adequacy decisions*, 2017, available at https://ec.europa.eu/info/law/law-topic/data-protection/international-dimension-data-protection/adequacy-decisions_en (last accessed 16 December 2022); for an overview of the countries that have obtained adequacy decisions thus far, *supra* n 33 Hennemann/Lienemann/Spirkl, section I01 on Adequacy Decisions by the European Commission.

[338] See the many (implicit and explicit) warnings in n 63.

for Ghana and other African countries to build strong partnerships domestically and with other countries in order to reap maximum benefits from the digital economy and to promote economic development on the continent.

Bibliography

Ademuyiwa/Adeniran, Assessing Digitalization and Data Governance Issues in Africa, *CIGI Paper* 112
(2020), available at https://www.cigionline.org/publications/assessing-digitalization-and-data-governance-issues-africa/ (last accessed 16 December 2022)

African Platform on Access to Information, *Right to Information Act 2019 [Act 989]* https://www.africanplatform.org/fileadmin/user_upload/Ghana-RTI-Act-__1_.pdf (last accessed 16 December 2022)

African Union, *African Union leading on Data Economy in Africa … for Africa*, 2022, available at https://au.int/en/pressreleases/20201006/african-union-leading-data-economy-africa-africa (last accessed 16 December 2022)

African Union, *Agreement Establishing the African Continental Free Trade Area*, 2018, available at https://au.int/en/treaties/agreement-establishing-african-continental-free-trade-area (last accessed 16 December 2022)

African Union, *AU Data Policy Framework*, 2022, available at https://au.int/en/documents/20220728/au-data-policy-framework (last accessed 16 December 2022)

African Union, *Malabo Convention Status List*, 2022, available at https://au.int/sites/default/files/treaties/29560-sl-AFRICAN_UNION_CONVENTION_ON_CYBER_SECURITY_AND_PERSONAL_DATA_PROTECTION.pdf (last accessed 16 December 2022)

African Union, *The Digital Transformation Strategy for Africa (2020–2030)*, 2020, available at https://au.int/en/documents/20200518/digital-transformation-strategy-africa-2020-2030 (last accessed 16 December 2022)

African Union, *Treaty Establishing the African Economic Community*, 1991 https://au.int/en/treaties/treaty-establishing-african-economic-community (last accessed 16 December 2022)

Attafuah, *Profile of Ghana's National Identification System (NIS)*, available at https://www.cryptovision.com/wp-content/uploads/2022/05/20220519_Mindshare_Kenneth_Agyeman_Attafuah_Ghana_NIS.pdf (last accessed 16 December 2022)

Avbelj, Supremacy or Primacy of EU Law-(Why) Does it Matter?, 17(6) *European Law Journal* 2011, 744

Babalola, Nigeria's data protection legal and institutional model: an overview, 12(1) *International Data Privacy Law* 2022, 44

Bank of Ghana, Payment Systems and Services Act 2019 [Act 987], available at https://www.bog.gov.gh/wp-content/uploads/2019/08/Payment-Systems-and-Services-Act-2019-Act-987-.pdf (last accessed 16 December 2022)

Better Than Cash Alliance, *About the Better Than Cash Alliance*, available at https://www.betterthancash.org/about (last accessed 16 December 2022)

Ghana Launches New Policies to Speed Up Financial Inclusion and Digital Payments to Transform the Economy, 2020, available at https://www.betterthancash.org/news/ghana-launches-new-policies-to-speed-up-financial-inclusion-and-digital-payments-to-transform-the-economy (last accessed 16 December 2022)

bilaterals.org, *Trade in services in the AfCFTA*, 2019, available at https://www.bilaterals.org/?trade-in-services-in-the-afcfta&lang=en (last accessed 16 December 2022)

Boshe/Hennemann/von Meding, African Data Protection Laws – Current Regulatory Approaches, Policy Initiatives, and the Way Forward, 3(2) *Global Privacy Law Review* 56 (2022)

Bradford, *The Brussels effect: How the European Union rules the world*, 2021

BusinessGhana, *NIA achieves over 80 percent registration target* 2021, available at https://www.businessghana.com/site/news/general/241494/NIA-achieves-over-80-percent-registration-target (last accessed 16 December 2022)

Centre for Strategic and Defence Studies Africa, *Cybersecurity Act 2020 (Act 1038)*, available https://csdsafrica.org/wp-content/uploads/2021/08/Cybersecurity-Act-2020-Act-1038.pdf, (last accessed 16 December 2022)

Collaboration on International ICT Policy in East and Southern Africa (CIPESA), *Challenges and Prospects of the General Data Protection Regulation (GDPR) in Africa*, 2018, available at https://cipesa.org/2018/08/challenges-and-prospects-of-the-general-data-protection-regulation-gdpr-in-africa/ (last accessed 16 December 2022)

Collins, Kenya and Ghana lead world in mobile money, *African Business*, 2021, available at https://african.business/2021/07/technology-information/kenya-and-ghana-lead-world-in-mobile-money/ (last accessed 16 December 2022)

Constitute Project, *Ghana 1992 Constitution (rev. 1996)*, available at https://www.constituteproject.org/constitution/Ghana_1996?lang=en (last accessed 16 December 2022)

Council of Europe, *Convention 108 and Protocols – Parties*, available at https://www.coe.int/en/web/data-protection/convention108/parties (last accessed 16 December 2022)

Cyber Security Authority, *Cybersecurity Act 2020 [Act 1038], available at* https://www.csa.gov.gh/resources/cybersecurity_Act_2020(Act_1038).pdf (last accessed 16 December 2022)

Daigle, Data Protection Laws in Africa: A Pan-African Survey and Noted Trends, *Journal of International Commerce and Economics,* 2021, available at https://usitc.gov/journals (last accessed 16 December 2022)

Daniel, *Data protection laws in Africa: What you need to know*, 2021 https://www.cio.com/article/191345/data-protection-laws-in-africa-what-you-need-to-know.html (last accessed 16 December 2022)

Data Protection Commission Ghana, '*Downloads – Data Protection Act*', 2019, available at https://www.dataprotection.org.gh/resources/downloads/data-protection-act (last accessed 16 December 2022)

Data Protection Principles, 2022, available https://www.dataprotection.org.gh/index.php/data-protection/data-protection-principles (last accessed 16 December 2022)

East African Community, *Draft Legal Framework for Cyberlaws*, 2008, available at http://repository.eac.int:8080/bitstream/handle/11671/1815/EAC%20Framework%20for%20Cyberlaws.pdf (last accessed 16 December 2022)

Economic Community of West African States, '*Supplementary Act A/SA.1/01/10 on Personal Data Protection Within ECOWAS*', 2010, available at https://ictpolicyafrica.org/es/document/z69cbq7b51? (last accessed 16 December 2022)

Engels, Data portability among online platforms, 5(2) *Internet Policy Review* 2016

European Commission, *Joint Programming Ghana 2021–2027*, available at https://international-partnerships.ec.europa.eu/system/files/2022-01/mip-2021-c2021-9368-ghana-annex_en.pdf (last accessed 16 December 2022)

Adequacy decisions, 2017, available at https://ec.europa.eu/info/law/law-topic/data-protection/international-dimension-data-protection/adequacy-decisions_en (last accessed 16 December 2022)

European Union, *Ghana | Team Europe Initiative and Joint Programming tracker*, 2016, available at https://europa.eu/capacity4dev/tei-jp-tracker/ghana?tab=jpt> (last accessed 16 December 2022)

Financial Intelligence Centre, *Anti-Money Laundering Act 2020 [Act 1044]*, available at https://fic.gov.gh/AML%20ACT%202020%20(ACT%201044).pdf (last accessed 16 December 2022)

Freedom House, *Ghana: Freedom on the Net 2021 Country Report | Freedom House*, 2022, available at https://freedomhouse.org/country/ghana/freedom-net/2021#footnoteref4_nyq3t8l (last accessed 16 December 2022)

Ghana Business Regulatory Reforms Portal, *Credit Reporting Act 2007 [Act 726]*, available at https://bcp.gov.gh/acc/registry/docs/Credit%20Reporting%20Act,%202007%20(Act%20726)%20.pdf (last accessed 16 December 2022)

GP Business Consulting, *Ghana's Digitization Drive: Report*, 2021, available at https://www.ghanapremiumconsultant.com/wp-content/uploads/2021/12/GP-Business-Consulting-Report-Ghanas-Digitization-Drive.pdf (last accessed 16 December 2022)

Greenleaf, Global Data Privacy Laws: 89 Countries, and Accelerating, [Special Supplement] *Privacy Laws & Business International Report* 2012

Greenleaf/Cottier, Comparing African Data Privacy Laws: International, African and Regional Commitments, *University of New South Wales Law Research Series* 2020

Greenleaf/Georges, African regional privacy instruments: Their effects on harmonization, 19 *Privacy Laws & Business International Report* 2014

Hennemann, *Wettbewerb der Datenschutzrechtsordnungen* (2020) 84(4) RabelsZ 864

Hennemann/Lienemann/Spirkl, Mapping Global Data Law: Part I: Data Protection Legislation, *University of Passau IRDG Research Paper Series* 2022, available at https://www.jura.uni-passau.de/fileadmin/dokumente/fakultaeten/jura/lehrstuehle/hennemann/Mapping_Global_Data_Law/Kartensatz_August_2022_v1.6.pdf (last accessed 16 December 2022)

Hoffmann, Data Protection Act(ion) – Report on the Law of Data Disclosure in Ghana, *University of Passau IRDG Research Paper Series* 2022, available at https://www.jura.uni-passau.de/irdg/publikationen/research-paper-series/ (last accessed 16 December 2022)

Ilori, *Data protection in Africa and the COVID-19 pandemic: Old problems, new challenges and multistakeholder solutions | African Declaration on Internet Rights and Freedoms*, 2020, available at https://africaninternetrights.org/en/updates/data-protection-africa-and-covid-19-pandemic-old-problems-new-challenges-and (last accessed 16 December 2022)

International Association of Privacy Professionals, *LinkedIn Live: 'Privacy Around the Globe: Ghana' – Interview with Patricia Adusei-Poku*, 2021, available at https://iapp.org/news/video/linkedin-live-privacy-around-the-globe-ghana/ (last accessed 16 December 2022)

International Labour Organization, *The Children's Act 1998 [Act 560]*, available at https://www.ilo.org/dyn/natlex/docs/ELECTRONIC/56216/101251/F514833765/GHA56216.pdf (last accessed 16 December 2022)

Internet Society, *Personal Data Protection Guidelines for Africa – Internet Society*, 2018, available at https://www.internetsociety.org/resources/doc/2018/personal-data-protection-guidelines-for-africa/ (last accessed 16 December 2022)

Issah Armstrong, The Impact of Ghana's Right to Information Act, 2019 (ACT 989) on Public and Private Institutions, *LinkedIn* 2020, available at https://www.linkedin.com/pulse/impact-ghanas-right-information-act-2019-989-public-issah-armstrong/ (last accessed 16 December 2022)

Judicial Service of Ghana, *Security and Intelligence Agencies Act 2020 [Act 1030]*, available at http://elibrary.jsg.gov.gh/fg/laws%20of%20ghana/2%20REP/Security%20and%20Intelligence%20Agencies%20Act,2020%20Act%201030.pdf (last accessed 16 December 2022)

Kerber, Digital markets, data, and privacy: competition law, consumer law and data protection, 11(11) *Journal of Intellectual Property Law & Practice*, 2016, 856

Koomson, Developing without a Competition Legislation: An Analysis of Competition Law in Ghana and Its Impact on Competition and Development, *MIPLC Master Thesis Series* 2019/20

Laws of Ghana, *National Identity Register Act, 2008 [Act 750]*, available at http://elibrary.jsg.gov.gh/fg/laws%20of%20ghana/2%20REP/NATIONAL%20IDENTITY%20REGISTER%20ACT,%202008%20ACT%20750.htm (last accessed 16 December 2022)

Macdonald, *Ghana telcos trying to facilitate biometric SIM registrations as diverse concerns grow' BiometricUpdatecom*, 2022, available at https://www.biometricupdate.com/202202/ghana-telcos-trying-to-facilitate-biometric-sim-registrations-as-diverse-concerns-grow (last accessed 16 December 2022)

Makulilo, Myth and reality of harmonisation of data privacy policies in Africa, 31(1) *Computer Law & Security Review* 2015, 78

Media Foundation for West Africa, *Essentials of the Right to Information Law (989): A Guide Book – Ghana*, available at https://www.mfwa.org/wp-content/uploads/2021/02/RTI-Toolkit-book-final.pdf (last accessed 16 December 2022)

Ministry of Communications, *Ghana National Cyber Security Policy and Strategy*, 2015, available at https://www.itu.int/en/ITU-D/Cybersecurity/Documents/Country_Profiles/National-Cyber-Security-Policy-Strategy-Revised_23_07_15.pdf (last accessed 12 October 2022)

Ministry of Finance, *Toward a Cash-Lite Ghana – Building an Inclusive Digital Payments Ecosystem: Digital Payments Roadmap*, available. at https://mofep.gov.gh/sites/default/files/acts/Ghana_Cashlite_Roadmap.pdf (last accessed 16 December 2022)

National Financial Inclusion and Development Strategy (NFIDS): 2018–2023, 2018, available at https://mofep.gov.gh/sites/default/files/acts/NFIDs_Report.pdf (last accessed 16 December 2022)

Digital Financial Services Policy, 2020, available at https://mofep.gov.gh/sites/default/files/acts/Ghana_DFS_Policy.pdf (last accessed 16 December 2022)

National Communications Authority, *Legal Instruments*, available at https://nca.org.gh/regulatory-framework/ (last accessed 16 December 2022)

Legal Instruments – Guidelines, Codes & Others, available at https://nca.org.gh/regulatory-framework/#guide (last accessed 16 December 2022)

National Development Planning Commission, *National Medium-Term Development Policy Framework: 2022–2025*, 2021, available at https://ndpc.gov.gh/media/MTNDPF_2022–2025_Dec-2021.pdf (last accessed 16 December 2022)

National Identification Authority, *National Database Management*, available at https://nia.gov.gh/national-database-management/ (last accessed 16 December 2022)

National Identity Register (Amendment) Act, 2017 [Act 950], available at https://nia.gov.gh/wp-content/uploads/2021/05/act_950.pdf (last accessed 16 December 2022)

National Identity Register Regulations, 2012 [L. 2111], available at https://nia.gov.gh/wp-content/uploads/2021/05/registration_act.pdf (last accessed 16 December 2022)

Our History, available at https://nia.gov.gh/our-history/ (last accessed 16 December 2022)

Synopsis of the National Identification System Project, available at https://nia.gov.gh/2018/05/29/synopsis-of-the-national-identification-system-project/ (last accessed 16 December 2022)

Press Briefing by NIA on the National Identification System Project, 2021, available at https://nia.gov.gh/2021/07/01/press-briefing-by-nia-on-the-national-identification-system-project/ (last accessed 16 December 2022)

The GhanaCard, 2022, available at https://nia.gov.gh/the-ghanacard-introduction/ (last accessed 16 December 2022)

NATO Cooperative Cyber Defence Centre of Excellence, *African Union*, available at https://ccdcoe.org/organisations/au/ (last accessed 16 December 2022)

African Union Adopts Conventions on Cyber Security, available at https://ccdcoe.org/incyder-articles/african-union-adopts-convention-on-cyber-security/ (last accessed 16 December 2022)

News Ghana, *$200M Approved By WB For Ghana's Digital Transformation Agenda*, 2022, available at https://newsghana.com.gh/200m-approved-by-wb-for-ghanas-digital-transformation-agenda/ (last accessed 16 December 2022)

Owusu-Darko, *The National Signals Bureau Bill and the constitutional right to be left alone*, 2020, available at https://thebftonline.com/2020/11/10/the-national-signals-bureau-bill-and-the-constitutional-right-to-be-left-alone/ (last accessed 16 December 2022)

Presidency of the Republic of Ghana Communications Bureau, *Time for a Digital Roadmap For Ghana – VP Bawumia*, 2019, available at https://presidency.gov.gh/index.php/briefing-room/news-style-2/1181-time-for-a-digital-roadmap-for-ghana-vp-bawumia (last accessed 16 December 2022)

Republic of Ghana, *The Ghana ICT for Accelerated Development (ICT4AD) Policy:* , available at https://nita.gov.gh/theevooc/2017/12/Ghana-ICT4AD-Policy.pdf (last accessed 16 December 2022)

Safo, *Register with Data Protection Commission or face prosecution – Adusei-Poku*, 2022, available at https://www.graphic.com.gh/news/general-news/register-with-data-protection-commission-or-face-prosecution-adusei-poku.html (last accessed 16 December 2022)

Songwe, *The Role of Digitalization in the Decade of Action for Africa*, 2020, available at https://unctad.org/fr/node/27711 (last accessed 16 December 2022)

Southern African Development Community, *Data Protection: Southern African Development Community (SADC) Model Law*, 2013, available at https://www.itu.int/en/ITU-D/Projects/ITU-EC-ACP/HIPSSA/Documents/FINAL%20DOCUMENTS/FINAL%20DOCS%20ENGLISH/sadc_model_law_data_protection.pdf (last accessed 16 December 2022)

The World Bank, *Project Appraisal Document on a Proposed Credit in the Amount of US$200 Million to the Republic of Ghana for a Ghana Digital Acceleration Project*, 2022, available at https://www.gtai.de/resource/blob/836976/e502e062a8950f68abf44c9dbfd5beaa/PRO20210201607694.pdf (last accessed 16 December 2022)

Turanskyi, Africa and Europe: Cyber governance lessons, *SAIIA Policy Insights*, 2020, available at https://saiia.org.za/research/africa-and-europe-cyber-governance-lessons/ (last accessed 16 December 2022)

Winn, Katz and the Origins of the Reasonable Expectation of Privacy Test, 40(1) *McGeorge Law Review* 2009, 1

WIPO IP Portal, *Ghana – Protection Against Unfair Competition Act, 2000 [Act 589]*, available at https://wipolex.wipo.int/en/text/157035 (last accessed 16 December 2022)

§ 7 CHINA'S DATA STRATEGIES: INSTITUTIONALISATION, ACTIVATION, AND LAYERING

Content

A. Introduction: Data Strategies on Paper and in Practice

1 This chapter asks the question: what are China's data strategies in practice? On paper the Communist Party of China (CPC) and state actors (the party-state[1]) have stipulated many data policies and laws with strategic goals. Yet this chapter uses doctrinal and qualitative evidence to argue that in practice, the Chinese party-state adopt data strategies that can be conceptualised as institutionalisation, activation and layering, which help co-produce a knowledge-based regulatory state and a national digital economy. This conceptualisation draws from an institutionalist approach to law and economics, which emphasises law's role in co-producing the economy[2], coding/contesting property[3], and the law's co-evolution with technology in a path-dependent, non-ergodic and historically layered fashion[4].

I. China's Data Strategies expressed on Paper/in Policies

2 China's data strategies on paper officially appeared in 2015 under the rise of big data, when the CPC for the first time raised the concept of 'national big data strategy' in its top-level policy report.[5] Soon the State Council (SC) – China's top executive branch – stipulated *The Action Plan for Promoting Big data Development* (2015), aimed at competing with Obama's 2012 *Plan on Big data.*[6]

3 In March 2016, the National People's Congress (NPC) – China's highest legislator – passed *China's 13th Five-Year Plan (2016–2020)*, with Chapter 27 named as 'Implementing the National Big-data Strategy'. It specifically required the state to 'accelerate the opening and sharing of government data' (sec. 1), and 'promote healthy development of the big data industry' (sec. 2).[7]

---

[1] This chapter uses the phrase 'party-state' to simply mean both the CPC and state actors, their meshed relationship in the policy-making and strategy-implementation processes and as evidenced below. Party-state here is used as a more descriptive term, without addressing the 'party-state' question in Chinese studies, for example, on China's unique model of party-state capitalism or the cadre responsibility system. See e.g. Pearson/Rithmire/Tsai, *Current History* (2021) 120 (827): 207–213. Edin, in: Critical Readings on the Communist Party of China (4 Vols. Set), 2017.

[2] See, e.g., Deakin et al., *Journal of Comparative Economics* 45.1 (2017), 188–200. Ostrom, *American Economic Review* 100.3 (2010): 641–72. Deakin/Meng, *Journal of Institutional Economics* (2021): 1–15.

[3] Pistor, *The code of capital*, 2019. Ostrom, Beyond markets and states: polycentric governance of complex economic systems, *American Economic Review* 100.3 (2010): 641-72. Deakin/Meng, Resolving Douglass C. North's 'puzzle' concerning China's household responsibility system, *Journal of Institutional Economics* (2021): 1–15.

[4] Deakin, 7 *Review of Law and Economics* (2011). Deakin/Markou, Evolutionary Law and Economics: Theory and Method, *Northern Ireland Legal Quarterly* 72.4 (2021). Peters, The ergodicity problem in economics, *Nature Physics* 15.12 (2019): 1216–1221. Zuo, Governance by Algorithm: China's Social Credit System, 2020.

[5] 授权发布:中国共产党第十八届中央委员会第五次全体会议公报-新华网 (xinhuanet.com) [Report of the Fifth Plenary Session of the 18th Communist Party of China (CPC) Central Committee, 2015.] (last accessed 16 December 2022).

[6] 国务院关于印发促进大数据发展行动纲要的通知国发〔2015〕50号）[State Council's instructions on the action plans for promoting big data development, 2015. SC [2015] 50.]; Obama administration unveils "big data" initiative: announces $200 million in new r&d investments (Executive Office of the President, 2012).

[7] 中华人民共和国国民经济和社会发展第十三个五年规划纲要 [The 13th Five-Year Plan of the People's Republic of China on economic and social development, 2016].

The State Council followed up accordingly that year by issuing the *Provisional Measures on Government Information Resources Sharing* (2016) with the aim to regulate and facilitate the data flows between governmental agencies.[8] In December 2016, *The Big Data Industry Development Plan (2016–2020)* was promulgated as a leading industrial policy for big-data and the digital economy by the Ministry of Industry and Information Technology (MIIT). It opens with the claim that 'data is a national and foundational strategic resource; and it is the "diamonds mine" in the 21st century.'[9] 4

Moreover, China's data strategy can be seen as a foundation for and against the background of China's other national development strategies (at least on paper/in policies). In 2017, the Central Committee of the CPC emphasised in its top-level policy document (the *19th Report)* the need to 'integrate the Internet, *big data*, and artificial intelligence (AI) into the real economy (*shiti jingji*)' in order to 'build a Strong Manufacturing Nation'.[10] 5

The 'Strong Manufacturing Nation' goal is listed under Chapter Five of the *Report* –'Implementing New Development Visions', which also includes Sec. 2 'building an Innovative Nation'. The Innovation Nation project envisages an accelerated application of China's fundamental research and critical technologies in order to support projects like 'Strength in Cyberspace', 'Digital China', and 'Smart Society'.[11] It was around the same time (2015–2017) that national projects like 'Social Credit' (2014), 'Smart Cities' (2016), and 'Smart Courts' (2017) were promoted by high-level policy documents and action plans. These projects all require data-sharing, building data centres, and innovating data applications[12]. 6

In 2019, China's data strategies on paper expanded to agriculture and geographically to the rural regions with its 'Digital Villages'[13]. This project is supposed to cover more than 540 million people living in rural areas (2020), i.e. around 38.5 % of China's entire population (2020) and more than 1.5 times of the U.S. population (2020).[14] It started with the central Party-state's joint policy document *Strategic Plan for Digital Villages Development (2019)*[15]. This *Strategic Plan* was followed by the *2019–2025 Development Plan (2020)*[16], *Key Working Points (2020)*[17] and most recently the *Directives 1.0* (2021) 7

---

[8] 国务院关于印发政务信息资源共享管理暂行办法的通知国发〔2016〕51号） [State Council on the provisional measures to government information resources sharing and management. 2016, SC [2016] 51.] (last accessed 16 December 2022).

[9] 工业和信息化部关于印发大数据产业发展规划20162020年）的通知 [MIIT on issuing the Big data Industry Development Plan. MIIT [2016] 412.] available at http://www.cac.gov.cn/2017-01/17/c_1120330820.htm (last accessed 16 December 2022).

[10] 习近平决胜全面建成小康社会 夺取新时代中国特色社会主义伟大胜利——在中国共产党第十九次全国代表大会上的报告[Xi, Jinping, Report Delivered at the 19th National Congress of the Communist Party of China – Secure a Decisive Victory in Building a Moderately Prosperous Society in All Respects and Strive for the Great Success of Socialism with Chinese Characteristics for a New Era, 2017.10.18], available at http://www.gov.cn/zhuanti/2017-10/27/content_5234876.htm (last accessed 16 December 2022).

[11] *Ibid.*

[12] E.g. 国务院关于印发社会信用体系建设规划纲要2014—2020年）的通知；最高人民法院关于加快建设智慧法院的意见；中共中央办公厅 国务院办公厅印发《国家信息化发展战略纲要》.

[13] 中共中央办公厅 国务院办公厅印发《数字乡村发展战略纲要》.

[14] Rural population – China | Data (worldbank.org); rural population (% of total population) – China | Data (worldbank.org); total Population – United States | Data (worldbank.org) 329,484,123 US population.

[15] 中共中央办公厅 国务院办公厅印发《数字乡村发展战略纲要》.

[16] 农业农村部 中央网络安全和信息化委员会办公室关于印发《数字农业农村发展规划2019–2025年）》的通知）》.

[17] 中央网信办等四部门联合印发《2020年数字乡村发展工作要点》.

for details of implementations[18]. These implementation policies and directives are all stipulated by the Cyberspace Administration of China (CAC) together with other top-level ministries, and they intend to shape China's rural data strategies and digital economy, for example by building public data platforms, big-data centres and introducing 'smart agriculture' applications, which are similar to their urban counterparts[19]. Some case studies were raised in the *Directives 1.0* (2021)[20], and practices like the *Blockchain Chicken Farm* also emerged[21].

8 While expanding agriculturally and geographically, China's data strategies also became more clearly market-oriented on paper. In 2020, the central Party-state for the first time jointly defined data as the fifth 'essential factor (of production)' following land, labour, capital, and technology in the top-level policy document *Instruction on Improving the Market Mechanism for Allocating Essential Factors (2020).* The document requires the state to 'foster a data factor market' by first, 'advancing open government data and sharing' (sec. 20), second, 'increasing the value of data resources' (sec. 21), and third, 'strengthening the integration and security protection of data resources' (sec. 22). Some emphases include to 'guide and cultivate the big-data trading market, and start data-trading according to laws and regulations' (sec. 26), and 'establish and improve mechanisms on data property transactions (*chanquan jiaoyi*) and self-governance by industrial associations' (sec. 27).[22]

II. Research Question and Gap of Understanding

9 While China's data strategies on paper have been laid out extensively, this chapter asks the question: what are China's data strategies in practice? Sub-questions include the following. Is data 'secured' and 'integrated' as the Party-state required in 2020? To whom and what extent do governments share data? Is data trading or 'property transaction' working well? Has the 'value of data' been realised?

10 For example, in contrast to the policy vision of data 'property transaction', as of January 2022, Chinese national laws in practice (deliberately) leave a grey zone for data property transactions and ownership, which encourages local and industrial experimentations (see below the Activation strategy)[23]. In fact, China's new Civil Code (2021) reaffirms that there is no clear data 'property' or 'ownership' at the national level (yet), which means doctrinally Chinese courts still cannot enforce traditional contractual clauses that cover data transactions[24]. Shenzhen also failed to write 'data property

---

[18] www.cac.gov.cn/rootimages/uploadimg/1632256402882582/1632256402882582.pdf (last accessed 16 December 2022).

[19] See, e.g. chapter 3 and 4 of the Directive 2021, available at www.cac.gov.cn/rootimages/uploadimg/1632256402882582/1632256402882582.pdf (last accessed 16 December 2022).

[20] *Ibid.*

[21] See Wang, Xiaowei. *Blockchain chicken farm: and other stories of tech in China's countryside*, 2020.

[22] 中共中央 国务院关于构建更加完善的要素市场化配置体制机制的意见 [CPC central committee and State Council: Instruction on Improving the Market Mechanism for Allocating Essential Factors, 2020.3.30.].

[23] See Part D.

[24] For a literature review of Chinese legal debates on data property rights, see 孔祥俊商业数据权数字时代的新型工业产权，《比较法研究》，202201）pp 2–3; 彭辉数据权属的逻辑结构与赋权边界，《比较法研究》, 202201）. It is also worth noting that China's Civil Code Article 127 stated that 'abide by laws where data and internet virtual assets are protected'. This is understood more as a protection for virtual assets like coins in online game purchases rather than data sets.

rights' into its municipal data legislation (2021)[25]. Many Chinese scholars have in fact recently argued against a general data property rights.[26]

A potential alternative to 'property transaction' is to use licensing, sharing or 'contact' (*jiechu*) agreements under intellectual property (IP) laws to approximate data sets as IP objects. However, legal professionals have pointed out the risk is that current Chinese IP laws do not clarify data as IP objects[27]. Legal scholars recently raised possibilities for 'data compulsory licensing' (*qiangzhi xuke*) based on 'essential facilities' provisions in antitrust and IP laws[28]. However, the *2021 Antitrust Guideline on Platform Economy* in its final version scrapped the part on 'considering data as an essential facility' (*cf.* Draft 2020).[29] Kong (2022) recently argued that instead of a general data property, China should start by stipulating 'commercial data rights' under IP law which delineate industrial data from more sensitive data types like personal/public data. This is an attempt to specify data governance regimes and use trade/commercial secret law as an inspiration to create new 'industrial IP rights' categories[30]. **11**

Moreover, Feng argued for an unfair competition law approach to protect those data interests that do not qualify for IP protections.[31] For example, the Hangzhou Internet Court ruled (and Hangzhou Intermediary Court affirmed) in the 'Wechat/Tencent unfair competition case' (2019, 2020) that the two plaintiffs (corporations of Tencent) have 'competition interests (*jngzheng quanyi*)' with regards to their 'data resource totality (*shuju ziyuan zhengti*)'. It also explicitly ruled that these corporations are only limited to the right of use rights to their 'individual data units (*danyi shuju geti*)' rather than the whole bundle of property rights.[32] **12**

Besides property, IP, and compulsory licensing, and the unfair competition protection, legal professionals also discussed the potential of data service agreements (as a service, AAS) to help data transaction and flow, especially concerning increasing data localisation rules around the world[33]. There are also five local Data Exchanges as emerging data brokers who experiment new modes of data transactions as of January 2022 (Guizhou 2015, Shaanxi 2015, Beijing 2021, Shanghai 2021, Changsha 2022), where Beijing raised the idea of 'use without retaining' (similar to AAS)[34]. But, in short, China's data trading and 'property transaction' is still in a legal grey zone, and there is a gap of understanding on the rapidly evolving practices being experimented. **13**

Moreover, very few works in the existing literature have comprehensively examined China's data strategies in practice. Ding briefly discussed China's global data strategy based **14**

[25] See Part D. II. Also see legal scholar's discussions: 地方无权对"数据权"立法深圳数据条例意见稿引专家热议 available at https://www.xuehua.us/a/5f15cb4ce3809536eb952075?lang=zh-cn (last accessed 16 December 2022).

[26] See literature reviews in 彭辉数据权属的逻辑结构与赋权边界，《比较法研究》, 202201）. 孔祥俊商业数据权数字时代的新型工业产权，《比较法研究》，202201）.

[27] See e.g. . 数据交易合同的法律问题 | China Law Insight; 刘一民律师数据交易架构和数据许可.

[28] 曾彩霞，朱雪忠数字经济背景下构建数据强制许可制度的合理性，基本原则和监管思路.《电子政务》2021. 陈永伟: 数据是否应适用必需设施原则——基于"两种错误"的分析,《竞争政策研究》2021:4. 李世佳: 论数据构成必需设施的标准——兼评《关于平台经济领域的反垄断指南》第十四条之修改, 河南财经政法大学学报. 2021, 36 (05).

[29] *Cf.* Antitrust Guideline 2021 and 2020 draft.

[30] 孔祥俊商业数据权数字时代的新型工业产权，《比较法研究》，202201）.

[31] 冯晓青数据财产化及其法律规制的理论阐释与构建 《政法论丛》202104）.

[32] ((2019) 浙8601民初1987号 [2019, Zhejiang, 8601 Civil first instance case no. 1987]; 2020）浙01民终5889号 [2020, Zhejiang, 01 Civil appeal case no. 5889].

[33] 数据交易合同的法律问题 | China Law Insight; 刘一民律师数据交易架构和数据许可.

[34] See 中部地区唯一新型数据交易所在长沙试运营|长沙市_新浪财经_新浪网 (sina.com.cn); also see D. II.

on existing legal and policy documents.[35] Dai used a law and economics approach to conceptualise the government's strategies to use reputation in a 2x2 matrix of 'regulation', 'searchlight', 'incorporation' and 'institutionalization' (figure 1). This conceptualisation touches on China's data strategies in the case of the Social Credit System (SCS), where for example public data is shared and used by public authorities in public administration. But Dai's paper does not intend to systematically examine the data practices or strategies involved. He also suggests a deficit of empirical evidence in his research.[36]

	Private sector information	**Public sector information**
Private actors' decision-making	regulation	searchlight
Public authorities' decision-making	incorporation	institutionalization

Figure 1. Dai's 2x2 martix for the theorisations of state strategies in the SCS, see n 36

15 This chapter fills a gap of understanding on China's data strategies in practice. It builds on doctrinal and empirical evidence and adopts an institutionalist approach in order to provide better conceptual models. The chapter argues that China's data strategies can be understood in practice as:

(1) Institutionalisation[37], or the co-production of formal institutions by public and private actors to address data harms/risks and stabilise the expectations of these actors;
(2) activation, or the party-state's adoptions of flexible policies and practices in order to mobilise data sharing and use, and
(3) layering, or the construction of long-term data habitat/ecosystems in order to achieve high-value data use and interpretation.

16 These practical strategies emerged to deal with three real predicaments in China's data governance:

(1) Security and privacy concerns under concentrated corporate (and state) power;
(2) fragmented data access and use by private and public actors; and
(3) the lack of valuable data use, interpretation, and long-term scaling.

III. Scope and Structure of the Chapter

17 The chapter limits the scope of discussion to China's data strategies practised within its borders. It is worth noting that China does not have explicit laws or policies on its

[35] 丁晓东构建全球数据竞争的中国战略，学习时报，2020 [Ding, Xiaodong, Qiushi.cn (last accessed 9 October 2020)].

[36] Dai, Xin. "Toward A Reputation State: A Comprehensive View of China's Social Credit System Project." *Social Credit Rating: Reputation und Vertrauen beurteilen* (2020): 139–163.

[37] This is broader than Dai's definition of the state's 'institutionalization strategy' in 2018, which means the government's use of its own public data for reputational regulations (G2G), such as the Shanghai public credit information system that provides public risk-scores for corporations. In this chapter however, institutionalision means setting up formal legal frameworks as focal points in order to allow organisations and individuals to compete and coordinate, mostly for private actors but not for governments. The government's data sharing would be more relevant in the second strategy of *activation*. Institutionalisation in this chapter nevertheless includes Dai's other three state data strategies in terms of reputational governance, i.e. regulation (of private reputation data market like Uber and Airbnb, B2B), searchlight (public information used by private individuals and corporations for decision-making, G2B), and incorporation (private data used for public decision-making, B2G).

extra-territorial data strategy, except for a 'Global Data Security Initiative' published by the Chinese Foreign Ministry (2020)[38]. However, recent Chinese laws and regulations have in practice formed a territorially defensive data strategy that prevents certain data from crossing China's geographical border. These practices include the stipulation of data localisation rules[39] and security reviews for cross-border data transfer, which culminated in the 2021 CAC review of DiDi's IPO in New York (C.).

In contrast to this formally instituted defensive strategy of retaining data within Chinese borders, it can be argued that China in practice has informally carried out an extra-territorial data strategy under the name of the 'digital silk road' (DSR). The DSR idea was first raised in a speech given by President Xi Jinping to corporate and to government partners around the world at the '2017 Belt-and-Road Initiative (BRI) Summit'[40]. Since then, many public and private practices were identified as the DSR, including the early 'China-Myanmar land cable networks' (2014) built by China Unicom[41], the 2017 DSR summits respectively held between China and the Czech Republic, Hungary and Serbia, the 'Digital Hub' jointly set up by China's Alibaba and a Malaysian company in Kuala Lumpur (2018), the 'China-Philippine Data Harbour' (2018) and so on[42]. These practices, together with the recent expansion of Chinese big-tech companies abroad, contributed to the apprehensions on whether China's DSR would in practice 'control the global internet' and shape the order of global digital governance. Even without explicit state policies, China's investments, businesses, and ICT infrastructure constructions are viewed as practices of China's expansive data strategy in African, Asian, European, and Latin American countries via the BRI[43]. Some argued that these expansive practices constitute a hard 'Beijing effect' compared to the soft 'Brussels effect'[44]. 18

This chapter focuses on China's domestic data strategy in practice, and all qualitative evidence is collected in cities rather than villages, due to practical limits of the fieldwork and the scope of this chapter. 19

The chapter proceeds by first introducing its institutionalist framing and the conceptual models of institutionalisation, activation, and layering (B. Institutionalist Theory, Conceptual Model and Methodology). It then discusses these three data strategies respectively by analysing doctrinal and qualitative evidence (C. Institutionalisation: Data Security, Protection, and Antitrust, D. Activation: Data Property, Commons, or 'Party manages data'?, E. Layering: Data Cycles, Local Habitats, and Sustainable Design), and in the end concludes (F. Conclusion). 20

B. Institutionalist Theory, Conceptual Model and Methodology

The conceptual categories of institutionalisation, activation, and layering are inspired by institutionalist theories of law and economics. Institutionalisation draws from the state's 21

[38] 外交部全球数据安全倡议, Foreign Ministry, *Global Data Security Initiative*, 2020.

[39] See civil code 2021, and Personal Information Protection Law 2021, and Data Security Law 2021.

[40] 携手推进"一带一路"建设--时政--人民网 (people.com.cn) (2017).

[41] 大数据与"一带一路"--理论-人民网 (people.com.cn) (2016); 中国缅甸国际陆地光缆工程全线贯通_地方报道_新闻_中国政府网 (www.gov.cn) (2014).

[42] 中国大数据企业走上"一带一路" (xinhuanet.com) (2018).

[43] See e.g. https://leidenasiacentre.nl/wp-content/uploads/2021/01/LAC-IPCS-DSR-Report-Aug-2020.pdf; Will China Control the Global Internet Via its Digital Silk Road? – Carnegie Endowment for International Peace (2020); China's Digital Silk Road and the Global Digital Order – The Diplomat (2021).

[44] Erie/Streinz, *The Beijing Effect: China's 'Digital Silk Road' as Transnational Data Governance*, 2021.

instituting capacity that co-produces the economy.[45] The activation strategy derives from law's capacity to code/contest property rights and facilitate access, transaction, and pooling practices[46]. The layering strategy is inspired by theories of long-term law-tech co-evolution, where law and technologies are institutionally 'layered' and imprinted through time.[47] These groups of theories together hold that institutions are path-dependent, non-ergodic (time irreversible)[48], and embedded in history.[49] In such evolutionary processes, institutions retain shared cognition and knowledge of governance practices as the 'sediments of time'.[50] This part explains the conceptual models of institutionalisation, activation, and layering, and their groundings in institutionalist theories.

I. Institutionalisation: State-market Co-Production

22 First, 'institutionalisation' is used to describe the state's use of formal institutions and practices to initiate knowledge exchange with private actors and co-produce the economy. This conceptual category is inspired by institutionalist theories of state-market co-production. In early literatures, Ostrom and co-authors used 'co-production' to explain public services being carried out by both paid (public) and unpaid (private) labours[51]. For example, 'safety' as a public good achieved by both the police walking on beat and the communities' anti-crime efforts. Her case study in Indianapolis[52] and neighbourhoods of African Americans[53] shows that instead of large-scale patrolling in their cars, the police walking on the streets (as formal institutions) exchange informal/tacit knowledge with people in the communities, who despite unpaid, voluntarily contribute to local crime prevention and reduction. Her later case studies shows similar synergetic mechanisms of co-production in U.S. education policy[54], urban infrastructure policy in Brazil, and education in Nigeria[55]. Her collaborative empirical studies on common-pool resources further demonstrated how the state and private communities need each other to co-produce both formal and informal institutions. Law in her framework is thus not merely about legal rules, but also the constitutive processes and practices that facilitate public-private knowledge exchange and collective actions.[56]

---

[45] *Supra* n 1.

[46] *Supra* n 2.

[47] *Supra* n 3.

[48] The non-ergodic concept is drawn from an emerging school of ergodicity economics. See Peters, *Quantitative Finance* 11.11 (2011), 1593–1602. Peters, *Nature Physics* 15.12 (2019), 1216–1221.

[49] See, Deakin/Markou, *Northern Ireland Legal Quarterly* 72.4 (2021). Deakin, 7 *Review of Law and Economics* (2011). Deakin, 55 *Current Legal Problems* (2002). Deakin/Wilkinson, *The Law of the Labour Market: Industrialisation, Employment, and Legal Evolution*, 2005.

[50] Aoki, *Corporations in evolving diversity: Cognition, governance, and institutions,* 2010; Koselleck, *Sediments of Time: on possible histories*, 2018; Deakin/Meng, The Governance of Covid-19: Anthropogenic Risk, Evolutionary Learning, and the Future of the Social State, *Industrial Law Journal* 49.4 (2020): 539–594; Zuo, *Governance by Algorithm: China's Social Credit System* (working paper), 2020, available at https://www.finance.group.cam.ac.uk/system/files/documents/GovernancebyAlgorithm_CERF_Zhenbin6.16.2020.pdf (last accessed 16 December 2022).

[51] Parks/Baker/Kiser/Oakerson/Ostrom/Ostrom/Percy/Vandivort/Whitaker/Wilson, *Policy studies journal*, 9(7), (1981) 1001–1011.

[52] Ostrom/Whitaker, *American Journal of Political Science* (1973), 48–76.

[53] Ostrom/Whitaker, Community control and governmental responsiveness: The case of police in black neighborhoods, *Improving the quality of urban management* 10.4 (1974), 303-34.

[54] Davis/Ostrom, *International Political Science Review* 12.4 (1991), 313–335.

[55] Ostrom, *World development* 24.6 (1996): 1073–1087.

[56] Ostrom, *American Economic Review* 100.3 (2010): 641-72.

In more recent literatures, Aoki uses the concept of 'embedded cognition' to describe institutions' capacity to store and transmit knowledge through time. He argued that states and corporations are not 'bundles of contracts' but epistemic communities that maintain focal points and cognitive structures embedded in society.[57] Deakin et al. further raise 'legal institutionalism' as a law and economics paradigm to explain how the rule-of-law state co-produces the modern market economy at its current global scales.[58] They argue that industrialisation and modern economic development require a clear boundary between the state and market, where co-production of public service becomes possible between public and private actors working with complementarity.[59] **23**

Deakin, Chen and collaborators further used qualitative evidence to show that China's large scale industrialisation have been accompanied with the emergence of a rule-of-law state, which enforces contracts, property rights, corporate governance structures and so on. They argue that this recent rising rule-of-law state complements and constitutes China's traditional *guanxi*-based economy. Such state-market complementarity helps the Chinese economy to break from its previous limits, which come from traditional modes of cooperation and enforcement that heavily rely on informal social norms within close-knit groups and geographical regions. A Chinese rule-of-law state, at least by enforcing private and commercial laws, thus co-produces the Chinese modern market economy.[60] Deakin and Meng also use the case of COVID-19 governance in Wuhan to further illustrate how legal institutions at national and international levels helped retain public health knowledge and coordinated large-scale collective actions[61]. **24**

In the context of data strategy, evidence shows that in 2021 China has intensive legislation and enforcement practices on cyber/data security, data protection, and antitrust. They are examples where the state uses data institutionalisation to initiate state-market co-production of common knowledge to address data harms/risks, stabilise corporate expectations, and scale up the digital economy. **25**

II. Activation: Coding Property or Pooling Commons

Second, the term 'activation' is used to describe the experimental processes of state-market co-production before new forms of practices and knowledge are stabilised and coded into laws. In this dynamic period, the state strategically encourages or acquiesces the flexible legal and policy spaces that allow for competing practices to emerge and 'activate' new forms of market transactions, pooling and/or use of undefined things or assets, including data. It can be viewed as a strategy that often chronologically precedes the institutionalisation strategy, or is adopted in-between stabilised periods of 'punctuated equilibrium' to trigger change in legal evolution.[62] **26**

'Activation' is inspired by institutionalist theories that reveal the processes of legal 'coding' of things into property and capital, and the polycentric governance of common-pool resources (CPR) co-produced by the public and private actors. **27**

---

[57] Aoki, *Corporations in evolving diversity: Cognition, governance, and institutions*, 2010.

[58] Deakin et al., *Journal of Comparative Economics* 45.1 (2017): 188–200.

[59] *Ibid.*

[60] Chen/Deakin, *Law and Development Review* 8.1 (2015), 123–145. Chen et al., *Journal of Corporate Law Studies* 17.2 (2017), 257–290.

[61] Deakin/Meng, *Industrial Law Journal* 49.4 (2020), 539–594.

[62] See Deakin, 7 *Review of Law and Economics* (2011). Deakin, 55 *Current Legal Problems* (2002). Deakin/Wilkinson, *The Law of the Labour Market: Industrialisation, Employment, and Legal Evolution*, 2005.

28 Pistor describes how the law has historically 'coded' (or categorised) land, technology, financial instruments, and other tangible/intangible things into property, patents and/or capital. She argues that legal institutions and lawyer's innovative practices are always in the process of creating or contesting property rights and new forms of transactions. The legal community in this sense helps the state authorities to code/decode shared understandings and practices on coercive measures and exchange informal knowledge that allows for large-scale market transactions, global cooperation, as well as wealth and inequality.[63] This aligns with Ostrom's description of the state-market co-production process in the case of CPR governance. Her cases studies show that forests, fisheries, and other 'things' that trigger collective action problems can hardly be governed by a dichotomy of state monopoly or private property rights. Thus, the formal legal coding and arrangements of CPR need more dynamic and diverse considerations of the natures of the CPR and their specific community contexts. These context-specific formal legal practices require, while co-producing, informal local knowledge in the communities.[64]

29 Deakin and Meng, moreover, recently used the case of 'household responsibility system' that governs China's rural lands to argue that ownership should move beyond the concept of 'legally enforced private property rights'. Instead it should be understood as an 'emergent, diverse and complex institution'. Deakin and Meng's arguments draw from and emphasise Ostrom's theories of CPR governance and legal institutions capacity to code/contest property.[65]

30 In the context of data, there has been no consensus on how law can code 'data',as a new 'thing', into an existing or novel legal category. This leaves an elastic legal and political space for major jurisdictions including the U.S., the EU, and China to compete in innovating data ownership and access practices.[66] Evidence will show that the Chinese state uses the activation strategy to allow for legal innovations on data trading, sharing, and use against data fragmentation. These legal ingenuities include the Central Bank's provisional license to Ant Group on handling personal credit information, techno-legal arrangements in Beijing International Data Exchange (BIDE) in contrast to Shenzhen's local legislative attempts on data property rights, and Tianjin's emerging practice of 'Party manages data'.

III. Layering: Law-Tech Co-Evolution

31 Third, 'layering' is categorised as a strategy that describes the state's efforts to construct sustainable ecosystems of institutions for long-term public governance in changing environments. It requires the state to make timely adjustments to the often fragile fits between formal institutions and their environments layered in history with path-dependency. In the data context, layering means the state builds useful data cycles and sustainable data habitats/ecosystems for valuable data applications. It is concerned with better designs of law and technologies in order to achieve valuable and long-term data use in public governance. It is a strategy of sustainability which could complement the stabilising strategy of institutionalisation, and the contestation strategy of activation. This layering strategy is inspired by institutionalist and design theories that understand law as

[63] Pistor, *The code of capital*, 2019.

[64] Ostrom, *American Economic Review* 100.3 (2010), 641-72.

[65] Deakin/Meng, *Journal of Institutional Economics* (2021), 1–15.

[66] See theoretical discussions on data property, transaction and practices, e.g. Litman, *Stanford Law Review* (2000), 1283–1313. Evans, *Harv. JL & Tech.* 25 (2011), 69. Victor, *Yale LJ* 123 (2013), 513. Wiebe, *Journal of Intellectual Property Law & Practice* 12.1 (2017), 62–71. China has tried to raise the data property concept in Shenzhen for example, but failed in the end (see discussed below).

co-evolved with technology through time. In early literature, Deakin argued that juridical categories like 'employment' evolved in history with path-dependency.[67] Similar to the evolution of technologies such as the computer keyboard arrangement (QWERTY), these juridical concepts can have 'frozen accidents' and exhibit 'punctuated equilibrium' through time.[68]

Applying design and affordance theories to law, Hildebrandt argues that modern 32 positive law is made possible by printing technologies, and the emerging pervasive smart technologies are likely to afford the design of data-driven laws.[69] Deakin and Markou combine this observation with legal evolution theory. They use the case of recent machine-learning applications in law to reveal the co-evolution between law and technology as institutionally path-dependent and non-ergodic, i.e. embedded in irreversible time. They argue that machine-learning and other data-driven technologies can lock-in the past, just like law's path-dependency in evolution, but with even more closed ends. They present the risk that while law is afforded by natural language that allows for flexible interpretations and breaking from the past, the numbers and code presented in data can be more rigid and thus trap the society into its past once applied to law and governance.[70] Hildebrandt uses the term 'freezing' to describe shared apprehensions that pervasive data and code-driven technologies will exacerbate law's negative imprinting of the past.[71]

Zuo builds on these literatures to elaborate the concept of 'layering' in law-tech 33 co-evolution. He argues that data categories/abstractions, which are more formalised, are layered on less formalised legal and social categories in a path-dependent way. For example, the data-driven algorithms for employment status prediction (e.g. for tax returns purposes) must input data categories that are based on existing legal categories like 'employee', 'worker' or 'independent contractor'. When new forms of employment appear in society, the corresponding legal categories will change, which will require a change in the data categories in the predictive algorithms.[72]

For example, when the UK court decided to define drivers working on ride-hailing 34 platforms as 'workers' (like Uber drivers), new population will be added to existing data categories or require creating new data categories in the mathematical models. This requires timely updates of both data sets and the algorithms to prevent model decay caused by such 'concept drifts'. Otherwise as time passes by the shift in social reality will impede valuable long-term data interpretation and/or prediction, and the data use will not be sustainable or scalable.[73]

'Layering' as drawn from the law-tech evolutionary literatures is useful to illustrate 35 the need for long-term interpretation of data in a sustainable 'habitat/ecosystem'. Evidence in Shanghai and Qingdao is raised focusing on practices in Smart Court and social/financial credit systems, complemented by secondary sources from Huawei, Alibaba and research institutes.

[67] Deakin/Wilkinson, *The Law of the Labour Market: Industrialisation, Employment, and Legal Evolution*, 2005.

[68] Deakin, 55 *Current Legal Problems* (2002). Deakin, 7 *Review of Law and Economics* (2011). Deakin, *Historical Social Research/Historische Sozialforschung* (2015), 170–184.

[69] Hildebrandt, *The Modern Law Review* 79.1 (2016): 1–30.

[70] Markou/Deakin, in: Markou/Deakin (eds.), *Is Law Computable? Critical Perspectives on Law and Artificial Intelligence*, 2020.

[71] See Hildebrandt, in: Markou/Deakin (eds.), *Is Law Computable? Critical Perspectives on Law and Artificial Intelligence*, 2020. Hildebrandt, *Journal of Cross-disciplinary Research in Computational Law* 1.1 (2021).

[72] Zuo, *Governance by Algorithm: China's Social Credit System* (working paper), 2020; also see Supiot, *Governance by numbers: The making of a legal model of allegiance*, 2017.

[73] *Ibid.*

36 'Qualitative Method': Based on these conceptual models and theoretical groundings, the research combines doctrinal and qualitative methods. The doctrinal data include legislations, regulations, their drafts and legislative notes, administrative and judicial decisions, and other publicly available legal documents. The empirical data include archival or internal documents, and semi-structured interviews conducted in China between 12/2020 and 4/2021. Grey secondary sources such as news and reports were also used as evidence to triangulate findings. Interview data and documents collected are limited by time and available social networks. However, they can cover a certain in-depth understanding of the cases involved.[74]

C. Institutionalisation: Data Security, Protection, and Antitrust

37 Heldt and Hennemann argued that the 'Roaring Twenties' of EU technology regulations are dawning. Drafts of the EU *Digital Services Act* (2020), *Digital Markets Act* (2020), *Data Governance Act* (2020), and the *AI Regulation* (2021) are at the forefronts, which they described as a strategy of 'upward convergence' in regulatory standards similar to the Brussels Effect[75]. This part evidences a similar legislative and regulatory trend in China that started with the 'Roaring Summer of 2021'. The Chinese strategy is however conceptualised as 'institutionalisation'. In the data context this means the state's initiation of a market-state co-production of public services and common knowledge within epistemic communities of data governance, in order to stabilise and scale up a national digital economy. Three major institutionalisation efforts respectively addressed emerging forms of harms/risks in data security, privacy, and competition: (1) Cybersecurity review of the Chinese ride-hailing giant DiDi Chuxing after its IPO at the New York Stock Exchange (NYSE: DiDi Global Inc); (2) the completion of China's data protection legal framework featuring 'gatekeeper' and managerial liabilities; (3) antitrust actions that restrain data power and facilitate interoperability.

I. DiDi's 2021 Cyber/Data Security Review

1. Security Concerns over DiDi *before* its IPO in New York

38 In 2016, China's *Cybersecurity Law*[76] was passed as the first high-level law that regulates data security.[77] It created a new legal category the 'critical information infrastructure (CII) Operators' with high-level obligations on cyber/data security (Article 31) and localisation requirements (Article 37). These high-level compliance requirements on CII Operators are stipulated because they are, by name, 'critical' in handling/managing data and its infrastructures. The Cyberspace Administration of China (CAC) is the top-level party-state organ that oversees such high-level security compliance.[78]

---

[74] See case study methodology. Poteete/Janssen/Ostrom, *Working together*, 2010. Buchanan/Chai/Deakin, *Hedge fund activism in Japan: The limits of shareholder primacy*, 2012. Chen et al., *Journal of Corporate Law Studies* 17.2 (2017), 257–290.

[75] Heldt/Hennemann *Tagesspiegel Background*, 15 July 2021.

[76] Effective since June 1st 2017.

[77] 中华人民共和国网络安全法 [Cybersecurity Law of the People's Republic of China 2017].

[78] Cybersecurity Law 2017. Chapter 3, section 2 on CII operators. Including article 37 on storing important data in China. 中华人民共和国网络安全法_中国人大网 (npc.gov.cn).

Soon after DiDi Chuxing got listed at the NYSE in the U.S. in June 2021, the CAC 39
started a security review/investigation under the *Cybersecurity Law* (2017), which effectively deemed DiDi as a 'CII Operator'[79]. Such security review after an outbound IPO is arguably functionally similar (as it does not stop the IPO) to the U.S. national security review by The Committee on Foreign Investment in the United States (CFIUS) which can pause and stop cross-border mergers and acquisitions[80].

DiDi is a ride-hailing tech giant born in China, and a major competitor with Uber in 40
the global ride-hailing market.[81] DiDi claims in its SEC filing that between March 2020 and March 2021 it had 377 million annual active users (which is larger than the U.S. population) and 156 million monthly active users (MAU) in China[82], compared to Uber's 93 million MAU in the world (last quarter of 2020)[83].

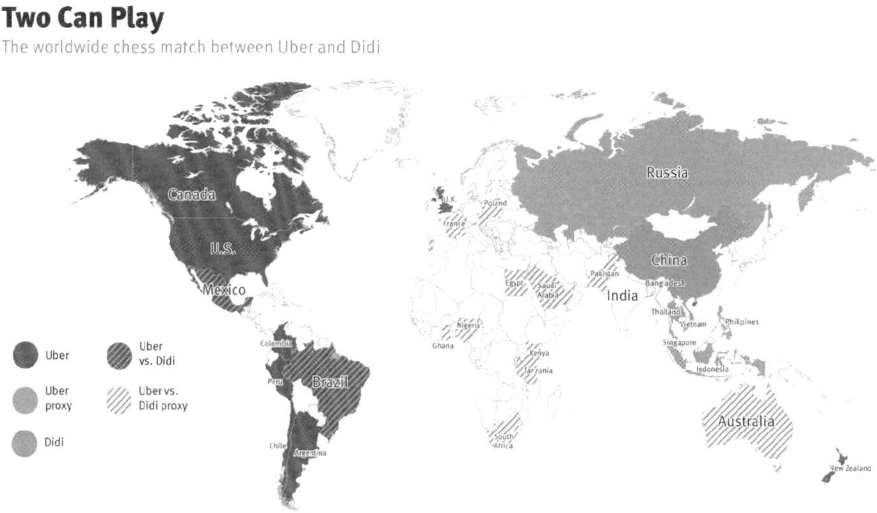

Figure 2. Uber and DiDi global market coverage (2018) supra n 81

Evidence shows that the regulatory agency had difficulty in addressing DiDi's cyber/ 41
data security issues long before DiDi's IPO in NYSE (June 2021). First, DiDi Shanghai was already investigated and raided by various Shanghai regulators based on security concerns in 2018. These include 'fake cars', illegal drivers and incomplete data filing to the ride-hailing regulatory agencies. But nothing was found when the enforcement team arrived. DiDi was reported to even have prepared several boxes of chaotic and useless files in advance for the enforcement team's third inspection.[84] Respondent X, a governmental official in Shanghai, complained in a closed group discussion that DiDi

[79] 2021a CAC announcement on DiDi.

[80] See e.g. Griffin, *Fordham L. Rev.* 85 (2016), 1757. Also see a classic case of Shuanghui's acquisition of Smithfield. China Inc. and the CFIUS National Security Review – The Diplomat, available at https://thediplomat.com/2013/12/china-inc-and-the-cfius-national-security-review/ (last accessed 16 December 2022).

[81] The New Global Order in Ride Hailing: Didi vs. Uber – The Information, available at https://www.theinformation.com/articles/the-new-global-order-in-ride-hailing-didi-vs-uber (last accessed 16 December 2022); *cf* below.

[82] Didi Global Inc Prospectus 424B4 (sec.report) 2021.

[83] Uber's users of ride-sharing services worldwide 2017–2020 | Statista, available at https://www.statista.com/statistics/833743/us-users-ride-sharing-services/ (last accessed 16 December 2022) *supra* n 81.

[84] 上海检查组第四次上门检查滴滴　数据已接入将复查|滴滴|检查组|上海_新浪科技_新浪网 (sina.com.cn).

is not concerned with their everyday fines from violations of regulations: 'they see such administrative fines as the cost in their financial reports'[85].

42 Second, Respondent Y raised in the same closed group discussion that

> *'the CAC is afraid of reviewing data security in cross-border transfers because they don't have the technical expertise yet.'*

43 This was especially acute with regards to the massive amount of geographical data generated each day on ride-hailing platforms like DiDi. Respondent Y claimed that one concern of the CAC was that such geographical big-data can be used to infer and reveal the locations of military bases or other sensitive places. However, the CAC did not have the technical team to understand how to evaluate such risks (Legal scholar Y, Shanghai, 2021).

44 Third, the sensory and audio-visual big-data collected by the cameras on self-driving cars were of particular concern with the rapid roll-out of autonomous vehicles like Tesla, and DiDi's robo-taxi in cities like Shanghai.[86] Respondent X and Y, for example, discussed the data risks of Tesla's self-driving cars in Shanghai. They claimed that Tesla's cameras and sensors collect an extensive amount of real-time visual data of its surroundings including people's faces, buildings, other vehicles and so on, and can transfer them abroad. Sensitive information can be inferred from such big-data where data security and privacy stakes are high (March 2021, Shanghai).

45 These security concerns over sensitive geographic data was later confirmed in May 2021 with the CAC's stipulation of *Several Provisions on the Management of Automobile Data Security (Draft for Comment).*[87] Article 3 listed six types of 'important data' which include for example,

- A3 (1) 'Data on the flow of people and traffic in military administrative areas, national defence science and industrial units or other units that involve state secrets, or sensitive, important areas of Party and government administrative units above the county level, etc.';
- A3 (3) 'Data on the operation of automobile charging networks'; and
- A3 (5) 'Audio-visual data of individuals' faces, voices, and license plates, etc., outside the vehicle'[88].

2. Institutionalisation in the DiDi Security Review 2021

46 DiDi's 2021 security review is not that surprising against the background of CAC and local regulators' security concerns. On July 2nd 2021, two days after DiDi's IPO at NYSE, the CAC announced its review of DiDi's cybersecurity compliance, and required that no new users be registered on DiDi's ride-hailing platform immediately. The announcement cited the *Cybersecurity Review Measure (2020)* as the applicable law, and used

---

[85] Government official X, Shanghai, 2021.3.

[86] AutoX launches its RoboTaxi service in Shanghai, competing with Didi's pilot program | TechCrunch 2020.

[87] Translation: Several Provisions on the Management of Automobile Data Security (Draft for Comment) | DigiChina (stanford.edu), available at https://digichina.stanford.edu/work/translation-several-provisions-on-the-management-of-automobile-data-security-draft-for-comment/ (last accessed 16 December 2022).

[88] (2) Survey and map data that is more precise than maps publicly issued by the state (4) Data on types and traffic volume, etc., of vehicles on the road (...); (6) Other data that might affect national security and the public interest, as specified by the state cybersecurity and informatization department and relevant departments of the State Council.

National Security Law (2015) and the *Cybersecurity Law (2017)* as the higher-level legal sources.[89] In this way CAC effectively deemed DiDi as a 'CII Operator' which is the only subject regulated under the scope of Article 1 and 2 of the current *Measure (2020)* ('national security risks were brought about by the CII Operators' procurement of network products and services'). Data security is listed in Art. 9 (1) as one of the risk factors for review ('theft, leak or damage of important data').[90]

On July 4th, CAC confirmed DiDi's 'severe violation of data regulations' and required all App Stores in China to delist DiDi's online ride-hailing app, despite allowing existing riders and drivers to keep using the app. It demanded DiDi to make changes to comply with the *Measure (2020)* and other security standards.[91] Two months after this sanction it was reported that DiDi's daily active users dropped by 30 % (comparing August to June).[92] **47**

Besides DiDi, on July 5th 2021 CAC initiated similar investigations and disciplines on three more Chinese tech giants that recently got listed in the U.S. These big-techs are all deemed as CII operators, which have cyber and data security concerns in their public listing abroad. Two other Chinese tech giants later cancelled their listing plans after the CAC's four reviews[93]. **48**

Within a week's time, on July 10th the CAC also released a new *Cybersecurity Review Measures (2021, Draft for Public Comments)* that has provisions targeting big-tech outbound IPOs. It requires any 'CII Operator with more than 1 million user information that wish to be publicly listed abroad, must file a cybersecurity review to the Cybersecurity Review Office' (Art. 6). **49**

Seven 'major factors' were listed concerning risks to national security (Art. 10), including the risk that 'after an IPO abroad is completed, the CII, core data, important data or massive amounts of personal information are influenced, controlled or maliciously used by foreign governments'. It also expanded the CAC's general review mandate to all 'data handlers' instead of just the 'CII Operators' (Art. 2).[94] More clarity would be provided regarding security concerns for both data handlers and CII operators when the revised *Measure 2021* is finalised and taken into effect. **50**

A more detailed *CII Security Protection Regulation (2021)* was also later passed in August 2021. This new *CII Regulation* (2021) adds granularity to the existing *Cybersecurity Law (2017)* and *Review Measure (2020)*, and clarifies important obligations for CII Operators to, first perform data security accountability and establish protection institutions (Art. 15); second, to prevent data leakage (Art. 2, 9, 18), and third, to maintain data completeness, confidentiality and usability (Art. 6). **51**

In addition, it is worth noting that China passed its long-due *Data Security Law (2021)* in June 2021, about three weeks before DiDi's IPO. It is a high-level legislation as important as the *Cybersecurity Law (2017)*, and came into effect on the same date with **52**

---

[89] 2021a CAC announcement on DiDi.

[90] See 2020 Review Measure.

[91] 2021a CAC announcement on DiDi.

[92] Didi loses 30 % of daily users after Beijing crackdown following IPO | Financial Times 2021 Sep, available at https://www.ft.com/content/13a768b0-1000-4cad-8a03-36a1e66f460b (last accessed 16 December 2022).

[93] See various analysis articles written by lawyers in China 从实施网络安全审查到APP下架，数据安全律师对滴滴事件梳理了八个核心问题-移动支付网 (mpaypass.com.cn) and in the U.S., After 5 Years, China's Cybersecurity Rules for Critical Infrastructure Come Into Focus | DigiChina (stanford.edu) 深度"滴滴"网络安全审查事件的全景分析与合规指引_腾讯新闻 (qq.com), available at https://new.qq.com/omn/20210710/20210710A087S900.html (last accessed 16 December 2022).

[94] 国家互联网信息办公室关于《网络安全审查办法修订草案征求意见稿）》公开征求意见的通知-中共中央网络安全和信息化委员会办公室 (cac.gov.cn).

the *CII Security Protection Regulation (2021)* on September 1st 2021[95]. Its Chapter IV detailed the 'Data Security Protection Obligations' for all 'handlers of important data' (a broader concept than CII Providers), where two articles are crucial:

53 (1) Article 27 requires 'The conduct of data handling activities using the Internet or other such information networks shall perform the data security protection obligations described above on the basis of the cybersecurity Multi-Level Protection System (MLPS)'.[96] The MLPS 1.0 was a ministerial standard for cybersecurity that functioned as early as 2007 before the big-data and algorithmic technologies took off in China[97]. Since 2019, the MLPS 2.0 is the revised standard in effect, which was updated by legal and technical communities entering the big-data era, and shall be used for more granular reviews on DiDi's data security issues[98].

54 (2) Article 31 stipulates the data security checks for 'outbound security management' for CII Operators and other data handlers working in China pursuant to the *Cybersecurity Law (2017)*.[99] This article raises data security concerns when data handlers change their corporate governance structures, e.g. by listing outside of China.

55 In DiDi's case the CAC cybersecurity review might be complicated if the U.S. regulatory authority Security Exchange Commission (SEC) requires data disclosure or access to third-party auditing due to DiDi's IPO at NYSE. For example, under the U.S. *Holding Foreign Companies Accountable Act 2020 (HFCAA),* the SEC and the Public Company Accounting Oversight Board (PCAOB) can access third-party audit papers of non-US firms listed in the U.S. required by the Sarbanes-Oxley Act 2002.[100] Besides, outbound data transfer concerns can also be triggered when the voting structure within the board changes and new decisions can be made on data transfer. Article 31 aligns with the latest proposed rules on security reviews of public listing abroad under the new *Cybersecurity Review Measures (2021, Draft for Public Comments).*

56 There are also rapid legislative moves on the security of cross-border data transfer. Most recently on October 29th 2021, the CAC also issued a new *Security Assessment Measures on the Cross-border Data Transfer (Draft for comments).* It specified the conditions, procedures, materials necessary for filing, and redress.[101] Shanghai's local legislature also passed a *Shanghai Data Regulation (Draft for comments 2021)* which requires the making of a 'low-risk catalogue' for certain types of cross-border data transfers in order to facilitate data flow in its *Lin Gang* free trade zone pilot (A66, 67).[102]

---

[95] 中华人民共和国数据安全法 [Data Security Law of the People's Republic of China 2021], available at http://www.npc.gov.cn/npc/c30834/202106/7c9af12f51334a73b56d7938f99a788a.shtml (last accessed 16 December 2022).

[96] Translation: Data Security Law of the People's Republic of China | DigiChina (stanford.edu).

[97] MLPS 2007.

[98] MLPS 2.0, 2019.

[99] 'The provisions of the Cybersecurity Law of the PRC apply to the outbound security management of important data collected or produced by critical information infrastructure operators operating within the mainland territory of the PRC; outbound security management measures for other data handlers collecting or producing important data within the mainland territory of the PRC are to be jointly formulated by the national cybersecurity and informatization department and relevant departments of the State Council.' 中华人民共和国数据安全法.

[100] 15 U.S.C. § 7211, Holding Foreign Companies Accountable Act 2020 (HFCAA); Congress Passes the "Holding Foreign Companies Accountable Act" (harvard.edu) 2021, available at https://corpgov.law.harvard.edu/2021/01/10/congress-passes-the-holding-foreign-companies-accountable-act/#1b (last accessed 16 December 2022); Senators call on US securities regulator to investigate Didi IPO | Financial Times (ft.com) 2021, available at https://www.ft.com/content/40c179f1-6450-43fd-9baf-f42425712016 (last accessed 16 December 2022).

[101] 国家互联网信息办公室关于《数据出境安全评估办法征求意见稿）》公开征求意见的通知.

[102] 上海人大 (spcsc.sh.cn); 《上海市数据条例草案）》解读一丨全国首提制定低风险跨境流动数据目录.

3. Co-Production of Knowledge in Cyber/Data Security

The above legislative and regulatory practices do not only establish rules, but more importantly shape new common knowledge within emerging cyber and data securities communities. As the evidence shows, the Shanghai local regulators had problems enforcing regulations against DiDi's massive real-time operations, and CAC started with little expertise facing new data security risks on such large-scale ride-hailing platforms and the roll-out of autonomous vehicles. 57

DiDi's security review thus became a point of institutionalisation where existing concerns are addressed by the state's legislative and enforcement practices. These CAC practices also initiate informal knowledge exchange with private actors to make more detailed regulations. DiDi's case sets an example for future security compliances by other private actors such as Tesla, whose autonomous vehicles collect massive amounts of data in China. 58

It is debatable whether DiDi's ongoing review is political in nature, but the process at least would help stabilise market expectations on: 59
(1) what is a 'CII operator' that should be reviewed,
(2) what are the review procedures and requirements;
(3) what knowledge and expertise the CAC needs and retains to review automobile data (including self-driving cars), foreign listing and cross-border data transfer.

This also enables the wider legal and technical community of cyber/data security to update common knowledge, for example, by revising the MLPS 1.0 (2007) standards to MLPS 2.0 in 2019 which aligns with high-level legislations and emerging technologies. The informal knowledge exchange within these epistemic communities engenders self-governance of data risks. Such private efforts evolve around but also shape the state's centralised instituting efforts to keep updating common knowledge and practices. In this sense, the CAC and regulators used the institutionalisation strategy to initiate the market-state co-production of knowledge on data security governance that stabilises corporate expectations and scales the digital economy. 60

II. Data Protection, Gatekeeper, and Managerial Liabilities

Besides security, data protection is the second area that shows extensive evidence of China's institutionalisation strategy. China's Personal Information Protection Law (PIPL) was recently passed in August 2021 and came into effect on 1st November.[103] It is considered as China's equivalent of the EU's General Data Protection Regulation (GDPR, 2018), but also features rather unique provisions such as gatekeeper and managerial liabilities inspired by/in competition with both the U.S. FTC decision on Facebook re third-party data violations (2020) and the EU's recent legislative proposals on digital markets and services (2020). 61

1. 'China's GDPR': Personal Information Protection Law (PIPL) 2021

To emphasise the importance of this legislation, the *National People's Congress (NPC) Legislative Note on PIPL (2020)* claims at the beginning that 'by March 2020 China's 62

[103] 中华人民共和国个人信息保护法 [Personal Information Protection Law of the People's Republic of China, 2021], available at http://www.npc.gov.cn/npc/c30834/202108/a8c4e3672c74491a80-b53a172bb753fe.shtml (last accessed 16 December 2022).

internet users reached 900 million.'[104] The *Note* followed, however, that data violations and harms on people's daily life are rampant and require change: 'an objective demand to enhance PI protection' and 'a real demand for maintaining a healthy ecosystem of the cyberspace'. To show this real predicament the *Note* cited reports and initiatives from the NPC with strong societal demands as well as the central Party's concerns over societal complaints.[105]

63 In addition to addressing the data privacy concerns, the PIPL is also considered as an 'important measure to promote healthy development of the digital economy'. The *Note (2021)* adopted the SC's understanding of 'data as an essential factor (of production)' and claimed that 'data competition becomes important in global competition, and PI is the core and foundation of big-data.'[106] It further raised that 'in coping with COVID-19', many big-data applications are useful and become more pervasive, but a comprehensive data protection framework needs to be built and applied.[107]

64 Doctrinally, the PIPL 2021 completes China's data protection framework. Its ultimate legal authority of data protection laws comes from the Chinese Constitution: Art. 33 on human rights, Art. 38 on human dignity, and Art. 40 on freedom and privacy in communication. In 2021, the *State Council's Human Rights Action Plan (2021–2025)* also highlighted in the protection of 'privacy rights' and 'personal information interests (PII , *geren xinxi quanyi*)'[108].

65 However, the earliest high-level data protection law in effect is the *Ninth Amendment of the Criminal Code (2015)*. It stipulates a maximum of seven years of prison for severe offences of stealing, selling or abusing people's personal information. This was targeted at the privacy concerns at that time with the rise of big-data technology. The *Ninth Amendment (2015)* was later followed by the *Judicial Interpretations on Personal Information Crime (2017)* issued by China's Supreme People's Court (SPC) and the Supreme People's Procuratorate (SPP). Some high-profile criminal cases have been reported for example, in Shanghai and Hangzhou where big-data companies illegally collect and store personal information. They were heavily fined and their legal representative and CTO were sentenced to three years of prison (but with reprieve periods).[109]

66 Besides the criminal code, China's new *Civil Code 2021* sets two layers of protection for personal information. First, Art. 1032 stipulates the 'privacy right' that is similar to the Art. 8 'right to private life' in the European Convention of Human Rights (ECHR). The Art. 1032 right protects private spaces, activities and communication at the right-level with human dignity as the foundation. Although privacy is afforded with higher-level protection, the scope of privacy is narrower compared to 'personal information interests' (PII).

67 Art. 1034 *Civil Code 2021* stipulates the protection of PII, which is not protected at the level of 'rights', but includes a larger scope of interests related to both private and non-private personal information. After the *PIPL 2021* came into effect, PII is protected in

---

[104] This is more than the total population of the EU, U.K. and U.S. combined, but only about 65 % of the Chinese population.

[105] 关于《中华人民共和国个人信息保护法草案）》的说明_中国人大网 (npc.gov.cn), 2020.

[106] *Ibid.*

[107] *Ibid.*

[108] 2021.9. Human Rights Plan Section chapter 2, section 3. 国家人权行动计划20212025年） (scio.gov.cn).

[109] See, e.g. (2020) 浙0106刑初437号 [2020, Zhejiang, 0106, Criminal Court, first instance case no. 437]. Also see 淘宝11.8亿条用户隐私被泄露 两男子被判刑 available at https://www.sohu.com/na/472780318_120957976 (last accessed 8 February 2023) [Taobao 1.18 billion pieces of user information leaked, two men sentenced. Sina news, 2021.6.17].

detail by this field-specific legislation. This completes the two-layer civil protection of personal information, and it is worth noting that as private information is part of personal information, it is doctrinally also protected under specific rules of the PIPL 2021[110].

Other important legislations on China's data protection include the *Cybersecurity* 68
Law 2017 and the *Data Security Law 2021,* together with other specific regulations concerning security issues. These security laws are excluded from and in parallel with the PIPL, and together cyber/data security and data protection form the two arms of China's data governance regime.[111]

The *Consumer Protection Law 2014* and *E-Commerce Law 2019* broadly touched 69
upon personal information with articles that link the jurisdictions to PIPL 2021.[112] There are also many low-level personal information protections standards (e.g. *Guidance for personal information security impact assessment 2020*)[113] and local legislations (e.g. *Shenzhen Data Regulation 2021*, *Shanghai Data Regulation 2021*).[114]

The Chinese courts are also active in the data protection regime where various 70
courts have made high-profile decisions. Even before the new Civil Code 2021, the Beijing Internet Court for example in 2020 had already made two decisions that WeRead (of Tencent, linked to Wechat) and TikTok (of Bytedance) respectively violated personal information protections laws. The court found WeRead had misled users to consent on displaying their favourite/liked books to Wechat friends and contacts, and required WeRead to stop accessing users' Wechat friendship list and delete all relevant information. It also required WeRead to stop showing users' data to the user's friends, such as favourite books, what is being read and so on. The Court also found violations of 'personal information interests' where TikTok's Beijing operator accessed the name and phone number of the plaintiff Ling via Ling's friend's contact book, but without consent from either Ling or Ling's contact. It ruled the deletion of related data including the name, phone number and the geographical data of Ling, and an apology with compensation of 1,000 RMB to Ling.[115]After the new Civil Code 2021, the first civil collective action case appeared where the Hangzhou Internet Court ruled both criminal punishment and civil liabilities to Sun who bought and then publicly sold more than 45,000 pieces of personal information online for profit.[116]

Recently, the Supreme People's Court also issued the *Judicial Interpretations on* 71
Facial Recognitions (2021).[117] The latest facial recognition related case also was accepted in Changsha on data protection basis, where a legal intern sued the building

---

[110] 中华人民共和国民法典 [Civil Code of the People's Republic of China 2021.] Art 1032, 1034, available at http://www.npc.gov.cn/npc/c30834/202006/75ba6483b8344591abd07917e1d25cc8.shtml (last accessed 16 December 2022).

[111] 中华人民共和国网络安全法 [Cybersecurity Law of the People's Republic of China 2017], available athttp://www.npc.gov.cn/ (last accessed 16 December 2022);. 中华人民共和国数据安全法 [Data Security Law of the People's Republic of China 2021], available at http://www.npc.gov.cn/npc/c30834/202106/7c9af12f51334a73b56d7938f99a788a.shtml (last accessed 16 December 2022).

[112] *Consumer Protection Law 2014*; *E-Commerce Law 2019.*

[113] 信息安全技术—个人信息安全影响评估指南(GB/T 39335-2020) [Information security technology – Guidance for personal information security impact assessment (GB/T 39335-2020)].

[114] 《上海市数据条例》; 深圳市第七届人民代表大会常务委员会公告第十号）(2021), available at http://www.sz.gov.cn/zfgb/2021/gb1218/content/post_9307139.html (last accessed 8 February 2023) [Shenzhen 7th People's Congress Plenary Committee Report No. 10. On passing the Shenzhen Economic Special Zone's Data Regulation, 2021. Effective 1st December 2022].

[115] 北京互联网法院微信读书、抖音侵犯个人信息权--法治--人民网 (people.com.cn).

[116] 民法典实施后全国首例个人信息保护民事公益诉讼案当庭宣判--法治--人民网 (people.com.cn).

[117] SPC 2021 on facial recognition.

management company of his law firm for imposing compulsory facial recognition entrance registrations (pending after the PIPL).[118]

72 The PIPL 2021 builds on these previous laws and practices, and completes China's data protection framework. Detailed practices and the empirical effects of PIPL await to be observed after it came into effect on 1st November 2021. Nevertheless, the following PIPL legislative process featuring gatekeepers and managerial liabilities to a certain degree manifests the institutionalisation strategy that deliberately clarifies the state and market divide in order to co-produce common knowledge in China's data protection practices.

2. Gatekeeper and Managerial Liabilities in the PIPL 2021

73 PIPL 2021 features 'gatekeeper' and managerial liabilities that require big-techs in China to take up more public enforcement obligations with regards to their third-party suppliers. The legislative process followed an international trend in regulatory practices of mandating big-techs to self-regulate their third-party suppliers or App developers.

74 First, after the Cambridge Analytica incident, the U.S. Federal Trade Commission (FTC) in 2020 required Facebook (U.S. v Facebook 2020) to take more public obligations of regulating its third-party developers/suppliers in terms of data protection. It not only deemed Facebook liable for third-party's breach of consumer data protection, but also stipulated managerial liability, so that Mark Zuckerberg can be held personally liable in the future with potential civil, regulatory, and even criminal punishment.[119]

75 Van Loo theorised this practice by the FTC as a move towards 'gatekeeper liability', where regulators like the FTC can require big-tech platforms to be law-enforcers that supervise and regulate their third-party suppliers. He argued that this liability originates from the vicarious/third-party liability in torts that can penetrate corporate protection of individual officers or the board of directors. The Facebook case manifests what he calls the 'revival or the *respondeat superior*': where gatekeeper liability re-emerged alongside the big-tech's rising power. Big-tech's control over third-party suppliers' data access means vicarious liability.[120]

76 The FTC's gatekeeper and managerial liabilities imposed on Facebook is a sanction-backed legal arrangement to clarify big-tech's obligations to self-govern and prevent systematic harms/risks. This approach aligns with Shanghai's 'cooperation and deterrence' attitude towards big-tech companies, as expressed by Respondent Z:

77 *'The Chinese state has historically adopted this cooperation and deterrence attitude towards large businesses … Render unto market what is the market's, and unto state what is the state's. Then we won't disturb the foundational ecosystems of the citizens.' (Government official Z, March 2021).*

78 However, gatekeeper liability was not in the first draft of China's PIPL (October 2020). Only personal liability for executives of data-handlers was stipulated in this draft with moderate fines and various years of bans from the profession. These managerial liabilities do not require the data-handlers to be large platforms or 'gatekeepers'[121].

[118] (2021) 湖南人脸识别第一案大楼强制"刷脸"，原告望促个保法落地_, available at https://www.163.com/dy/article/GJES9OT205129QAF.html (last accessed 16 December 2022), (2021) Shanghai Data Regulation 2021, effective 1st January 2022 (available at https://www.shanghai.gov.cn/nw12344/20211129a1a38c3dfe8b4f8f8fcba5e79fbe9251.html, last accessed 8 February 2023).

[119] United States v. Facebook, Inc., No. 19-2184 (TJK), 2020 WL 1975785 at *5 (D.D.C. 23 April 2020)

[120] Van Loo, *Geo. LJ* 109 (2020): 141. Van Loo, *Va. L. Rev.* 106 (2020), 467.

[121] See PIPL first legislative draft for comments.

Comparatively, while the GDPR does not stipulate personal/managerial liabilities, the UK Data Protection Act (2018) has 'Liability of directors etc.' that penetrate the corporate protection.[122] Many other Chinese laws that focus on risk-related security compliance also have managerial liabilities, including the *Food Safety Law 2019, Cybersecurity Law 2017,* and *Data Security Law 2021.*[123]

Nevertheless, Art. 58 featuring gatekeeper liabilities appeared in the second draft of China's PIPL (April 2021). It stipulated a group of obligations onto big-techs which are similar to those in EU's *Digital Services Act (DSA, Draft 2020)* on 'very large online platforms' (VLOPs).[124] Art. 58 and the DSA share similar requirements on transparency, compliance structures and audits for big-tech companies in order to prevent systemic risks and to better regulate third-party suppliers or App developers[125]. Besides, The MIIT also accompanied the PIPL second draft with an *APP Personal Information Protection Regulations (Draft for comments)* in April 2021, which proposed more details on how to regulate third-party APPs on gatekeepers.[126] 79

It is worth noting that the Chinese legal academia and legislators became more aware of the term 'gatekeeper' after the EU's *Digital Markets Act (DMA, Draft 2020)* explicitly proposed 'gatekeeper obligations' for big-tech platforms in December 2020.[127] The focus of the *DMA (Draft 2020)* however is on fair competition for third-party developers/suppliers and interoperability, which is different from the obligations on VLOPs stipulated by the EU's *DSA (Draft 2020)* and the FTC's mandated gatekeeper's liabilities concerning data protection.[128] 80

The third and final version of the PIPL (August 2021) solidified Art. 58 as obligations for 'personal information handlers that provide important internet services, with very large amounts of users and complex business categories'. It added two more sections which further specified gatekeeper liabilities: 81

(i) 'platforms should set internal compliance institutions', and
(ii) 'platforms should obey transparent, just and fair principles, and should set platform rules that specify third-party's obligations on handling data.'[129]

These provisions to some extent established the state-market boundary and the division of labours and in regulating third-party providers.

Legal scholars' efforts are also considerable in the PIPL's drafting gatekeepers liabilities. For example, a comparative law article by Professor Zhang Xinbao at Renmin Law School introduced the concept of gatekeeper obligations in 2021 after the second draft of PIPL and the EU 2020 DMA and DSA proposals.[130] Professor Wang Xixin at Peking Law School advocated for a 'state protection obligation' from public law 82

---

[122] Data Protection Act 2018 c.12. Section 198.

[123] See China's *Food Safety Law 2019, Cybersecurity Law 2017,* and *Data Security Law 2021.*

[124] 《个人信息保护法草案二次审议稿）》[Second draft PIPL 2021.].

[125] COM (2020) 825: Proposal for a REGULATION OF THE EUROPEAN PARLIAMENT AND OF THE COUNCIL on a Single Market For Digital Services (Digital Services Act) and amending Directive 2000/31/EC, Procedure 2020/0361/COD.

[126] 公开征求对《移动互联网应用程序个人信息保护管理暂行规定征求意见稿）》的意见 [MIIT Mobile Internet Application Personal Information Protection Provisional Regulations (Draft for Comments), 2021.4.26], available at http://www.gov.cn/hudong/2021-04/26/content_5602780.htm (last accessed 16 December 2022).

[127] See Zhang Xinbao. 2021.

[128] COM (2020) 842: Proposal for a REGULATION OF THE EUROPEAN PARLIAMENT AND OF THE COUNCIL on contestable and fair markets in the digital sector (Digital Markets Act) Procedure 2020/0374/COD.

[129] See PIPL.

[130] 张新宝互联网生态"守门人"个人信息保护特别义务设置研究，《比较法研究》，2021年第3期。[Zhang Xinbao, *Comparative Law Journal*, 2021 (3)].

perspective which requires the state to take up its protection role on personal information and coordinate both public and private efforts in data protection.[131] Professor Zhou Hanhua at the Chinese Academy of Social Science has also been deeply involved in the 15 year-long legislative process and the three versions of PIPL since 2020.[132]

3. State-market Co-Production of Data Protection and a soft 'Beijing Effect'

83 The above evidence describes China's legislative and regulatory processes on data protection, in particular featuring gatekeeper and managerial liabilities. Together they show the state's institutionalisation strategy that deliberately provides a division of labour between the state and market actors, which clarifies separate spaces for the co-production of common knowledge in data governance communities.

84 Data protection practices before the PIPL 2021 already started addressing data violations using criminal punishments which established redlines for data-handling activities. They did not however provide stable private expectations on what constitutes compliant data handling practices in daily operations. PIPL 2021 is the institutionalisation effort that tries to stabilise these accumulated practices and knowledge. The PIPL's gatekeeper provisions in particular provided the state with new tools to enforce data protection through big-techs like Alibaba and DiDi. This aligns with the state's 'cooperation and deterrence' attitude that involves big-techs in the daily data governance of their third-party supplies and users.

85 PIPL also competes with the EU's digital governance framework – GDPR (2018), DMA and DSA (drafts 2020) – for high standards of privacy and data protection. Respondent Z in Shanghai claimed that 'by implementing the law well at home, we can set good examples and reach our laws beyond China as best practices (Government official X, Shanghai, 2021.3). This raises the potential of a 'Beijing Effect' in data protection practices in competition with the 'Brussels Effect'.[133] More accurately, this can be a soft 'Beijing Effect' (which is more similar to the 'Brussels Effect') that does not necessarily require expansive foreign investments or infrastructure constructions, as compared to the 'hard' Beijing Effect as recently argued through the case of the Digital Silk Road.[134]

III. Antitrust: Data Power and Interoperability

86 The Chinese state also started an antitrust movement against big-tech companies during 2020–2021 alongside its institutionalisation on security and data protection. Major cases include first, the Central Bank's 2020 investigation of Ant Group (affiliate of Alibaba Group). Ant is China's Fintech giant for e-payment and consumer loans, and claims to have more than 1 billion annual active users within China. Second, the $2.75

---

[131] 王锡锌个人信息国家保护义务及展开，《中国法学》，2021年第1期。[Wang Xixin, *China Legal Science*, 2021 (1)].

[132] See e.g. Top Scholar Zhou Hanhua Illuminates 15+ Years of History Behind China's Personal Information Protection Law | DigiChina (stanford.edu).

[133] See Bradford, *The Brussels effect: How the European Union rules the world*, 2020.

[134] *Cf* Erie/Streinz, The Beijing Effect: China's 'Digital Silk Road' as Transnational Data Governance, available at https://papers.ssrn.com/sol3/papers.cfm?abstract_id=3810256 (last accessed 16 December 2022).

billion fine (comparable to $2.8 billion EU antitrust fine on Google[135]) issued by China's antitrust agency State Administration for Market Regulation (SAMR) on Alibaba Group in April 2021. Alibaba is China's e-commerce tech-giant and equivalent of Amazon.[136] Third, the SAMR $530 million fine of Meituan, which is China's food delivery tech-giant and a rough equivalent of Deliveroo/Uber Eats (food delivery) plus Yelp (consumer rating and booking). It serves 340 million annual transacting users by 2018 as claimed in its 2018 IPO at the Hong Kong Stock Exchange (HKEX).[137]

First, on November 3rd 2020 the Shanghai Stock Exchange paused the public listing plan of Ant Group after China's Central Bank and other financial regulators launched a joint investigation[138]. The Central Bank later in its press conference listed 'using market advantage status to exclude competitors' as one of the problems of Ant Group. It also raised 'breaking monopolies … and maintaining a fair and competitive market order' as the first principle of the future regulations of big-tech platforms.[139] **87**

Soon, in November 2020, data became an important factor in the *Antitrust Guideline on Platform Economy (Draft for comments, 2020)* issued by the State Council Antitrust Committee at the SAMR. This top-level *Antitrust Guideline (2021)* was passed in February 2021, which listed 'the capacity to hold and process relevant data' as a determining factor in the evaluation of a platform's market dominance under the category of the platform's 'financial and technical conditions' (Art. 11 sec. 3).[140] **88**

'Platform's data occupation situation (平台占有数据情况)' also became a 'considering factor' in defining whether a platforms can be deemed as an 'essential facility' (*bixu sheshi*) (Art. 14). Whether data itself can be deemed as an 'essential facility', however, is not clear under the *Antitrust Guideline 2021*. In fact, the 2021 Guideline explicitly deleted the part on 'deeming data as essential facility' in Art. 14 of the 2020 draft. Data was instead added as a new factor for deeming whether platforms are essential facilities (*cf* 2020 draft).[141] **89**

Nevertheless, data is listed as one of the 'essential resources and facilities' (必要资源和必需设施) among 'technology, IP', 'channel (*qu dao*), and user' in the consideration of platform-related merger controls (Art. 20). These mixed signals imply the regulator's **90**

[135] Google loses challenge against EU antitrust ruling, $2.8-bln fine | Reuters 2021.11.10, available at https://www.reuters.com/technology/eu-court-upholds-eu-antitrust-ruling-against-google-2021-11-10/ (last accessed 16 December 2022).

[136] China fines Alibaba record $2.75 bln for anti-monopoly violations | Reuters, available at https://www.reuters.com/business/retail-consumer/china-regulators-fine-alibaba-275-bln-anti-monopoly-violations-2021-04-10/ (last accessed 16 December 2022); 市场监管总局依法对阿里巴巴集团控股有限公司在中国境内网络零售平台服务市场实施"二选一"垄断行为作出行政处罚 (samr.gov.cn) 2021 April 10th.

[137] China Fines Meituan $530 Million in Second Tech Antitrust Case – The New York Times (nytimes.com); 市场监管总局依法对美团在中国境内网络餐饮外卖平台服务市场实施"二选一"垄断行为作出行政处罚 (samr.gov.cn) 2021; 3802297-t01hkpo (todayir.com).

[138] 关于暂缓蚂蚁科技集团股份有限公司科创板上市的决定 | 上海证券交易所 (sse.com.cn).

[139] 央行联合约谈蚂蚁集团情况公布指出存在问题与5大整改要求_监管 (sohu.com).

[140] 国务院反垄断委员会关于平台经济领域的反垄断指南 [State Council Antitrust Committee [2021] 1, Antitrust Guideline on Platform Economy (2021)], available at http://www.gov.cn/xinwen/2021-02/07/content_5585758.htm (last accessed 16 December 2022).

[141] 《关于平台经济领域的反垄断指南征求意见稿）》 (china-cer.com.cn) 2020. '认定相关数据是否构成必需设施，一般需要综合考虑数据对于参与市场竞争是否不可或缺，数据是否存在其他获取渠道，数据开放的技术可行性，以及开放数据对占有数据的经营者可能造成的影响等因素。' 认定相关平台是否构成必需设施，一般需要综合考虑其他平台的可替代性、是否存在潜在可用平台、发展竞争性平台的可行性、交易相对人对该平台的依赖程度、开放平台对该平台经营者可能造成的影响等因素。国务院反垄断委员会关于平台经济领域的反垄断指南_部门政务_中国政府网 (www.gov.cn).

ambiguous attitudes towards considering data as an essential facility, and have triggered debates among Chinese antitrust scholars.[142]

91 'Data and algorithms' were also listed as technical tools to 'restrict transactions' (Art. 15), and added as ways to form horizontal (Art. 6), vertical (Art. 7) or 'Hub-and-spoke' agreements that are monopolistic (Art. 8). 'Depriving of data' (Art. 21 sec. 1) and 'opening data infrastructure' (Art. 21 sec. 2) were added as antitrust enforcement tools.[143]

92 After the passing of this *Guideline (2021)*, two massive antitrust fines were respectively issued to Alibaba and Meituan. Among others, the use of 'technical tools of data and algorithms' was deemed by SAMR as conducive to Alibaba and Meituan's abuses of market dominance that excluded competitors by forcing suppliers to 'choose only one (platform) between two (options) (*er xuan yi*)'. Besides these two fines, SAMR also issued two similarly drafted 'administrative guidance' that respectively prohibits Alibaba and Meituan's future anticompetitive behaviours including those that involve 'the use of data and algorithms'[144].

93 It is worth noting that SAMR, the antitrust agency, did *not* claim that data or algorithmic power were considered as defining factors for Alibaba or Meituan's market dominance. Therefore, no antitrust measures on firm structures were taken.[145]

94 Another high-profile antitrust practice focused on data and platform interoperability. In September 2021, the MIIT (the industrial regulator but not the antitrust agency) held an administrative guidance joint-meeting with big-tech companies including Douyin (the Chinese TikTok), Taobao (Alibaba), Wechat (Tencent) and others. The MIIT required these tech-giants to stop blocking each other's links and data flow on their platforms or affiliated companies within a week in order to improve interoperability.[146] This is similar to the EU's *DMA (2020 Draft)* which requires gatekeepers to ensure fair competition for their third-party suppliers.[147] While Wechat is still reported to be partly resisting Taobao (Alibaba) links[148], major platforms including Wechat, Alibaba and Douyin changed their technical architectures to comply with this administrative guidance.[149]

95 These antitrust practices combine new legislative efforts with state enforcement and administrative guidance, which together require big-techs to develop self-governance rules and help maintain a competitive digital market order. These practices institute a new antitrust regime in the digital economy and co-produce common knowledge in the new epistemic communities of antitrust agencies and private actors.

---

[142] 王健 吴宗泽论数据作为反垄断法中的必要设施 (shupl.edu.cn) 2021 ; 陈永伟: 数据是否应适用必需设施原则——基于"两种错误"的分析,《竞争政策研究》2021:4. 李世佳: 论数据构成必需设施的标准——兼评《关于平台经济领域的反垄断指南》第十四条之修改, 河南财经政法大学学报. 2021,36(05).

[143] 国务院反垄断委员会关于平台经济领域的反垄断指南_部门政务_中国政府网 (www.gov.cn).

[144] 市场监管总局依法对阿里巴巴集团控股有限公司在中国境内网络零售平台服务市场实施"二选一"垄断行为作出行政处罚, available at https://www.samr.gov.cn/xw/zj/202104/t20210410_327702.html (last accessed 16 December 2022); 市场监管总局依法对美团在中国境内网络餐饮外卖平台服务市场实施"二选一"垄断行为作出行政处罚, available at https://www.samr.gov.cn/xw/zj/202110/t20211008_335364.html (last accessed 16 December 2022).

[145] Id.

[146] 工信部召开"屏蔽网址链接问题行政指导会", available at http://tech.china.com.cn/internet/20210911/380718.shtml (last accessed 16 December 2022).

[147] COM (2020) 842: Proposal for a REGULATION OF THE EUROPEAN PARLIAMENT AND OF THE COUNCIL on contestable and fair markets in the digital sector (Digital Markets Act) 2020/0374/COD.

[148] 互联网行业如何"拆墙""安全"成焦点 乱码现象仍存在, available at http://news.hsw.cn/system/2021/1001/1377522.shtml (last accessed 16 December 2022).

[149] 微信能跳转淘宝了，互联网围墙"潜规则"将成往事, available at http://www.eeo.com.cn/2021/0917/504983.shtml (last accessed 16 December 2022).

Summary – State-Market Co-Production via Institutionalisation: The above evidence shows that the Chinese state has in recent years intensively adopted formal institutions in the fields of data security, data protection and antitrust to deal with data harms/risks in the rising digital 'economy'. This institutionalisation strategy co-produces and stabilises common knowledge in the epistemic communities of data governance in order to scale a national digital economy. Co-production means the efforts from both the state's formal practices and the private actors' informal knowledge exchange and self-governance at scales. The data security, privacy, and competitive market order in China's digital economy are provided by both formal and informal labour from public and private actors. **96**

D. Activation: Data Property, Commons, or 'Party manages data'?

Evidence in China manifests data fragmentation at all levels. Public and private data handlers keep data to themselves and lack the incentives to share data as an 'essential factor' in the market. To deal with data fragmentation, the Chinese state adopted what this chapter calls the 'activation' strategy since 2015. **97**

In the context of China's data governance, activation is used to contest data access and ownership, where the state innovates ways to 'activate' data flow and use by experimenting data licensing, ownership, 'use without retaining', and Party management. These different legal, technical or political arrangements 'code' or contest the socio-legal nature of data, before stabilised institutions and common knowledge can be co-produced. **98**

Evidence of 'activation' is drawn from three cases. First, the push and pull between Ant Group and Central Bank over personal credit information, second, the contrasting approaches to data property between Shenzhen and Beijing, and third, Tianjin's case of 'Party manages data'. **99**

I. Ant Group v the Central Bank–Licensing or Commons?

1. Central Bank's license to Ant Financial (2015–2018)

Between 2015–2018 the Chinese Central Bank used private licensing to activate the market use of personal financial credit information (which are different from personal public credit information or 'social credit'). Before 2015, the consumer credit-reporting (*geren zheng xin*) business was monopolised by the Central Bank, which meant that only public reporting of personal credit information was legal. This meant first, only the Central Bank's database can be analysed to provide risk-assessment services for commercial banks loan decisions (though commercial banks can always build their own risk models based on internal data for internal use). Second, the data types are also strictly limited, for example including, personal credit cards payment, mortgages payment, and other financial information. **100**

However, in 2015 the Central Bank for the first time granted eight provisional licenses of consumer credit-reporting to Big-Techs including Ant Financial (before changing its name to Ant Group in 2020) and Tencent (whose consumer credit product **101** was never effectively online)[150]. This gave birth to Sesame Credit (of Ant Financial), which uses people's behavioural data to produce financial/social risk-scores.[151]

102 Central Bank's licenses in 2015 brought two main changes in terms of the use of personal information. First, it allowed private actors to handle personal credit information that they privately collected or acquired, giving up the Central Bank's monopoly on consumer credit-reporting. Second, the types of data being handled expanded from the narrow consumer credit data to the use of 'alternative data' including social networks, consumer habits, and other information collected by the FinTech giants.[152]

103 It is worth noting that in 2015 there were very few data protection laws in China except for the *Ninth Amendment of the Criminal Code* which served as a redline of deterrence towards novel data practices.[153] Meanwhile the 2013 *Regulation on Credit-reporting Industry* (similar to the U.S. *Fair Credit Reporting Act 1970*) only provides the legal framework for handling traditional consumer credit data in the credit-reporting industry.[154] The big-techs' handling of 'alternative data' for multiple analytical purposes was thus left in a legal grey zone, before the Central Bank's 2015 licenses granted them with more degrees of regulatory certainty and protections.

104 Respondent A, a law firm partner in Beijing, argued that these provisional licenses were taken not so much as an opening of the private consumer credit-reporting market, but as a regulatory haven for big-techs to collect data and innovate new technologies.

> *'The tech giants were desperate to get the Central Bank's provisional licenses not because of the consumer credit-reporting business itself. They wanted to have regulatory protections in collecting and analysing new data. That was a regulatory haven.'*[155]

105 In practice, Central Bank's 2015 provisional licenses provided a window period for data-driven and AI technological innovation. Sesame Credit (of Ant Financial) for example was able to experiment 'smart' projects on Alibaba's massive e-commerce ecosystem as well as collaborating with local governments in early social credit and smart city projects, though the real effects and normative aspects of these projects are debatable.[156]

2. Central Bank's Data Pooling Attempts after 2018

106 In 2018 however, the Central Bank did not renew the eight consumer credit-reporting licenses after realising the problem of data fragmentation and data silos created by these companies. It criticised the tech-giants like Ant and Tencent who kept their data strictly to themselves as 'data islands'.[157]

[150] 人民银行印发《关于做好个人征信业务准备工作的通知》, available at http://www.gov.cn/xinwen/2015-01/05/content_2800381.htm (last accessed 16 December 2022).

[151] See, explanation by sesame credit's former ITO 人民银行印发《关于做好个人征信业务准备工作的通知》 (antfin.com). Also see Dai, Xin, in: Everling (ed.), *Social Credit Rating: Reputation und Vertrauen beurteilen* (2020), 139–163.

[152] *Ibid.* See Sesame Credit's ITO explains how different types of data are used besides traditional financial credit-reporting data.

[153] *Ibid.*

[154] State Council's Regulation on Credit-reporting Industry 2013. No.631. 征信业管理条例 (www.gov.cn).

[155] Law firm partner A. Beijing, 2021.4

[156] See, e.g. Dai, Xin, in: Everling (ed.), *Social Credit Rating: Reputation und Vertrauen beurteilen*, 2020, 139–163. 刷芝麻信用"进"杭图借还图书 2017, available at https://zj.zjol.com.cn/news/621587.html (last accessed 16 December 2022).

[157] 万存知演讲全文八家个人征信试点机构无一合格，合格机构应该是这样, available at https://www.leiphone.com/category/fintech/9OZUYsGKPrV6I4fm.html (last accessed 16 December 2022).

The Central Bank instead established a fully licensed joint-venture, Baihang Credit in Shenzhen, with a shareholding structure that gave Ant Financial, Wechat (Tencent) and other seven companies each 8 % shareholdings. The goal was to incentivise these private tech giants to pool their personal credit data into this joint venture. However, such pooling effort is reported to have stagnated as of 2019.[158] This may have contributed to the motivation of the state to use antitrust measures against Ant Group as discussed above. **107**

In December 2020, the Central Bank fully licensed another consumer credit-reporting company, Pudao Credit, which situates in Beijing and is also a joint venture between state and corporate holders, including big-techs in China like JD.com (25 %), Xiaomi (17.5 %), and Kuangshi Technology (17.5 %)[159]. It is reported to be trialling new ways of big-data innovation for micro-finance, but it is unclear if data pooling is arranged between these shareholders as of 2021.[160] **108**

This history of the central bank v Ant Group since 2015 shows the push and pull between the state and corporations trying to deal with data fragmentation by activation. Moreover, the following section presents a local competition between Beijing's 'data pooling' approach, and Shenzhen's attempted data property right approach. **109**

II. Beijing v Shenzhen: 'Use without Retaining' or Property Right?

1. Data Fragmentation due to Ownership and Compliance Uncertainties

Respondent X, a Shanghai official, claimed that it is very difficult for local governmental agencies with share data with each other because there are risks that internal mistakes would be made known to another public department. There are not many incentives to share data, while sharing means potential exposure of one's weaknesses.[161] **110**

Respondent C complained about lack of data access as a data scientist and product manager in a state-affiliated credit-reporting company in Qingdao. The Central Bank's credit payment data is the most important data type to train and test the prediction accuracy of the algorithms. Machine learning (ML) techniques like back-propagation cannot work without this crucial data set. **111**

> *'My team cannot train useful machine-learning models because we don't have the data on loan paybacks from the Central Bank's Qingdao branch. Without that data we cannot label our algorithmic predictions as good or bad.'*[162]

The access to credit payment data was expected to be done by negotiation between the Qingdao's municipal (horizontal state) and the local central bank (vertical state). However respondent C was uncertain about the progress during the time of the interview. **112**

Respondent C also mentioned that other important public data like financial reports, tax, and payment for employees' social insurance, all needed negotiation with powerful local governmental agencies like the SAMR, tax agency, and the social security agency. **113**

[158] 百行征信僵局，腾讯阿里困兽之斗，available at https://www.jiemian.com/article/3542916.html (last accessed 16 December 2022).

[159] 央行发放第二张个人征信业务许可 2020, available at http://www.xinhuanet.com/fortune/2020-12/25/c_1126908900.htm (last accessed 16 December 2022).

[160] 朴道征信错位发展，采集信贷之外的信用数据) 2021, https://www.163.com/dy/article/GC2OIQ6F053257CG.html (last accessed 16 December 2022).

[161] Government official X, Shanghai, 2021.3.

[162] Manager C, Qingdao, 2021.2.

Meanwhile accessing electricity usage data was expensive because large state owned enterprises (SOEs) like the State Grid Corporation of China already charges fees based on data access entries.[163]

114 There were also greater uncertainties of data ownership as well as data protection by the time of the interviews before PIPL 2021 was passed in August 2021 (but still left the data ownership problem unanswered).

> *'Without clear ownership arrangements and data protection rules how do we access public data? Can we keep the data we used in our hard drives?'*[164]

115 In spite of these difficulties, this state-affiliated credit-reporting company took an innovative method called 'use without retaining the data'. The technical team basically goes to different local branches of the ministries, accesses their public data and finish the calculation in their office, and takes away the software product/algorithms with some predictive capacities without taking the data away. But the problem was that they need to go to the offices and update the algorithms quite often.[165]

116 The above interview evidence only reveals the data fragmentation experienced by this particular firm in relation to public information access in Qingdao. However, Respondent C claimed that they have extensively consulted and learnt from practices in other cities like Hangzhou and Shanghai. There has been active informal knowledge exchange between local state and firms on how to access and trade data.[166]

117 Respondents at an internal discussion in Shanghai also showed their burning concerns on how to define data property and transaction under uncertain compliance regimes, especially concerning the Shanghai's big-data centre and the pilot of *Lingang* free trade zone with the aim to be a data harbour (Shanghai, 2021.3).[167] Interviews with officials at Hefei's big-data centre also show similar questions regarding data ownership and data protection (Hefei, 2021.3). The reported rise of China's big-data centres and companies also evidence the local attempts to 'activate' data use when data is actually fragmented without clear legal coding on data ownership and protection.[168]

118 Beijing and Shenzhen are two poles within these myriads of local activation experiments. Beijing adopts a commons approach to data access, while Shenzhen tried to formally establish data property right and interest in its legislation (yet without success).

2. Beijing: 'Use without Retaining'– a Data Pooling Approach

119 The Beijing International Data Exchange (BIDE) was established in March 2021 under the Beijing Municipality.[169] It partly functions as a traditional trading centre for big-data products like analytics instruments, their future financial gains, i.e. securitised data assets, and cross border data transactions (Art. 5 sec. 2).[170]

---

[163] Manager C, Qingdao. 2021.2.

[164] Manager C, Qingdao, 2021.2.

[165] Manager C, Qingdao, 2021.2.

[166] Manager C, Qingdao, 2021.2.

[167] Also see Shanghai Data Regulation (Draft for comments) 2021.

[168] 大数据中心互联网时代的"粮仓", available at http://www.cac.gov.cn/2020-03/18/c_1586070965007725.htm (last accessed 16 December 2022); 关于加快构建全国一体化大数据中心协同创新体系的指导意见 (发改高技〔2020〕1922号), available at https://www.ndrc.gov.cn/xxgk/zcfb/tz/202012/t20201228_1260496.html?code=&state=123 (last accessed 16 December 2022).

[169] 北京国际大数据交易所 (bjidex.com).

[170] 北京市地方金融监督管理局 北京市经济和信息化局关于印发北京国际大数据交易所设立工作实施方案的通知 2020.9.29, 2020.9.29, available at http://www.beijing.gov.cn/zhengce/gfxwj/202103/t20210331_2341258.html (last accessed 16 December 2022).

But more importantly, BIDE features the 'use without retaining' approach to data access (Art. 5 sec. 2) that is similar to the informally adopted method in Qingdao.[171] The difference is that in Beijing the BIDE is expected to functions as a 'pool' that helps gather data from different data handlers, while in Qingdao's case the data scientist had to go to each different branches of the government to 'use without retaining' the data[172]. 120

Experts have commented that BIDE is better than previous data trading centres (e.g. in Guizhou) because the 'use without retaining' method circumvents the ownership question and replaces it with the 'right to use' question. It also creates a safe environment for public and private actors to access data and run their computer programs based on specific needs. The fees charged are based on the entries of data access and quantity. It is safe both in terms of data security and data protection, which adopts a 'regulatory sandbox' approach inspired by the UK's financial regulations. The sandbox environment creates a virtual space to experiment the release of data or financial instruments before taking these practices into the real market environment.[173] 121

This chapter calls these BIDE's practices attempts towards 'data pooling', where data are being collectively governed by data communities who regularly contribute and use such data commons, with the state backing its security and compliance regimes. This categorisation is inspired by Ostrom's polycentric governance of common-pool resources (CPR), which defies a dichotomy of state v privatisation on the governance of commons like forests or fisheries.[174] 122

The effects of Beijing's data pooling practices, however, still need to be observed in the long-run. Like Qingdao, the 'use without retaining' practices can also face the problems of regular data updates and data fragmentation when critical data providers like the Central Bank refuse to share data. 123

3. Shenzhen: Data Property Right and Interest?

Beijing's 'use without retention' is in contrast to Shenzhen's (unsuccessful) attempt to code 'data rights' into its local legislation, which leaned towards a property rights approach. In October 2020, the central Party-state issued an implementing plan (2020–2025) which instructed Shenzhen to start piloting data property and transaction institutions, and data protection mechanisms.[175] 124

As a result, in July 2020, Shenzhen proposed its first draft of *Shenzhen Data Regulations (2020)*. It was the first time in China a formal legislation draft that tried to stipulate 'data right' articles. They include Art. 4 on a personal data right to 'self-determination, control, processing/disposal, benefit and redress', and Art. 52 which protects 'data rights' that are exclusive to its collector or generators.[176] This triggered constitutional debates on whether the local laws could establish such data rights even before higher national laws allowed, and on whether this 'data right' would prevent the flow of data.[177] It was also argued that in the 'Wechat unfair competition case' (2020) 125

[171] Manager C, Qingdao, 2021.2.

[172] *Ibid.*

[173] Expert opinions in 2021 news article; http://jrj.beijing.gov.cn/jrgzdt/202104/t20210401_2342064.html 2021.4.1 北京国际大数据交易所成立.

[174] See e.g. Ostrom, *American Economic Review* 100.3 (2010): 641-72.

[175] http://www.gov.cn/zhengce/2020-10/11/content_5550408.htm 中共中央办公厅 国务院办公厅印发《深圳建设中国特色社会主义先行示范区综合改革试点实施方案20202025年)》.

[176] 深圳市司法局关于公开征求《深圳经济特区数据条例征求意见稿)》意见的通告, available at http://sf.sz.gov.cn/hdjlpt/yjzj/answer/5748 (last accessed 16 December 2022).

[177] 地方无权对"数据权"立法深圳数据条例意见稿引专家热议. (2020), available at https://www.xuehua.us/a/5f15cb4ce3809536eb95207b?lang=zh-cn (last accessed 16 December 2022).

the Hangzhou Internet Court decided that personal data is protected as a 'right of control' at the individual level, but the corporations only have competition rights with regards to the 'data pool'[178]. This was used by legal scholars as evidence against writing 'data rights' into the latter two versions of the *Shenzhen Data Regulation (2021).*[179]

126 In July 2021, Shenzhen passed its final version of the *Data Regulation* (effective January 2022) after the second draft (May 2021). It deleted all articles regarding data rights, and explained in a companion legislative note that there has been 'no consensus on data rights', and it is difficult to create this 'new right category' in local legislation. However, in Article 4 it does recognise the property right of data products and services made by natural and legal persons, which is not controversial in the existing legal framework.[180]

127 Shenzhen's data legislation saga is to some extent similar to the Central Bank's 2015–2018 private licenses, though Shenzhen's early efforts were rejected in later drafts. The state started by proposing privatised legal arrangements that incentivised corporations to innovate new ways of using their data, but later challenged by needs of better data access and flow. In contrast, the data pooling idea also appeared in both the Central Bank's post-2018 approach on consumer credit information and the Beijing 'use without retaining' cases.

III. Tianjin: 'Party manages data'

128 A final form of the activation strategy is by resorting to the Party's leadership. It is more politically flexible than the Central Bank's licensing and the experiments on data access or ownership (Beijing v Shenzhen).

129 In Tianjin Municipality, the party-vanguard raised the idea of 'Party manages data' (*dangguan shuju*) since 2019, which so far only focuses on facilitating the use of public information collected by local government agencies.[181] News reported that this strategy is crucial for data security and improving governance performances. For example, it was reported to be very useful in the COVID-19 pandemic governance. Public big data were used in conjunction with the 'grid management' in streets and neighbourhoods. The 'red, orange and green QR code' system was claimed to be effective where civil servants and community workers use these systems in respective 'grids' (streets) to help identify risks.[182]

130 Wang Yun, the chief officer of the Tianjin Big Data Centre (a public department in Tianjin government) argued in a news report that 'Party members should have some spaces and immunity to trial and error in their innovative use of data for the public good'.[183] In 2020 the Tianjin Big Data Centre passed an *Implementation Measure* (2020)

---

[178] (2019) 浙8601民初1987号 [2019, Zhejiang, 8601 Civil first instance case no. 1987] 2020）浙01民终5889号 [2020, Zhejiang, 01 Civil appeal case no. 5889].

[179] 地方无权对"数据权"立法深圳数据条例意见稿引专家热议, available at https://www.xuehua.us/a/5f15cb4ce3809536eb95207b?lang=zh-cn (last accessed 16 December 2022).

[180] 深圳市第七届人民代表大会常务委员会公告第十号）(2021), available at http://www.sz.gov.cn/zfgb/2021/gb1218/content/post_9307139.html (last accessed 8 February 2023) [Shenzhen 7th People's Congress Plenary Committee Report No. 10. On passing the Shenzhen Economic Special Zone's Data Regulation, 2021. Effective 2022.1.1].

[181] 坚持党管数据建设数字天津 [Insist on the Party manages data method to build digital Tianjin, www.cac.gov.cn, last accessed 15 April 2019].

[182] http://stdaily.com/index/kejixinwen/2021-09/08/content_1218450.shtml "党管数据"是保证数据安全的必由之路; http://www.xinhuanet.com/2021-01/05/c_1126949362.htm "党管数据"天津样本——专访天津市委宣传部副部长、市委网信办主任王芸.

[183] http://www.xinhuanet.com/2021-01/05/c_1126949362.htm "党管数据"天津样本——专访天津市委宣传部副部长、市委网信办主任王芸.

to list certain immunity measures to promote the local party cadres to take more responsibilities and adopt new technologies in governance. This is a follow-up policy of the Tianjin Municipality's 2018 *Action Plan (2018-2020)* which aimed to tackle the problem of party members' 'inaction and not taking responsibilities'.[184]

Wang also claimed that Party's leadership is important to break 'information islands' 131
and 'data chimneys', and big data is crucial to the Party's governance capacity and performance. She categorised the major achievements of this strategy since 2019 as enhancing top-level designs of governmental data, 'promoting the development of digital economy' and 'services to the people'. Wang provided some examples. (1) Governmental data sharing with national and ministerial agencies to coordinate financial and market regulations and building risk-models and emergency management systems. (2) Using data to help with economic recovery after the COVID-19 pandemic in 2020 by analysing economic data (e.g. on tax) to help private companies decide when to get back to work and alleviate their pressures on cash-flow and loan payback. The Tianjin Big Data Centre also designed a technology called 'code for frozen food'. It traces the supply of frozen food from sea ports to the serving tables, as COVID-19 virus proved to survive in frozen environments via the supply chain. (3) Providing public information to the local communities on daily life, including municipal construction plans, environment concerns, fire safety, noise pollution, police alerts, community disputes and so on.[185]

Outside of Tianjin, this 'Party manages data' approach has also been advocated, for 132
example by large state-owned enterprises in their data security compliance work in general.[186]

Despite its emphasis on a political and flexible handling of data, Tianjin's 'Party 133
manages data' strategy still need to comply with data laws including the PIPL 2021 that regulates both public and private 'data handlers'. The party-state most likely can only legally access and use public information collected by state agencies themselves under legal procedures. Against private actors, Tianjin is actually one of the first few cities that passed a local legislation (effective January 2021) that bans the private collection of biometric data including facial data (Art. 16).[187] Government news also claim that the city is at the forefront of personal data protection practices against abusive private information collection and processing.[188] Nevertheless, there is rather limited information on the protection against public abuse. The empirical and normative aspects of Tianjin's 'Party manages data' practices still require further fieldwork and long-term observations.

Sectional conclusion – Legal coding/pooling of data assets via activation: Attempts 134
have been made to 'code' data with legal arrangement in China, yet without conclusive agreements among stakeholders. Data fragmentation is revealed at different ministerial (vertical), regional (horizontal) and corporate levels. To cope with data fragmentation,

---

[184] http://www.gov.cn/xinwen/2018-04/03/content_5279425.htm 关于深入开展不作为不担当问题专项治理三年行动方案2018—2020年）.

[185] http://www.cac.gov.cn/2021-08/18/c_1630875756964401.htm 党管数据的津门"智"理，光明日报, last accessed 18 August 2021.

[186] http://theory.people.com.cn/n1/2021/0830/c40531-32212137.html 坚持党管数据 保障数据安全.

[187] 天津市社会信用条例天津市第十七届人民代表大会常务委员会公告，第63号）available at https://flk.npc.gov.cn/detail2.html?ZmY4MDgwODE3NTI2NWRkNDAxNzYzYzc1Zjg0ZTU3MWY%3D (last accessed 5 May 2023) [Tianjin Social Credit Regulations, Tianjin 17th People's Congress Plenary Committee Report, No 63. Effective on 1 January 2021].

[188] 天津扎实开展数据安全和个人信息保护工作 [Tianjin steadily develops work on data security and personal information protection, www.tjcac.gov.cn, last accessed 20 August 2020]; 天津市开展APP违法采集个人信息集中整治 [Tianjin works on regulating APP illegal collections of personal information, www.gov.cn, last accessed 23 November 2019].

the Chinese party-state adopted different forms of activation strategies as shown in case studies. These include the cases of Central Bank v Ant Group, Beijing v Shenzhen and Tianjin's 'Party manages data'.

135 In these three case studies the state provided legal and policy spaces for the coding and contestation of data's ownership and access. If we borrow Roman law's concept, data so far, in its individual form, seems to be *res nullius* – physical things that have not or have never had an owner. This legal category includes the individual 'wild animal', or *ferae naturae*, which will not become property until being captured/killed.

136 Following this metaphor, the activation strategy allows individual units of data, i.e. the new 'wild animal', to be captured in a window period by public and private 'hunters'. The strategy allows them to try ways that best use the captured data in privatised or collective ways. The competition between ministerial (vertical), regional (horizontal) and corporate interests jointly contest the technical-legal arrangements of data access and use, with informal knowledge exchange happening in data governance communities including scholars, lawyers, and social groups across geographic or administrative regions.

137 While the activation strategy provides dynamic periods of state-market co-production of new practices and knowledge, this paper also observes an emerging 'data pooling' approach from these practices. Instead of hunting 'wild animals', China's data governance in practice may lead towards a common-pool resources (CPR) governance approach, similar to the governance of forestry or fisheries studied by Ostrom. If so, activation may transit into institutionalisation which could solidify a CPR-based practice of data governance.

E. Layering: Data Cycles, Local Habitats, and Sustainable Design

138 As required in the party-state's top-level data policies, data security, data markets, access and transaction are all foundations for the ultimate goal to 'increase the values of data resources'[189]. Evidence however finds a lack of valuable and sustainable use of data in governance settings, which the local public actors try to address.

139 This chapter 'Layering' describes the local state actors' attempts to build sustainable data cycles and habitats with in-depth understanding of data's local institutional contexts. This can be seen as a data strategy that is concerned with better designs of laws and technologies in order to achieve valuable and sustainable data use in governance. The strategy provides an insight that data cycles are generated locally and data scaling is limited by institutional layering. Evidence is mainly drawn from empirical observations of China's smart court and the social/financial credit risk-assessment projects.

I. Smart Court: National v Local Practices

140 The 'Smart Court' project in China has experienced difficulties when applying data-driven technologies to the court's daily operations. Not only did such difficulties happen

---

[189] 中共中央 国务院关于构建更加完善的要素市场化配置体制机制的意见 [CPC Central Committee and State Council: Instruction on Improving the Market Mechanism for Allocating Essential Factors, 2020.3.30.], available at http://www.gov.cn/zhengce/2020-04/09/content_5500622.htm (last accessed 16 December 2022).

at the Supreme People's Court's (SPC) national case recommendation system, but also many provincial High Courts' databases and models. Evidence shows limitations in these efforts that use China's judicial big-data with the goal to help judges make consistent judgements and accelerate the proceedings.

More specifically, the national (SPC) and provincial (High Court) case recommenda- **141** tion systems are not effective enough to gain popularity among judges because the recommended cases were not always very relevant. This low relevance in matches can be partly due to the insufficiency of digitised court judgments before the 1990s/2000s to form long-term time series, and sometimes the concentrated caseloads in certain years or regions that were weighted over-heavily in the algorithmic models.[190] Respondent B, a judge and court administrator in a Shanghai Intermediary Court, said:

> *'While technology can improve efficiency of the court, the quality of judgments cannot be rushed in the Smart Court progress.'*[191]

The judges in this Shanghai court use another locally designed 'typical case' system, **142** instead of the national system, Respondent B also mentioned. This local system is built by more traditional ways of human-selection, i.e. senior judges come together to discuss what new cases can be seen as important and typical, and circulate these cases to the entire court and lower courts.[192]

These 'typical cases', without any high-tech involved, are claimed to be more helpful **143** in the long-term. It alludes to the temporal aspects of layering – data and its knowledge accumulated through time within institutions with path-dependency. Local courts can have their own concerns and ways of generating judicial data which can be difficult when scaling to the national level. This means data-driven technologies in governance contexts might be more effective at local level with longer time-scales.

Another example is the 'algorithmic case allocation' system used in this Shanghai **144** intermediary court to automate the process of case assignment. It claims to help prevent judges from arbitrarily picking cases they wish to decide, and also makes more efficient division of labour by sending simple cases to junior judges while the complex ones to senior judges.[193] This local court practice gained much support by judges at the court, which is largely due to the active participation of judges in the design and updates of this algorithmic system. At the initial design of this system, data scientists and judges sit together to discuss the data categories and the labelling of the cases' cause of actions. Periodically the senior judges come back to evaluate the system's performance, following the operational cycles of the court and the time when legal institutions change. For example, when new types of cases emerge due to legal amendments or new judicial interpretations, the senior judges would make decisions on how to change data categories in terms of the cause of actions, and ask the court's information team (with computer scientists) to update the system. This also follow the court's own judgement cycles which determine the data lifecycle of generation, processing and use.[194]

The smart court cases show that legal institutions operated at the local level are coded **145** into the data cycle construction and modelling. These legally and historically embedded technologies retain shared knowledge and practices, like the 'sediments of time', shaped by interactions between lawyers, judges, administrators and the wider legal epistemic

[190] 左卫民，如何通过人工智能实现类案类判，《中国法律评论》，2018年第2期。[Zuo, Weimin, *Chinese Legal Commentaries*, 2018 (2).]
[191] Judge and Court Administrator B, Shanghai, 2021.
[192] *Ibid.*
[193] Judge and Court Administrator B, Shanghai, 2021.3.
[194] Judge and Court Administrator B, Shanghai 2021.3.

community.[195] These technologies, like laws, thus require timely updates and alignments to the changes of external environments, including their legal institutional context and the court's own operational environments. Both legal and tech epistemic communities are crucial in such law-tech co-evolution process.

II. Social/Financial Credit: Public Information for Risk-assessment

146 'Data sediments' were first referred to in official documents in the State Council's E-Government instructions 2017. In that context, data sediments mean the long-term accumulation of public data in government practices. This temporal strategy is important in the use of public information for risk-assessment in the state project of social and financial credit systems. Cases in Shanghai and Qingdao are discussed below. Respondent D, a civil servant in Shanghai, made an illuminating point on the state's layering practice as building 'data habitats' when discussing the ways forward for the Shanghai's use of public credit information:

> *'We need to build a habitat for data, like raising fish in a garden pond. It takes time for the fish to grow and then you can draw useful information from this data.'*[196]

147 The fish pond analogy interestingly echoes with Ostrom's case studies on the governance of fisheries, i.e. the common-pool resources (CPR). The data habitat analogy reveals the commons or pooling aspects of data, which has sustainability and time concerns with regards to its own data cycles in its long-term institutional environments (similar to CPR regeneration cycles in polycentric governance)[197].

148 This idea of data habitat was raised when discussing the challenges in some of the risk-assessment practices in Shanghai. Respondent D said that the risk scores generated for businesses sometimes are not very useful for an experienced regulator when deciding how to allocate inspection resources.

> *'[... The regulators] don't need our risk models that much data because they already have a deep understanding of the places to safeguard the market order. Our public credit information is not that often useful for them'.*[198]

149 Respondent D also mentioned that the depth of the data requires understanding of the data habitat, because data interpretation has different layers through time.

> *'You also need a habitat to understand the depth of the data. If someone has a criminal record, but because of over-defending himself or others in a violent crime, then maybe he can be seen as brave. To understand him you need more data over a period of time and context.'*[199]

150 The standardisation of data meant the losing of certain depth of understanding of the data which should be interpreted in its context. Data layering means to understand data not just as numbers or digits, but also the embedded meaning of those data in the environments where it was generated and construed. In this way the data applica-

---

[195] A concept borrowed from Koselleck, 2018. Also see Zuo, Zhenbin, *Governance by Algorithm: China's Social Credit System* (working paper), 2020, available at https://www.finance.group.cam.ac.uk/system/files/documents/GovernancebyAlgorithm_CERF_Zhenbin6.16.2020.pdf (last accessed 16 December 2022).

[196] Civil servant D, Shanghai, 2021.3.

[197] See e.g. Ostrom, *American Economic Review* 100.3 (2010), 641-72.

[198] Civil servant D, Shanghai, 2021.

[199] *Ibid.*

tions can provide more accurate and helpful use in the long-run without being locked-in its path-dependency.

To achieve deeper knowledge in the field and in its context, human expertise or tacit knowledge is also required to pass on informal knowledge alongside formalised institutional knowledge. Respondent D mentioned that: **151**

> *'In market regulations, the local authorities usually are already quite familiar with the business situation because they have been there for years. They know who the major players are and how to regulate them, while smaller shops come and go (…).'*[200]

Layering thus requires human expertise to pass on informal knowledge and provide a larger picture of the data contexts. This hybrid between human expertise (regulators' informal knowledge) and formal data support (institutionalised public credit-reporting) together shapes the technology and their actual use in Shanghai's public credit information centre. Moving from Shanghai to Qingdao, Respondent C who works at a state-affiliated credit-reporting company in Qingdao also described the rooms for improvements on their risk-prediction products in the longer term: **152**

> *'Each commercial bank has its own way of collecting and accumulating data. They have their own risk models for lending decisions built after for a long time, and often use our data analytics products as an auxiliary that often needs to be recalibrated according to their own understanding (…) They have been in the field for much longer, and knows how to recalibrate polluted or distorted data. What we could do is to provide more comprehensive data models for them, and their own insights acquired through time can correct our models and predictions.'*[201]

This shows that even at local levels, useful data applications are hard to achieve without understanding the specific needs and tacit context over time. Informal knowledge retained and exchanged in private actors like banks thus are crucial for the in-depth application of standardised and large-scale data in the long run. They are epistemic communities that help retain the embedded cognition/knowledge through time. **153**

Data cycles and their path-dependence on the legal institutions was also discussed by Respondent C: **154**

> *'The data on quarterly financial reports is not helpful because many small businesses don't even survive that long. The data disclosure cycle follows certain administrative practices established in the past. You need to changes those then we can extract useful information.'*[202]

This highlights the importance of legal institutions like financial disclosure rules on the generation and update of data in its habitat. The data cycles are path-dependent on how law regulates the periodical publication of for example the firm's financial reports. This could be extended to other situations where public data are restrained by each regulatory agency's own mandate, such as tax, social insurance paid for the employees, electricity usage etc. These different institutions and organisational operations create various time frames at local levels and thus diverse data cycles. **155**

---

[200] *Ibid.*
[201] Staff C, Qingdao, 2021.2.
[202] Staff C, Qingdao, 2021.2.

III. Law-tech Co-Evolution and Layering in Design

156 The above qualitative evidence reveals aspects of the practical hurdles that need to be surpassed before achieving sustainable data governance for data applications. Compared to industrial big-data, the massive amount of public information (including court judgements) and personal information may not be as easy to use for example in judicial and social/financial governance settings.

157 As a result, data assets are hard to evaluate, especially when the legal contestation on data property and commons are still ongoing. Alibaba and Deloitte's joint report (2019) also pointed out that data is not yet deemed as assets in accounting, and thus cannot be represented in financial reports.[203]

158 Some secondary grey sources also reveal emerging trends to make use of the public 'data sediments'. Huawei for example claimed that 'we help government have its data assets sedimented'.[204] It also tries to provide services on big data ecosystems.[205] Various businesses and reports also actively use terms like 'awakeing the sleeping data sediments'.[206] Although these slogans can be corporate marketing strategies, they share common themes of releasing the value of long-term accumulated public information in governance, which requires building a better data habitat.

159 Moreover, Shi's research on COVID prediction puts 'emphasis on heterogeneous, unstructured data (…) and let unfiltered data become sediments.' He explained that medical and socio-economic data need to be accumulated over time to achieve a good prediction of COVID-19 cases. 'Only high quality data can have good results'.[207] The big-data predictions in turn shapes laws and policies on COVID governance. This can also be seen as data layering practices that utilise long-term institutional data for governance and shape new data cycles of generation and use.

160 Attempts have been made to layer data institutions and build data habitats in Smart Court, social and financial credit systems, and some corporate or research use of public data. These emerging cases demonstrate a law-tech co-evolution process where layering is a key strategy to the timely adjustment between institutions and the technological design and prevent pathological path-dependencies. For example, data cycles can be co-designed and updated by judges, regulators and data scientists in areas like market regulations and disclosure cycles. In specific industries like banking for instance, market regulators and commercial banks can be involved in the design of public data infrastructures that helps update data cycles and bank's lending decisions and financial regulations.

---

[203] Deloitte and Alibaba Research Institute, Path towards data assetization, 2019. 德勤携手阿里研究院联合发布《数据资产化之路——数据资产的估值与行业实践》报告 (deloitte.com).

[204] 田林一: 沉淀政府数据资产，实现数据随需共享 – 华为期刊 (huawei.com) [Tian, Linyi. Sediments of government data assets, realising data sharing upon demands. Huawe.com] (last accessed 16 December 2022).

[205] 大数据生态系统-华为云 (huaweicloud.com) [Theme on Big data ecosystem, see Huawei Cloud website] (last accessed 16 December 2022).

[206] See e.g. WakeData惟客数据-唤醒沉睡的数据 (wakecloud.com) [Awake the sleeping data, wakecloud.com]; 我国大数据快速发展，唤醒"沉睡"的数据赋能各行各业(ruiec.com) [Rapid development in big-data, awakening the 'sleeping' data to empower all industries, ruiec.com] (last accessed 16 December 2022); 数据"沉睡"制约大数据产业发展 _ 经济参考网 (jjckb.cn) [Wu, Shuaishuai, jjckb.cn, 2017.3.23].

[207] 任芳言让数据沉淀的人—新闻—科学网 (sciencenet.cn) [Ren, Fangyan: a person that lets data precipitate. 2021.1.5.] Reporting on Shi Yong's work in predicting COVID case growth in Wuhan (last accessed 16 December 2022).

Public and private epistemic communities in this sense can generate new knowledge and practices for valuable data use. They can help provide a deeper understanding of how past data is locally layered through time and shaped by law-tech co-evolution. With emerging evidence of layering, this chapter conceptualises it as a strategy that helps better design institutional data habitats/ecosystems. **161**

F. Conclusion

The chapter conceptualises three data strategies of the Chinese party-state in practices: institutionalisation, activation and layering. It concludes that the Chinese party-state uses these strategies to co-produce a data-driven regulatory state and a national digital market. It contributes to the more general theoretical debate on state-market relationship, and argues that a rising rule-of-law state in China co-produces the digital economy, shapes data 'property' and commons, and co-evolves with new technologies. More specifically, the three state strategies are conceptualised based on institutionalist theories of law and economics, and are examined by doctrinal and qualitative evidence drawn from China's recent developments since 2010s. **162**

Institutionalisation is shown to works as a stabilising strategy. It facilitates state-market co-production of common knowledge by stabilising formal institutions that deal with data security, data protection and antitrust concerns. Cases are drawn from DiDi's IPO security review, the legislative process of PIPL featuring gatekeeper and managerial liabilities, and the antitrust actions on Ant Group, Alibaba, Meituan and other big-techs. These cases together show the rise of stabilising legal institutions and a knowledge-based regulatory state co-produced with a national digital market. They also reinforce a public-private divide that facilitates division of labours between state and market actors in co-producing security, data protection and market order facing a rapidly evolving digital society. **163**

Activation is observed to serve as a contestation strategy. It triggers co-production of epistemic communities which experiment data commons, ownership, or political leadership approaches to tackle data fragmentation. Activation allows for dynamic and provisional ways of activating the data market and use, while also exhibiting tendencies to be later institutionalised into stabilised common knowledge and coded into formal laws. Cases of the Central Bank v Ant Group, Beijing v Shenzhen, and the Tianjin's 'Party manages data' were provided. They demonstrate a dynamic data commons/pooling approach is emerging, while data property is highly contested. These cases also show that data property or commons thus do not emerge by themselves, but require legal-political contestations. **164**

Layering is evidenced to function as a sustainable development strategy. It only recently emerged as a strategy to build data cycles and long-term habitats that facilitate the in-depth understanding of data and the use of valuable data. It reveals that while big data is useful in large-scale governance projects, news data technologies are layered, i.e. path-dependent on existing socio-legal institutions. Cases of China's Smart Court, the social and financial credit systems, and other grey resources provide initial evidence on the state's layering approach towards co-design of data cycles and habitats for more valuable applications and deployments of data technologies. **165**

The conceptual model of institutionalisation, activation and layering contributes to an institutionalist understanding of China's data law, policy and practices in relation to China's digital market and data-driven technologies. It is also intended as a common **166** theoretical framework that can be applied beyond its data context and to analyse other countries' legal systems and practices. This strategy model and its theoretical foregrounding pave the way for more comparative studies and empirical research which is beyond the scope of this chapter. The normative implications of these strategies and data governance practices also requires further examination, ideally based on more empirical evidence.

Bibliography

I. Major books and articles

167 Aoki, *Corporations in evolving diversity: Cognition, governance, and institutions*, 2010

Chen/Deakin/Siems/Wang, Law, trust and institutional change in China: evidence from qualitative fieldwork, 17(2) *Journal of Corporate Law Studies* 257 (2017)

Chen/Deakin, On Heaven's lathe: state, rule of law, and economic development, 8(1) *Law and Development Review* 123 (2015)

Dai, Toward A Reputation State: A Comprehensive View of China's Social Credit System Project, *Social Credit Rating: Reputation und Vertrauen beurteilen* 139 (2020)

Davis/Ostrom, A public economy approach to education: Choice and co-production, 12(4) *International Political Science Review* 313 (1991)

Deakin/Gindis/Hodgson/Kainan/Pistor, Legal institutionalism: Capitalism and the constitutive role of law, 45(1) *Journal of Comparative Economics* 188 (2017)

Deakin, Evolution for Our Time: A Theory of Legal Memetics, 55 *Current Legal Problems* (2002)

Deakin, Juridical ontology: the evolution of legal form, *Historical Social Research/Historische Sozialforschung* 170 (2015)

Deakin, Legal Evolution: Integrating Economic and Systemic Approaches, 7 *Review of Law and Economics* (2011)

Deakin/Markou, Evolutionary Law and Economics: Theory and Method, *Northern Ireland Legal Quarterly* 72.4 (2021)

Deakin/Meng, Resolving Douglass C. North's 'puzzle' concerning China's household responsibility system, *Journal of Institutional Economics* 1 (2021)

Deakin/Meng, The Governance of Covid-19: Anthropogenic Risk, Evolutionary Learning, and the Future of the Social State, 49(4) *Industrial Law Journal* 539 (2020)

Deakin/Wilkinson, *The Law of the Labour Market: Industrialisation, Employment, and Legal Evolution*, 2005

Griffin, CFIUS in the Age of Chinese Investment, 85 *Fordham L. Rev.* 1757 (2016)

Hildebrandt, Code Driven Law. Scaling the Past and Freezing the Future, in: Markou/Deakin (eds.), *Is Law Computable? Critical Perspectives on Law and Artificial Intelligence*, 2020

Hildebrandt, Law as Information in the Era of Data-Driven Agency, 79(1) *The Modern Law Review* 1 (2016)

Hildebrandt, The adaptive nature of text-driven law, 1(1) *Journal of Cross-disciplinary Research in Computational Law* (2021)

Koselleck, Sediments of Time on possible histories, 2018

Markou/Deakin, Ex Machina Lex: Exploring the Limits of Legal Computability, in: Markou/Deakin (eds.), *Is Law Computable? Critical Perspectives on Law and Artificial Intelligence*, 2020

Ostrom, Beyond markets and states: polycentric governance of complex economic systems, 100(3) *American Economic Review* 641 (2010)

Ostrom, Crossing the great divide: Coproduction, synergy, and development, 24(6) *World development* 1073 (1996)

Ostrom/Whitaker, Community control and governmental responsiveness: The case of police in black neighborhoods, 10(4) *Improving the quality of urban management* 303 (1974)

Ostrom/Whitaker, Does local community control of police make a difference? Some preliminary findings, *American Journal of Political Science* 48 (1973)

Parks/Baker/Kiser/Oakerson/Ostrom/Ostrom/Percy/Vandivort/Whitaker/Wilson, Consumers as coproducers of public services: Some economic and institutional considerations, 9(7) *Policy studies journal* 1001 (1981)

Peters, Optimal leverage from non-ergodicity, 11(11) *Quantitative Finance* 1593 (2011)

Peters, The ergodicity problem in economics, 15(12) *Nature Physics* 1216 (2019)

Pistor, The code of capital, 2019

Supiot, *Governance by numbers: The making of a legal model of allegiance*, 2017

Victor, The EU general data protection regulation: Toward a property regime for protecting data privacy, 123 *Yale LJ* 513 (2013)

Zuo, Governance by Algorithm: China's Social Credit System (working paper), 2020, Governance by Algorithm_CERF_Zhenbin 6.12.2020.docx (cam.ac.uk), available at https://www.finance.group.cam.ac.uk/system/files/documents/GovernancebyAlgorithm_CERF_Zhenbin6.16.2020.pdf (last accessed 16 December 2022)

坚持党管数据建设数字天津 [Insist on the Party manages data method to build digital Tianjin, 2019.4.15]

淘宝11.8亿条用户隐私被泄露 两男子被判刑 [Taobao 1.18 billion pieces of user information leaked, two men sentenced. Sina news, 2021.6.17]

天津市开展APP违法采集个人信息集中整治 (2021), available at http://www.gov.cn/xinwen/2019-11/23/content_5454795.htm (last accessed 8 February 2023) [Tianjin works on regulating APP illegal collections of personal information, www.gov.cn, 2019.11.23]

天津扎实开展数据安全和个人信息保护工作 [Tianjin steadily develops work on data security and personal information protection, www.tjcac.gov.cn, 2020.8.20]

王锡锌个人信息国家保护义务及展开，《中国法学》，2021年第1期。[Wang Xixin, "Personal information's state protection obligations and its implications." *China Legal Science*. 2021 (1).]

张新宝互联网生态"守门人"个人信息保护特别义务设置研究，《比较法研究》，2021年第3期。[Zhang Xinbao. "Research on Internet ecosystem's Gatekeepers special protection obligations to personal information." Comparative Law Journal. 2021 (3)

左卫民如何通过人工智能实现类案类判，《中国法律评论》，2018年第2期。 [Zuo, Weimin. 2018. "How to achieve similar case with similar judgements by AI". *Chinese Legal Commentaries*. 2018 (2).]

II. Laws, policies and cases

1. Major Laws and regulations (including drafts)

COM (2020) 842: Proposal for a REGULATION OF THE EUROPEAN PARLIAMENT AND OF THE COUNCIL on contestable and fair markets in the digital sector (Digital Markets Act) Procedure 2020/0374/COD

COM (2020) 825: Proposal for a REGULATION OF THE EUROPEAN PARLIAMENT AND OF THE COUNCIL on a Single Market For Digital Services (Digital Services Act) and amending Directive 2000/31/EC, Procedure 2020/0361/COD

中华人民共和国民法典 [Civil Code of the People's Republic of China 2021], available at http://www.npc.gov.cn/npc/c30834/202006/75ba6483b8344591abd07917e1d25cc8.shtml (last accessed 16 December 2022)

中华人民共和国个人信息保护法 [Personal Information Protection Law of the People's Republic of China, 2021], available at http://www.npc.gov.cn/npc/c30834/202108/a8c4e3672c74491a80-b53a172bb753fe.shtml (last accessed 16 December 2022)

中华人民共和国网络安全法 [Cybersecurity Law of the People's Republic of China 2017], available at http://www.npc.gov.cn/ (last accessed 16 December 2022)

中华人民共和国数据安全法 [Data Security Law of the People's Republic of China 2021], available at http://www.npc.gov.cn/npc/c30834/202106/7c9af12f51334a73b56d7938f99a788a.shtml (last accessed 16 December 2022)

信息安全技术—个人信息安全影响评估指南(GB/T 39335-2020) [Information security technology – Guidance for personal information security impact assessment (GB/T 39335-2020)]

国务院征信业管理条例 国务院令631号）State Council's Regulation on Credit-reporting Industry 2013. No.631, available at http://www.gov.cn/zwgk/2013-01/29/content_2322231.htm (last accessed 16 December 2022)

国务院反垄断委员会关于平台经济领域的反垄断指南 [State Council Antitrust Committee [2021] 1, Antitrust Guideline on Platform Economy (2021.2.7)], available at http://www.gov.cn/xinwen/2021-02/07/content_5585758.htm (last accessed 16 December 2022)

公开征求对《移动互联网应用程序个人信息保护管理暂行规定征求意见稿）》的意见 [MIIT Mobile Internet Application Personal Information Protection Provisional Regulations (Draft for Comments), 2021.4.26], available at http://www.gov.cn/hudong/2021-04/26/content_5602780.htm (last accessed 16 December 2022)

天津市社会信用条例天津市第十七届人民代表大会常务委员会公告，第63号 2020） [Tianjin Social Credit Regulations, Tianjin 17th People's Congress Plenary Committee Report, No 63. Effective on 1st January 2021], available at http://credit.sc.gov.cn/xysc/c100016/202205/fa2757b27c104200a868f49cca46f7d6.shtml (last accessed 8 February 2023)

深圳市第七届人民代表大会常务委员会公告第十号）[Shenzhen 7th People's Congress Plenary Committee Report No. 10. On passing the Shenzhen Economic Special Zone's Data Regulation, 2021. Effective 2022.1.1], available at http://www.sz.gov.cn/zfgb/2021/gb1218/content/post_9307139.html (last accessed 8 February 2023)

2. Policies

习近平决胜全面建成小康社会　夺取新时代中国特色社会主义伟大胜利——在中国共产党第十九次全国代表大会上的报告 [Xi Jinping: Report Delivered at the 19th National Congress of the Communist Party of China – Secure a Decisive Victory in Building a Moderately Prosperous Society in All Respects and Strive for the Great Success of Socialism with Chinese Characteristics for a New Era, 2017.10.18], available at http://www.gov.cn/zhuanti/2017-10/27/content_5234876.htm (last accessed 16 December 2022)

中共中央 国务院关于构建更加完善的要素市场化配置体制机制的意见 [CPC central committee and State Council: Instruction on Improving the Market Mechanism for Allocating Essential Factors, 2020.3.30.], available at http://www.gov.cn/zhengce/2020-04/09/content_5500622.htm (last accessed 16 December 2022)

授权发布:中国共产党第十八届中央委员会第五次全体会议公报-新华网 (xinhuanet.com) [Report of the Fifth Plenary Session of the 18th Communist Party of China (CPC) Central Committee. 2015.]

中华人民共和国国民经济和社会发展第十三个五年规划纲要，available at http://gov/cn/xinwen/2016-03/17/consent_5054992.htm (last accessed 8 February 2023 [The 13th Five-Year Plan of the People's Republic of China on economic and social development, 2016]

国务院关于印发促进大数据发展行动纲要的通知国发〔2015〕50号 2015, available at http://www.gov.cn/zhengce/content/2015-09/05/content_10137.htm (last accessed 8 February 2023) [State Council's instructions on the action plans for promoting big-data development, 2015. SC [2015] 50.]

国务院关于印发政务信息资源共享管理暂行办法的通知国发〔2016〕51号） [State Council on the provisional measures to government information resources sharing and management. 2016. SC [2016] 51.], available at http://www.gov.cn/zhengce/content/2016-09/19/content_5109486.htm (last accessed 16 December 2022)

工业和信息化部关于印发大数据产业发展规划20162020年）的通知 [MIIT on issuing the Big-data Industry Development Plan. MIIT [2016) 412.], available at http://www.cac.gov.cn/2017-01/17/c_1120330820.htm (last accessed 16 December 2022)

外交部全球数据安全倡议 [Foreign Ministry: Global Data Security Initiative (2020)], available at http://www.xinhuanet.com/world/2020-09/08/c_1126466972.htm (last accessed 16 December 2022)

Obama administration unveils "big data" initiative: announces $200 million in new r&d investments (Executive Office of the President, 2012), available at https://obamawhitehouse.archives.gov/sites/default/files/microsites/ostp/big_data_press_release_final_2.pdf (last accessed 16 December 2022)

3. Cases and administrative actions

United States v. Facebook, Inc., No. 19-2184 (TJK), 2020 WL 1975785 (D.D.C. April 23, 2020)

2019）浙8601民初1987号 [2019, Zhejiang, 8601 Civil Court, First instance case no 1987]

2020）浙01民终5889号 [2020, Zhejiang, 01 Civil appeal case no. 5889]

2020）浙0106刑初437号 [2020, Zhejiang, 0106, Criminal Court, first instance case no. 437]

§ 8 THE REGULATORY LEVEL PLAYING FIELD(S) – GLOBAL COMPLIANCE EFFORTS OF AND GLOBAL STANDARD-SETTING BY INTERNATIONAL CORPORATIONS

Content

A. Introduction

For companies operating internationally, the various data regulations evolving world- 1
wide pose both an enormous challenge and a great opportunity. Compared to the 2000s, where only around 30 comprehensive data protection laws existed worldwide, and even compared to 10 years ago, the number of data protection laws[1] have increased tremendously[2] – by now there are around 130 omnibus privacy laws in place worldwide.[3] These are comprehensive data protection laws which do not only regulate personal information on a sectoral basis but rather in a general way.[4] Especially, the EU General Data Protection Regulation (GDPR)[5] has being a catalyst for numerous new data protection laws around the globe.[6] Some countries, however, still have only sector-related or no data protection laws in place.[7] However, this number is shrinking almost on a weekly basis.

[1] The term used, 'data protection law', shall not be understood as excluding, but including laws named – for several reasons – data privacy laws, privacy laws, or the like.

[2] *Cf* Greenleaf, 169 *Privacy Laws & Business International Report* 23–27 (2021).

[3] *Cf* Morrison Foerster, World Privacy Map (2021) and the University of Passau Research Centre for Law and Digitalisation's Global Data Law Maps.

[4] Most prominently, however, the U.S. has – to a large extent – only sectorial laws in place. See in more detail below sub B. IV.

[5] Regulation (EU) 2016/679 on the protection of natural persons with regard to the processing of personal data and on the free movement of such data, and repealing Directive 95/46/EC (General Data Protection Regulation).

[6] *Cf* in this regard Hennemann, *RabelsZ* 84 (2020), 864; Greenleaf, 169 *Privacy Laws & Business International Report*, 1, 3–5 (2021). E.g. Brazil (LGPD).

[7] E. g. in parts of Africa (*cf* Hennemann/Boshe/Meding, *ZfDR* 2021, 193 = *GPLR* 2022, 56 as well as Bryant, 24 *Stan. Tech. L. Rev.* (2021), 389) as well as most of the U.S. states.

2 This development is first and foremost a challenge for globally acting companies. Besides other legal and compliance requirements, corporations have to design their products, processes and functionalities in line with approximately 130 data protection laws worldwide. Against this background, this chapter tries to give a global overview over the state of global data protection playing fields. This includes five categories of data protection laws worldwide. Additionally, practical experience, especially from the perspective of a globally acting eCommerce company, will be shared. In this context, it shall be demonstrated that the engagement of large international corporations cannot be reduced to global compliance efforts. Rather, it will be shown that large corporations are actually setting their own global *de facto* standards by responding to the demands of numerous law makers and national data protection regulators. Thereby, the practices of international companies also contribute to the emergence of transnational data protection standards[8] – and lay a path for possible global privacy harmonisation perspectives.

B. Global Data Protection Playing Field(s)

3 It shall be differentiated between five global data protection playing fields: (1) the European Union (EU) with its well-known GDPR; (2) third countries and its data protection laws that have been classified by the EU as offering an adequate level of protection (so called adequate third countries); (3) non or not yet adequate third countries with data protection laws similar to or modelled after the GDPR; (4) the U.S. with mostly (sectoral) data protection laws on federal and state level; and (5) countries with data protection laws that include specific data localisation requirements.

I. European Union/European Economic Area

4 The first global data protection playing field is the EU/EEA with its GDPR. The EU's GDPR, which also applies to the countries of the European Economic Area (EEA), took effect in May 2018. Back then, many businesses were concerned about the new harmonised EU data protection law – not only regarding its hefty fines but also regarding the numerous wide and unclear general definitions. With time, it has become clear(er) which parts of the law are working smoothly and which parts are not.

5 First, it is significant from a corporation's perspective that since 2018, the number of data protection rights requests has increased significantly. Those requests come from users as well as from data protection authorities. Especially, ever since the GDPR has been applicable, users seem well-educated regarding the existence of their new data protection rights. An increased data protection awareness, not only in Europe but also across the globe, can be spotted. Consequently, data protection issues have become a strategic aspect for corporations, especially in the digital economy.

6 Secondly, there is still a lot of uncertainty about the exact interpretation and application of GDPR. The abstract terms and general definitions of GDPR increased the need for interpretation. Even though the law is now already four years applicable, central terminology such as 'legitimate interest', 'transparency', and 'unambiguous consent' are still not entirely clear. There is obviously some guidance by data protection

---

[8] *Cf* generally for the prospects of transnational commercial law and a corresponding *lex mercatoria* formed by (practice of) private actors Goode/Kronke/McKendrick, *Transnational Commercial Law*, 2nd ed., 2015.

authorities[9] and already first court rulings[10] regarding some use cases, but many terms and general definitions are still far away from being interpreted precisely enough for every day's practice. In addition, the interaction of GDPR with other laws is not practically settled in specific areas, e.g. the interplay between GDPR, EU ePrivacy Directive[11], as well as national ePrivacy and cookie laws[12].

Thirdly, the existing structure and interplay of data protection authorities in the EU **7** has clear down-sides. Different regulatory guidance and different enforcement levels exist across the EU – leaving aside the fact that authorities seem to have the tendency to 'compete' with each other when it comes to considering themselves as lead supervisory authorities imposing sanctions. Additionally, the consistency mechanism is not working properly in practice. EU-wide alignments on specific terminology or definitions are rare to find. Differing requirements for the use of cookies and respective cookie banners under the EU GDPR and under national cookie laws is an obvious example. The German system of state data protection authorities (of the German *Länder*) does not make the situation any easier – and adds to the number of member states' authorities 16 state regulators that a corporation has to monitor. Additionally, the one-stop-shop privilege (Art. 56 GDPR) did not fulfil the hopes its introduction went along with. In the early days of the GDPR, it seemed to be one of the most attractive factors for companies. The privilege aimed for one competent lead authority for a corporation in the EU. The respective corporation 'choose' this authority by their main establishment within the EU. Recent court decisions, however, shape more and more exemptions from the privilege.[13] Consequently, a growing number of data protection authorities start to 'regulate' corporations even in those countries where they do not have their main establishment. For example, the French regulator is very active and has (successfully) claimed competence for corporations seated inter alia in Ireland.[14] Additionally, regulators have shortened deadlines in order to test whether companies have the respective records at hand to fulfil their accountability requirements.

The overall development around the interpretation and implementation of the GDPR **8** leads to constant uncertainty in the market. This situation is to some extend inevitable after the implementation of an EU-wide catch-all law applicable to corporations of any size. However, the main reason for the continuing unclarity, uncertainty and inconsistency of the interpretation and implementation of the GDPR is the fact that an EU-wide harmonized law is being enforced by numerous national (and in Germany even state level) data protection authorities with respectively diverging political agendas, resources, and different cultural and legal backgrounds. A growing amount of data protection litigation – involving corporations, data protection authorities, and users – is likely to bring more clarity.

---

[9] *Cf* for example EDPB, Guidelines 05/2020 on consent under Regulation 2016/679.

[10] *Cf* for example ECJ Case C-507/17 Google LLC v Commission nationale de l'informatique et des libertés (CNIL) [2019] ECLI:EU:C:2019:772.

[11] Directive 2002/58/EC of 12 July 2002 concerning the processing of personal data and the protection of privacy in the electronic communications sector (Directive on privacy and electronic communications).

[12] E.g. the (German) Telecommunications and Telemedia Data Protection Act (Telekommunikation-Telemedien-Datenschutz-Gesetz – TTDSG) and the (French) Deliberation No. 2020-091 of September 17, 2020 adopting guidelines on the application of article 82 of the law of January 6, 1978, as amended, to operations and writing operations in a user's terminal (including 'cookies and other tracers') and repealing the deliberation n° 2019-093 of July 4, 2019.

[13] E.g. ECJ Case C-507/17 Google LLC v Commission nationale de l'informatique et des libertés (CNIL) [2019] ECLI:EU:C:2019:772 and ECJ Case 645/19 Facebook Ireland Ltd and Others v Gegevensbeschermingsautoriteit [2021] ECLI:EU:C:2021:483.

[14] ECJ Case C-507/17 Google LLC v Commission nationale de l'informatique et des libertés (CNIL) [2019] ECLI:EU:C:2019:772.

II. Adequate Third Countries

9 The second global data protection playing field consists of the so called adequate third countries. Data protection laws of non-EU/non-EEA countries differ greatly from the GDPR – even if they have been classified by the European Commission as offering an adequate level of protection (Art. 45 GDPR). The European Commission came to a respective classification only with respect to a limited number of countries since 2000. Switzerland, for example, received this status very early, i.e. back in 2000[15], while Japan only recently received it in 2019 after amendments were made to the Japanese data protection law.[16] The UK received an approval in 2021 after lengthy negotiations – and continuing doubts as to the sustainability of the decision (analogue to the ECJ-rulings in Schrems I and II[17] with regard to the U.S.).[18] Furthermore, it becomes visible that countries approved as adequate are very much aware of the fact that the European Commission is obliged to check the status constantly (Art. 45 para 4 GDPR) – and are consequently considering amendments to their (older) data protection laws. Switzerland is a prime example.[19] In the last years, Switzerland has been working to update its data protection law in order to uphold the adequacy decision. It is remarkable that – even after its revision – the new Swiss data protection law will follow a slightly more liberal approach to data protection than the actual GDPR. For example, under the Swiss data protection law data processing activities are generally allowed. This is conceptionally different to the GDPR. Under the GDPR, data processing activities are generally prohibited and need a legal basis to be exceptionally lawful (Art. 6 GDPR). This brief example underlines the fact that an adequate level of protection does not mean that the law has to 'copy' the GDPR but leaves at least some leeway in this regard.[20]

10 In addition to the current set of adequate third countries, many countries outside the EU are currently preparing themselves for such an adequacy decision.[21] Adequacy has just been granted to South Korea.[22] Brazil is another potential candidate – as Brazil has recently introduced a new data protection law which is very similar to the GDPR.[23] In addition, it must be noted that the GDPR (Art. 45 para 1) leaves room to declare just a single state or a part of a country as adequate.[24] This option is, for example, considered for the leading U.S. state in data protection regulation, California. Such a decision is

[15] Commission Decision of 26 July 2000 pursuant to Directive 95/46/EC, *Official Journal* L 215, 1–3.

[16] *Cf* Wang, 33 *Harvard Journal of Law & Technology* (2020), 661 and Commission Implementing Decision (EU) 2019/419 of 23 January 2019 pursuant to Regulation (EU) 2016/679, *Official Journal* L 76, 1.

[17] ECJ Case C-362/14 Maximillian Schrems v Data Protection Commissioner [2015] ECLI:EU:C:2015:650 – Schrems I and ECJ Case-311/18 Data Protection Commissioner v Facebook Ireland Ltd and Maximillian Schrems [2020] ECLI:EU:C:2020:559 – Schrems II.

[18] Commission Implementing Regulation (EU) 2021/1772 of 28 June 2021 pursuant to Regulation (EU) 2016/679, *Official Journal* L 360, 1.

[19] For a detailed discussion see Hennemann, in: Paal/Poelzig/Fehrenbacher (eds.), *Festschrift Ebke*, 2022, 371.

[20] But see the rather strict interpretation by the Article 29 group Adequacy Referential (2020), available at https://ec.europa.eu/newsroom/article29/items/614108.

[21] *Cf* for the respective 'push effect' the instrument of an adequacy decision goes along with in favour of the GDPR Hennemann, in: Paal/Poelzig/Fehrenbacher (eds.), *Festschrift Ebke*, 2022, 371; Hennemann, *RabelsZ* 84 (2020), 864.

[22] Commission Implementing Decision (EU) 2022/254 of 17 December 2021 pursuant to Regulation (EU) 2016/679, *Official Journal* L 44, 1.

[23] Infra sub B. III.

[24] For example, done for Canada (only commercial organisations), Isle of Men, and Guernsey.

likely to create a political churn in the U.S., especially on a federal level. However, from a compliance perspective and with regard to the requirements to be fulfilled, the current Californian Consumer Privacy Act (CCPA) is almost as strict as the EU's GDPR.[25]

III. Non-Adequate Countries with GDPR-like Data Protection Laws

The third 'family' to be considered are those countries that have not yet received an adequacy decision but have installed GDPR-like data protection laws. Brazil is a good example in this regard.[26] The Brazilian Lei General de Proteção de Dados (LGPD), the Brazilian data protection law, follows various requirements of GDPR quite strictly. It even installs some stricter requirements (e.g. the answer-period for data subject's rights is significantly shorter). Fines, however, are not as high as under EU data protection law. In addition, it is noteworthy that the Brazilian regulator also shows a key interest in understanding how the GDPR actually works in practice, and especially what lessons can be learned.[27] Different African and Asian countries also serve as examples of this category. Kenya, Mauritius, Nigeria, and South Africa as well as New Zealand have enacted laws mirroring the GDPR. **11**

IV. The U.S.

Another separate regulatory category of global data protection playing fields is formed by U.S. privacy laws, especially on state level. U.S. state privacy laws have a very different historic background compared to the aforementioned settings. The U.S. are traditionally known for its very sectorial-based approach to privacy. This approach has been heavily discussed in the last couple of years – also with respect to the Snowden revelations. However, since California implemented a comprehensive data protection law, things are dramatically changing. The California Consumer Privacy Act (CPPA) came into force in January 2020. It contains new user rights, some even stricter than GDPR. The requirement of a 'do not sell my data'-button is the most prominent example. Corporations must implement this button in case they sell data. The driving force of this rule were the Facebook Cambridge Analytica revelations. The Californian legislator wanted to ensure that consumers have a say in the sale of their data to any third party. In addition, the style of the California law differs from GDPR. Although the requirements are ultimately relatively similar, the act is much more descriptive, based on examples, longer, and less principle-based. In 2023, the even stricter California Privacy Rights Act (CPRA) will come into force – requiring corporations to comply with a new Californian Privacy law a second time within relatively short time. The CPRA additionally creates a new Privacy regulator, the California Privacy Protection Agency (CPPA). **12**

The enactment of the Californian Consumer Privacy Act in 2020 started a nationwide development. The act served as a U.S. wide catalyst for privacy laws. Data protection law drafts are currently going through legislative processes in multiple states[28] – and **13**

[25] The new Californian law, California Privacy Rights Act (CPRA), coming into force in 2023, pursues in most instances an even stricter approach than the GDPR.

[26] *Cf* Hoffmann/Vargas, 06 *IRDG Research Paper Series* (2022).

[27] *Cf* also DataGuidance by OneTrust/Baptista Luz Advogados, Comparing privacy laws: GDPR v. LGPD, 2021.

[28] *Cf* IAPP, US State Privacy Legislation Tracker.

most of them derive from the current Californian Consumer Privacy Act. New privacy laws have been enacted recently, for example, in Colorado and Virginia – both laws are less strict than CCPA, but with many similarities. Other states (e.g. Washington State, Texas, and Arizona) are passing similar privacy legislation.[29] At the same time, a similar discussion about a U.S. Privacy Framework has been going on at the federal level for years. However, according to recent news, such law-making efforts are on a perpetual pause, at least until the Federal policy community discusses a possible deal on the key issues of pre-emption and private rights of action.

14 These developments challenge the assumption that there is no comprehensive federal privacy law in the U.S. – yet. Corporations across the globe, but especially in the U.S., are very much lobbying for a respective federal privacy framework. The current patchwork of state privacy laws puts a significant, inconsistent, and complicated compliance burden onto corporations doing business across the U.S. A 'gap analysis' for each and every single law, which comes into force in the U.S., is required. The different state law approaches also vary contentwise. Regarding the desired U.S. federal privacy framework, some voices prefer a federal privacy law close to the GDPR. The main argument is that a similar set of rules in the EU and the U.S. would be beneficial to companies doing business in both economies. Other voices promote a Californian design as this state is the primary location of most of U.S. tech companies. A mix of the GDPR and the Californian law as well as completely new designs are also being discussed.

V. Data Protection Laws with Special Data Localisation Requirements

15 Finally, the fifth category of data protection laws encompasses data protection laws with specific data localisation requirements.[30] Two major examples are Russia and China. The two countries have implemented respective regulation in the context of data protection laws, data security, and/or cyber security laws. The Russian personal data law came into force in 2015[31]. It requires, for example, that data collected from Russian citizens be stored in databases located in Russia. In the beginning, it was an open question whether corporations must store data in Russia only or whether a copy of the data in question suffices. The Russian regulator clarified that the database in Russia must at all times contain more or at least an equal amount of data compared to the database abroad. It is suspected that it was Russia's reaction to secure data vis-à-vis potential U.S. sanctions because of the Crimea Crisis. LinkedIn, for example, has been hit with enforcement in 2016 as their services were blocked by Russia.

16 Over the last years, China developed data protection laws in a quite similar fashion. However, in China, requirements for data localisation cannot only be found in one specific privacy law but are rather scattered throughout different laws (e.g. the cyber security law, the data security law as well as other sectorial regulations).[32] There was some hope that the

---

[29] *Ibid.*

[30] Data localisation requirements in a wider sense might also be spotted in the EU. The entire concept of specific requirement for a transfer to a third country (Art. 44 et seq. GDPR) can be regarded as an indirect or soft form of data localisation.

[31] Russian text available at http://pravo.gov.ru/proxy/ips/?docbody&nd=102375717 (last accessed 4 January 2023).

[32] *Cf*, amongst other things, the Cybersecurity Law of the People's Republic of China which became effective on 1 June 2017 as well as the Data Security Law of the People's Republic of China which became effective on 1 September 2021. A translation of the cybersecurity law is available at https://digichina.stanford.edu/work/translation-cybersecurity-law-of-the-peoples-republic-of-china-effective-june-1-2017/ (last accessed 4 January 2023) and a translation of the data security law is available at

new Personal Information Protection Law (PIPL)[33], in force since November 2021, would resolve this patchwork, but that is not the case. A sectorial approach still exists in China. Two types of data are subject to data localisation: personal information and important data. While the former is understandable from an EU perspective, the latter refers to political strategic information including state secrets and mapping data (traffic, traffic streams, and mapping data related to the energy network). These two types of data must be kept within the country's territory. It is a further factor for Chinese data localisation law whether a corporation is a critical information or infrastructure operator – a reference point linked to energy providers, telecommunication providers, etc. Both types of laws are very much driven by a political agenda.

C. Global Standard-Setting

Despite the different regulatory playing fields, the global interplay between data protection laws, regulators, enforcement agencies, corporations, users, and privacy activists – counter-intuitively – has fed prospects of global standard-setting. **17**

I. Legislators and Enforcement Agencies

From a legislator's viewpoint, first the EU Data Protection Directive (DPD)[34] and second the EU GDPR have evolved as an influential data protection standard worldwide.[35] It might not have proven to be the most consistent enforcement set up or the global 'gold standard'[36] so far, but the instruments have been *de facto* boosters of harmonisation – even influencing evolving U.S. state privacy laws (in California followed now by Colorado, Virginia, and several others). However, it is too early to speak of an all-encompassing global standard as mixed approaches as well as data protection laws with specific data localisation requirements can be observed. Consequentially, and especially after the Schrems II court ruling of the ECJ, the legislators' focus currently lies on international data transfers. Countries are interested in keeping 'their' data within their country's territory or at least safe and secure. The EU has used the instrument of (strict) adequacy decisions respectively in order to facilitate an 'upward convergence'[37]. One must, however, be aware of the fact that this approach might backfire on the European Union. As stricter data protection laws emerge (and EU states are also pursuing intelligence activities), other non-EU and non-EEA countries and regions might declare the European Union as not adequate in return. The blueprint character of the GDPR including its (strict) adequacy requirement is therefore not without risk. **18**

---

https://digichina.stanford.edu/work/translation-data-security-law-of-the-peoples-republic-of-china/ (last accessed 4 January 2023).

[33] A translation of the Chinese PIPL is available at https://digichina.stanford.edu/work/translation-personal-information-protection-law-of-the-peoples-republic-of-china-effective-nov-1-2021/ (last accessed 4 January 2023). *Cf* also the contribution by Zuo in this volume § 7, pp. 119–159.

[34] Directive 95/46/EC of 24 October 1995, *Official Journal* L 281, 31.

[35] Greenleaf, 169 *Privacy Laws & Business International Report*, 1, 3–5 (2021).

[36] Albrecht, *CR* 2016, 88, 98.

[37] Communication from the Commission to the European Parliament and the Council of 10 January 2017 COM(2017) 7 final, 18. *Cf* also Proposal for a Regulation of the European Parliament and of the Council on harmonized rules on fair access to and use of data (Data Act) of 23 February 2022 COM/2022/68 final.

19 With respect to data protection enforcement, a parallel development and trend can be observed. The increased global activity of enforcement agencies goes along with significant and prominently placed sanctions. Facebook for example, received an enormous fine from the FTC in the U.S.[38] Fines against Amazon[39], Google[40], YouTube[41], Facebook[42], and WhatsApp[43] were issued in Europe in 2021 and 2022. More significant privacy fines around the globe are soon to come. Especially, since enforcement agencies have received more rights under more 'aggressive' data protection laws – and are willing to demonstrate their power on the global privacy playing field.

II. Corporations

20 Corporations have to navigate through this fast-evolving environment. First and foremost, corporations are bound by the aim to ensure compliance with all the different (new) data protection laws. Second – and more than noteworthy –, driven by this aim, corporations incrementally create a whole set of their 'own' high-watermark data protection requirements – standards that fit for many similar, but in detail slightly different, data protection rules around the globe. Consequently, globally acting corporations might even grant users more data protection rights than specific jurisdictions would afford. That may sound surprising at first glance but is a consequence of weighing pragmatic global and consistent approaches against more costly regional solutions. eBay, for example, implemented the GDPR globally in 2018, and added, for example, in 2020 the Californian Consumer Privacy Act (CCPA) requirements to their global privacy program. It has proven too complicated to distinguish efficiently, for example, whether a user is a European resident on holiday in California buying a pair of sneakers from a seller in Brazil, and then traveling to Singapore. Practical evidence therefore supports the notion of a 'race to the top'[44] – as international operating corporations seem to aim for the strictest data protection law including (or in addition to) special local data protection requirements to stay compliant. This approach tends to guarantee more data protection also from another perspective: not distinguishing between the actual location, residency, or citizenship of specific users (where, according to the applicable law, possible) means that corporations require less data of the user in the first place; identifying the one and only applicable law could mean having to collect data (passport data, residency data etc.) that corporations might not actually be willing to keep (and secure).

21 Consequentially, it is more than understandable that corporations support the development of pan-regional and even global data protection standards on a policy

---

[38] Federal Trade Commission, 27.4.2020, C-4365, Facebook, Inc., In the Matter of.

[39] The decision of 15 July 2021, referenced under n° 26FR/2021 of the commission nationale de la protection des donnees (CNPD), imposed an administrative fine of €746 million on Amazon Europe Core S.à r.l., *cf* Tribunal administratif du Grand-Duché de Luxembourg, n° 46630 du rôle, inscrit le 29 octobre 2021.

[40] The Commission fines Google € 4.34 billion, *cf* Summary of Commission Decision of 18 July 2018 (Case AT.40099 – Google Android), *Official Journal* C 402, 19.

[41] *Cf* ECJ Case C-682/18 Frank Peterson v Google LLC and Others and Elsevier Inc.v Cyando AG [2021] ECLI:EU:C:2021:503.

[42] *Cf* European Parliament resolution of 25 October 2018 (2018/2844(RSP)), *Official Journal* C 345/58, 58.

[43] The decision 1/2021 of the EDPB of 28 July 2021 imposed a fine of € 225 million on WhatsApp Ireland Ltd, *cf* Case T-709/21: Action brought on 1 November 2021 – WhatsApp Ireland v EDPB, *Official Journal* C 2, 50.

[44] *Cf* Hennemann, *RabelsZ* 84 (2020), 864.

level.[45] Truly global data protection standards are yet to come, but at least a pan-regional law in the U.S. is not entirely unlikely to be enacted in the coming years. Ideally, such a law would offer a consistent, comprehensive, and especially pre-emptive privacy rights on the federal level. From a corporation's perspective, rules resembling CCPA (or even CPRA) and GDPR would offer mostly harmonised, non-fragmented standards – and therefore a significant step forward.

D. Summary and Outlook

The above-described data protection laws in the five different global data protection playing fields only represent a small portion of legislative efforts in the privacy space. New data protection laws are evolving around the globe almost on a weekly basis – currently, especially on the state level in the U.S. and on a country-level in the Asia-Pacific region. From a global perspective, it is important to note that the EU and its GDPR are not in the data protection spotlight anymore. **22**

Besides these observations, there have been further developments in the area of data regulation recently. More and more countries propose or actually pass laws which regulate not only the collection and use of *personal* information, but rather the collection and use of data in general.[46] Also, globally, data protection regulation might slowly but steadily be replaced by data regulation. With these developments in mind, we will soon see even more global data regulation playing fields for personal and non-personal information alike. **23**

Bibliography

Albrecht, Das neue EU-Datenschutzrecht – von der Richtlinie zur Verordnung, *CR* 2016, 88 **24**

Bryant, Africa in the Information Age: Challenges, Opportunities, and Strategies for Data Protection and Digital Rights, 24 *Stan. Tech. L. Rev.* (2021), 389

DataGuidance by OneTrust/Baptista Luz Advogados, Comparing privacy laws: GDPR v. LGPD, 2021, available at https://www.dataguidance.com/sites/default/files/gdpr_lgpd_report.pdf (last accessed 4 January 2023)

dpa, Apple-Chef: DSGVO Vorbild fur globalen Datenschutz, *ZEIT ONLINE* (21 October 2018), available at https://www.zeit.de/news/2018-10/21/apple-chef-dsgvo-vorbild-fuer-globalen-datenschutz-181021-99-467914 (last accessed 4 January 2023)

dpa, Facebook-Chef fordert weltweite Internet-Regulierung nach DSGVO-Vorbild, *heise online* (31 March 2019), available at https://www.heise.de/newsticker/meldung/Facebook-Chef-fordert-weltweite-Internet-Regulierung-nach-DSGVO-Vorbild-4356615.html (last accessed 4 January 2023)

dpa, Microsoft lobt die Datenschutz-Regeln, *FAZ.net* (11 May 2018), available at https://www.faz.net/aktuell/wirtschaft/digitec/satya-nadella-microsoft-lobt-die-dsgvo-15584713.html (last accessed 4 January 2023)

EDPB, Guidelines 05/2020 on consent under Regulation 2016/679, 2020, available at https://edpb.europa.eu/sites/default/files/files/file1/edpb_guidelines_202005_consent_en.pdf (last accessed 4 January 2023)

[45] *Cf* dpa, *FAZ.net* (11 May 2018); dpa, *ZEIT ONLINE* (21 October 2018); dpa, *heise online* (31 March 2019).

[46] E.g. EU Data Act, EU Data Governance Act, India Data Protection Law, etc.

EDPB, Recommendations 01/2021 on the adequacy referential under the Law Enforcement Directive, 2021, available at https://edpb.europa.eu/sites/default/files/files/file1/recommendations012021onart.36led.pdf_en.pdf (last accessed 4 January 2023)

European Commission, A European strategy for data, 19 February 2020, available at https://eur-lex.europa.eu/legal-content/EN/TXT/PDF/?uri=CELEX:52020DC0066&from=EN (last accessed 4 January 2023)

European Commission, Adequacy decisions, available at https://ec.europa.eu/info/law/law-topic/data-protection/international-dimension-data-protection/adequacy-decisions_en (last accessed 4 January 2023)

European Commission, Decision on the adequate protection of personal data by the Republic of Korea with annexes, 17 December 2021, available at https://commission.europa.eu/system/files/2021-12/1_1_180366_dec_ade_kor_new_en.pdf (last accessed 4 January 2023)

European Commission, Decision on the adequate protection of personal data by the United Kingdom with annexes, 28 June 2021, available at https://commission.europa.eu/system/files/2021-06/decision_on_the_adequate_protection_of_personal_data_by_the_united_kingdom_-_general_data_protection_regulation_en.pdf (last accessed 4 January 2023)

Federal Trade Commission, 27.4.2020, C-4365, Facebook, Inc., In the Matter of, available at https://www.ftc.gov/legal-library/browse/cases-proceedings/092-3184-182-3109-c-4365-facebook-inc-matter (last accessed 4 January 2023)

Goode/Kronke/McKendrick, *Transnational Commercial Law*, 2nd ed., 2015

Greenleaf, Global Data Privacy Laws 2021: Despite COVID Delays, 145 Laws Show GDPR Dominance, 169 *Privacy Laws & Business International Report*, 1, 3–5 (2021), also available at https://papers.ssrn.com/sol3/papers.cfm?abstract_id=3836348 (last accessed 4 January 2023)

Greenleaf, Global Data Privacy Laws 2021: Uncertain Paths for International Standards, 169 *Privacy Laws & Business International Report* 23–27 (2021), also available at https://papers.ssrn.com/sol3/papers.cfm?abstract_id=3836408 (last accessed 4 January 2023)

Hennemann, Schweizer Datenschutzrecht im Wettbewerb der Rechtsordnungen, in: Paal/Poelzig/Fehrenbacher (eds.), *Festschrift Ebke*, 2022, p. 371

Hennemann, Wettbewerb der Datenschutzrechtsordnungen, 84 *RabelsZ* (2020), 864

Hennemann/Boshe/Meding, African Data Protection Laws – Current Regulatory Approaches, Policy Initiatives, and the Way Forward, *Global Privacy Law Rev.* 3 (2022), available at https://papers.ssrn.com/sol3/papers.cfm?abstract_id=3947664 (last accessed 4 January 2023), (German version *ZfDR* 2021, 193)

Hoffmann/Vargas, LGPD Et Al. – Report on the Law of Data Disclosure in Brazil, 06 *University of Passau IRDG Research Paper Series* (2022)

IAPP, US State Privacy Legislation Tracker, available at https://iapp.org/resources/article/us-state-privacy-legislation-tracker/ (last accessed 4 January 2023)

Morrison Foerster, World Privacy Map, 2021, available at https://www.mofo.com/resources/insights/210127-data-privacy-day.html (last accessed 4 January 2023)

University of Passau Research Centre for Law and Digitalisation's Global Data Law Maps, available at https://www.jura.uni-passau.de/en/faculty/institutes-and-centres/fredi/global-data-law/ (last accessed 4 January 2023)

Wang, 33 *Harvard Journal of Law & Technology* (2020), 661

§ 9 'DATA COLONIALISM'? BIG DATA'S ADVERSE IMPACT ON THE (GLOBAL) SOUTH

Content

A. Replacing 'Castiron Chains' with 'Invisible Chains'?

In May 2021, the conclusion of the German Namibian Reconstruction and Reconciliation Agreement brought more than five years of negotiations between the former colonial power and its former colony to an end. In the agreement, Germany committed to investing roughly one billion Euros in Namibian reconstruction and development projects. More importantly perhaps, it agreed to classify the atrocities committed by German imperial forces against the Herero and Nama in the early 20th century as a genocide, and to ask the Namibian descendants of its victims for forgiveness.[1] Politicians in both countries were quick to praise the deal. German foreign minister Maas stated in a press release: 'I am pleased and indeed grateful that we have agreed with Namibia on how to deal with the darkest chapter of our shared history.'[2], and Namibian 1

[1] Federal Foreign Office, 28 May 2021.
[2] Federal Foreign Office, 28 May 2021.

president Geingob called the agreement 'historic'[3].Their sentiment was not shared by all, however. Representatives of the Herero and Nama criticised the deal harshly, with Paramount Chief of the Herero Rukoro declaring: 'That's a black cat in the bag instead of reparations for a crime against humanity'[4], and describing the agreement as 'an insult'[5]. These reactions show that the effects of historical colonialism are still clearly discernible in the formerly colonised countries of the Global South.

2 Now, some scholars warn of a similar phenomenon which is gaining momentum in the Global South: Its 'citizens [who] historically have been forced into castiron chains'[6] may be facing 'a future in invisible chains consisting of 0's and 1's'[7], they state. These chains symbolise 'data colonialism', the practice which is examined in this chapter. In its first section, the chapter provides a definition of 'data colonialism'. Its second part presents the parallels as well as the differences between 'data colonialism' and colonialism's historical manifestation. Its third section examines possible regulatory responses.

B. Defining 'Data Colonialism'

3 From the manifold contributions on various aspects of 'data colonialism',[8] two stand out for their detailed description of the phenomenon: Couldry and Mejias' 2019 paper 'Data Colonialism: Rethinking Big Data's Relation to the Contemporary Subject'[9] and Thatcher, O'Sullivan and Mahmoudi's 2016 paper 'Data colonialism through accumulation by dispossession: New metaphors for daily data'[10]. Their respective definitions of 'data colonialism' are summarised in this section, and a description for the purposes of this chapter is derived from it.

I. 'Data Colonialism' as a Frame

4 In their paper, Couldry and Mejias use colonialism as a frame for approaching Big Data and its impact on society.[11] They argue that '[d]ata colonialism combines the predatory extractive practices of historical colonialism with the abstract quantification methods of computing.'[12] 'Data colonialism' as they understand it presupposes the quantification of all of human life which occurs as vast amounts of data relating to every aspect of life are first produced and then collected on social media platforms, in the workplace and through self-tracking practices.[13] These individual data can then be combined and analysed by corporations in order to generate profits, thereby turning the data – and, as a consequence, human life itself – into a commodity.[14]

---

[3] Reuters Staff, *Reuters*, 28 May 2021.
[4] Jolaso, *The African Courier*, 30 May 2021.
[5] Jolaso, *The African Courier*, 30 May 2021.
[6] Marker/Vestergaard/Hendricks, *African Statistical Newsletter* 2019, 6.
[7] Marker/Vestergaard/Hendricks, *African Statistical Newsletter* 2019, 6.
[8] *Cf* in particular the contributions to *Television & New Media's* special issue on 'Big Data from the South' in 2019 and Couldry/Mejias foundational book *The Costs of Connection*, 2019, pt. 1 ch. 1–3.
[9] Couldry/Mejias, *Television & New Media* 2019, 336.
[10] Thatcher/O'Sullivan/Mahmoudi, *Environ Plan D* 2016, 990.
[11] Couldry/Mejias, *Television & New Media* 2019, 336 (336 f./338).
[12] Couldry/Mejias, *Television & New Media* 2019, 336 (337).
[13] *Cf* Couldry/Mejias, *Television & New Media* 2019, 336 (341 f.).
[14] *Cf* Couldry/Mejias, *Television & New Media* 2019, 336 (343).

Couldry and Mejias argue that this process is enabled by the popular narrative of data as 'the new oil'[15]. It creates the incorrect impression that individual data are merely raw materials which do not belong to anyone, and that neither the data nor the process of their generation have any inherent value for which the data subjects would need to be compensated. Data hence only become valuable once they are acquired by the corporations able and willing to collect and process them on a large scale.[16] According to Couldry and Mejias, these corporations can rely on an ideology which frames society as the natural beneficiary of Big Data practices when, in reality, data are appropriated to the benefit of selected corporations in whose hands the profits are concentrated.[17] 5

II. 'Data Colonialism' as a Metaphor

Thatcher, O'Sullivan and Mahmoudi use the term 'data colonialism' as a metaphor to symbolise the power asymmetries surrounding Big Data in their paper.[18] They argue – as the title of their paper states – that 'data colonialism' occurs through 'accumulation by dispossession'. This requires the privatisation of something that was previously not private, in the sense that it was not owned by anyone.[19] When personal experiences such as eating out or dating occur with the help of information and communication technologies such as smartphones and Internet platforms, they are first quantified as individual data, then alienated, i.e. separated, from the data subjects and finally privatised by corporations which obtain sole legal control, thus dispossessing the data subjects of their data.[20] By combining the individual data they amassed, these corporations are then able to create the commodity of Big Data.[21] This enables them to mine these data sets in order to generate profits, for example by improving personalised advertisements.[22] 6

III. Datafication, Appropriation, and Profit Generation

Both seminal descriptions of 'data colonialism' refer to three processes which will be used to characterise the phenomenon in this chapter: datafication, appropriation, and profit generation. Datafication describes the practice of translating real-life events into data points on a large scale, using the sharing and measuring mechanisms described above. Appropriation refers to the corporate collection and combination of the individual data thus generated into Big Data sets under the respective corporation's control. Profit generation occurs where corporations use these data sets solely to their financial benefit, not (or at least not directly) to that of the data subjects. 7

---

[15] Couldry/Mejias, *Television & New Media* 2019, 336 (340).
[16] *Cf* Couldry/Mejias, *Television & New Media* 2019, 336 (339 f.).
[17] *Cf* Couldry/Mejias, *Television & New Media* 2019, 336 (340).
[18] Thatcher/O'Sullivan/Mahmoudi, *Environ Plan D* 2016, 990 (992).
[19] Thatcher/O'Sullivan/Mahmoudi, *Environ Plan D* 2016, 990 (995).
[20] *Cf* Thatcher/O'Sullivan/Mahmoudi, *Environ Plan D* 2016, 990 (995 ff.).
[21] Thatcher/O'Sullivan/Mahmoudi, *Environ Plan D* 2016, 990 (994).
[22] Thatcher/O'Sullivan/Mahmoudi, *Environ Plan D* 2016, 990 (995).

C. Comparing 'Data Colonialism' and Historical Colonialism

8 At first glance, the definition set out in the previous section bears more relation with capitalism than with colonialism.[23] However, there are a number of parallels between 'data colonialism' and colonialism's historical manifestation: the practice of extraction, the control over infrastructure, the narrative of the benefit and the claim of 'terra nullius'. These parallels are elaborated in the first of the following two subsections. In the second subsection, the two major differences – the actors who are involved and the means which are used – are expounded. This provides the basis for an answer to the question: Is 'data colonialism' a new manifestation of colonialism?

I. The Parallels

1. The Practice of Extraction

9 In former times, the colonisers usurped the land, natural resources, and labour which they encountered in the colonised territories. They claimed the land on which they landed as their own, they mined it for gold, diamonds or other raw materials and they forced the indigenous people to work for them, sometimes even enslaving them.[24] Under 'data colonialism', a different type of extraction occurs: Instead of raw materials, individual data are considered to be a valuable resource which may be 'mined' for commercial gain.[25] Like diamonds, gold, or oil under historical colonialism, data as the relevant resource under 'data colonialism' can in theory be extracted in the Global North as well as in the Global South. Its value in principle does not depend on the nationality or origin of the data subject. However, the Global South is more heavily affected by 'data colonialism' in practice because – unlike in the Global North – a vast amount of hitherto unused data still exists there. A comparison of the global levels of mobile Internet connectivity illustrates this: In 2019, roughly three quarters of all North Americans and 70 percent of the European and Central Asian populations were connected to the mobile Internet. At the same time, this could only be said for about a quarter of all inhabitants of Sub-Saharan Africa and a third of the South Asian population.[26] The unexploited commercial potential in the Global South becomes clear when its population is compared to that in the Global North: In 2019, close to 370 million people lived in North America, and Europe and Central Asia combined had a population of around 920 million. At the same time, 1.1 billion people lived in Sub-Saharan Africa and over 1.8 billion people inhabited South Asia.[27] If they connect these areas of the Global South to the mobile Internet more thoroughly, corporations can

[23] *Cf* in particular Zuboff's work on 'surveillance capitalism' which refers to colonialism as well, *cf* Zuboff, *The Age of Surveillance Capitalism*, 2019, pt. 1 ch. 6.

[24] *Cf* Coleman, *Mich. J. Race Law* 2019, 417 (419 f.); Couldry/Mejias, *Television & New Media* 2019, 336 (337); Milan/Treré, *Television & New Media* 2019, 319 (326).

[25] Coleman, *Mich. J. Race Law* 2019, 417 (428); Couldry/Mejias, *Internet Policy Rev.* 2019, 1 (3); Marker/Vestergaard/Hendricks, *African Statistical Newsletter* 2019, 6; Milan/Treré, *Television & New Media* 2019, 319 (326).

[26] GSMA Intelligence, *Connected Society*, 2020, 15.

[27] The World Bank, *Data: Population, total.*

greatly enlarge the pool of people whose lives they can datafy and whose data they can then appropriate and use to generate profits.

2. The Control over Infrastructure

In order to facilitate their extractive practices, some former colonisers established transportation infrastructures in the colonised territories. Railways and roads were needed to transport the raw materials to the harbours from where they were shipped to the colonial power's homeland. Such infrastructure was controlled by the colonial forces, and used to their benefit, not to the advantage of the colonised population.[28] Under 'data colonialism', tech corporations build information and communication infrastructures which enable the datafication of their users' lives, and the subsequent appropriation of their data for profit generation purposes.[29] **10**

In theory, this phenomenon can again affect the entire world. In practice, however, the impact of corporate control over information and communication infrastructure is greater in the Global South, as such infrastructure is scarcer in many of its regions. There is thus more room for corporations to establish it.[30] One software example of such an effort is Facebook's project 'Free Basics'. This is a mobile app which gives its users in regions with lacking mobile Internet connectivity an opportunity to browse selected websites free-of-charge.[31] A hardware example is provided by Apple's cheaper iPhones. They were introduced to target markets with less wealthy consumers, especially in the Global South.[32] **11**

Arguably, projects such as 'Free Basics' and cheaper iPhones hold some benefits for their participants who might otherwise not have had access to the mobile Internet or to a smartphone. For this reason, they are not quite the same as the roads and railways built and used by the colonisers in former times. However, corporations do not conduct these projects for purely altruistic reasons. There is a business case for them: If people use 'Free Basics' or a cheaper iPhone, for example, Facebook and Apple can use these infrastructures to datafy their lives, appropriate their data and generate profits for themselves. In addition, corporations who establish information and communication infrastructure have a first mover advantage in the markets of the Global South,[33] thus inhibiting local infrastructure efforts which might have provided an alternative to the corporately controlled infrastructure in the long run.[34] **12**

3. The Narrative of the Benefit

Historically, its perpetrators oftentimes justified colonialism with regard to the benefits it supposedly held for the indigenous people when, in reality, they themselves were the profiteers. The picture of the docile 'white saviour' was used to conceal the commercial and political gains which the colonisers hoped to make.[35] In a similar vein, 'data colonialist' practices today are framed as practices which benefit society and/or the **13**

---

[28] Coleman, *Mich. J. Race Law* 2019, 417 (420); Kwet, *Race Cl* 2019, 3 (7).

[29] Coleman, *Mich. J. Race Law* 2019, 417 (424/428 f.); Kwet, *Race Cl* 2019, 3 (7 f.); Marker/Vestergaard/Hendricks, *African Statistical Newsletter* 2019, 6.

[30] *Cf* Coleman, *Mich. J. Race Law* 2019, 417 (428).

[31] Facebook Connectivity.

[32] Bloomberg, *South China Morning Post*, 10 January 2013.

[33] Arora, *Int. J. Commun.* 2016, 1681 (1686).

[34] Coleman, *Mich. J. Race Law* 2019, 417 (430).

[35] *Cf* Arora, *Television & New Media* 2019, 366 (372).

data subjects whose data are collected.[36] This narrative deflects from the fact that the data are used to generate profits for the corporations which collected and assembled them.[37]

14 Once again, there is a difference between the historical manifestation of colonialism and 'data colonialism': Big Data and the machine learning processes these data sets enable can actually benefit those whose data are used as well as society as a whole. Alibaba, for example, has developed an algorithm which can detect COVID-19 in CT scans with a 96 percent accuracy.[38] This might be helpful in the fight against the global pandemic and would not have been possible without Alibaba's appropriation of vast amounts of data.

15 However, positive aspects of Big Data such as these tend to be overemphasised by the corporations which collect and use data.[39] Facebook, for example, states that its mission is 'to give people the power to build community and bring the world closer together'[40], and Google's aim is to organise the world's information and make it universally accessible and useful.[41] While the guidance these mission statements provide is not denied, they do not change the fact that neither Facebook nor Google nor any other corporation involved in the generation and use of Big Data are non-profit organisations. Instead they are private companies with obligations to their shareholders, and their main aim – with regard to 'data colonialist' as well as any other business practices – is to generate profits.

4. The Claim of 'Terra Nullius'

16 Lastly, colonial forces historically considered the territories they usurped to be 'terra nullius', believing both the land and its natural resources to be ownerless and therefore free for their taking. This negated the indigenous peoples' moral and legal rights to the territories and the raw materials.[42] Under 'data colonialism', individual data are considered ownerless, free for the taking of the corporations willing and able to collect and use them.[43]

17 To some extent, this phenomenon once again affects the Global North as well as the Global South. For example, a comprehensive property right to one's own data which would allow individuals to bar corporations from collecting their data exists neither in the EU nor in the US.[44] However, data protection laws provide a defence against some 'data colonialist' practices in many areas of the Global North. One example is the appropriation of individual data: Under the GDPR, corporations which collect personal data can never be entirely sure whether the data 'belong' to them, as Art. 17 GDPR provides data subjects in most cases with a so-called right to be forgotten. This gives them the power to demand the erasure of their data. Under Sec. 1798.105 CCPA, consumers have a similar right to request that businesses delete personal information which they collected on them.

---

[36] Couldry/Mejias, *Television & New Media* 2019, 336 (340).
[37] Coleman, *Mich. J. Race Law* 2019, 417 (430).
[38] Alibaba Cloud.
[39] *Cf* Arora, *Int. J. Commun.* 2016, 1681 (1686); Couldry/Mejias, *Internet Policy Rev.* 2019, 1 (9).
[40] Facebook Investor Relations.
[41] Google Search.
[42] Cohen, *Philos Technol* 2018, 213 (214 f.).
[43] Couldry/Mejias, *Television & New Media* 2019, 336 (340). *Cf* in addition Cohen, *Philos Technol* 2018, 213 (216).
[44] *Infra* mn. 42 et seq.

In contrast, while there are remarkable data protection efforts underway in various regions of the Global South,[45] a number of its nations have no or significantly weaker (or less enforced) data protection laws.[46] It is therefore easier, from a legal standpoint, for corporations to datafy their citizens' lives in order to appropriate their data and to generate profits for themselves.[47] 18

II. The Differences

1. The Actors Involved

Historically, colonialism built on the North/South divide: Countries in the Global North such as European nations and the US were the colonisers. Countries in the Global South such as African, Asian and South American nations were the colonised. Under 'data colonialism', both the 'colonisers' and the 'colonised' include different parties. 19

The 'data colonisers' certainly comprise companies seated in the Global North, especially in the US American Silicon Valley, such as Amazon, Facebook and Google. Increasingly, however, corporations from the Global South, namely from China, engage in 'data colonialism' as well.[48] Some examples are Baidu, Alibaba and TikTok. 20

The 'data colonised' on the other hand undoubtedly include nations of the Global South which are more heavily affected by 'data colonialist' practices than countries in the Global North for the reasons set out in the previous subsection. However, they also include what shall be referred to as the South-in-North.[49] This term stands for marginalised groups in the Global North which are disproportionally affected by 'data colonialist' practices, as they experience a double 'data colonialism'[50]: Their lives are datafied and their data are appropriated and used for profit generation like everybody else's, but the use of Big Data – for example for predictive data analyses – can serve to discriminate against them specifically.[51] With regard to 'data colonialism', the South is therefore not merely a place, but a metaphor: It includes the geographical area of the Global South as well as the South-in-North.[52] 21

2. The Means Used

In former times, colonialism relied on physical force and violence to enable its extraction of land, resources, and labour.[53] Horrific atrocities were performed by the 22

[45] *Cf* Dei-Tutu/Hoffmann, § 6, on the African data strategy and Zuo, § 7, on the Chinese data strategy.
[46] Arora, *Surveill. Soc.* 2019, 717 (718).
[47] Arora, *Television & New Media* 2019, 366 (368); Marker/Vestergaard/Hendricks, *African Statistical Newsletter* 2019, 6.
[48] Arora, *Television & New Media* 2019, 366 (372 f.); Couldry/Mejias, *Television & New Media* 2019, 336 (337); Ricaurte, *Television & New Media* 2019, 350 (356); Segura/Waisbord, *Television & New Media* 2019, 412 (417).
[49] This is a turn on the phrase 'North-in-South' which Mann/Daly, *Television & New Media* 2019, 379 (379 f.) use to describe Australia's position in the world.
[50] Mann/Daly, *Television & New Media* 2019, 379 (381). *Cf* in addition Couldry/Mejias, *Television & New Media* 2019, 336 (337/345); Ricaurte, *Television & New Media* 2019, 350 (353).
[51] *Cf* Arora, *Television & New Media* 2019, 366 (367); Arora, *Surveill. Soc.* 2019, 717 (721 f.).
[52] *Cf* Milan/Treré, *Television & New Media* 2019, 319 (321/325).
[53] Segura/Waisbord, *Television & New Media* 2019, 412 (416).

colonial powers, for example in the form of the genocide committed by the German imperial forces against the Herero and Nama.[54]

23 'Data colonialism' does not rely on these or any remotely comparable practices.[55] It is true – as Couldry and Mejias state to justify their use of the term 'colonialism'[56] – that the economic concentration of power in the hands of corporations serves as a 'muscle' to enforce their extensive data collection desires. However, this influence does not compare to the physical violence employed by colonisers in previous centuries. To call the practices of datafication, appropriation and profit generation colonialism – without the quotation marks used in this chapter – would thus trivialise the atrocities committed in the name of historical colonialism.

III. A Metaphor for the Adverse Impact on the South

24 The comparison between historical colonialism and 'data colonialism' has shown significant parallels as well as fundamental differences between the two phenomena. While 'data colonialism' should therefore not be considered a new manifestation of colonialism, the use of the term as a metaphor helps to illustrate the adverse impact which the datafication, appropriation, and profit generation practices surrounding Big Data may have on the South in particular.

D. Reacting to 'Data Colonialism'

25 Countering the adverse impact of 'data colonialism' on the South is a task for regulators across the globe, and across all legal disciplines. Consumer protection and competition law are two possible roads which could be taken to address the structural imbalances underlying 'data colonialist' practices.[57] The last section of this chapter focusses on another avenue: data law. It first analyses the (limited) potential which data protection law holds in this regard, and then proposes providing data subjects with discretionary power over their data.

I. Data Protection Law

1. The GDPR's 'Colonialist' Approach

26 As shown in the previous section, data protection law is able to prevent some 'data colonialist' practices.[58] Couldry and Mejias credit the GDPR specifically with disrupting such processes.[59] Nevertheless, regulators in the Global North – especially in Europe – should not be tempted to engage in 'data protection colonialism'[60] in order to address

---

[54] *Supra* mn. 1.

[55] Segura/Waisbord, *Television & New Media* 2019, 412 (416 f.).

[56] Couldry/Mejias, *Television & New Media* 2019, 336 (341).

[57] *Cf* Coleman, *Mich. J. Race Law* 2019, 417 (436); Hennemann/Boshe/von Meding, *ZfDR* 2021, 193 (213).

[58] *Cf* for its limitations *infra* mn. 30 et seq.

[59] Couldry/Mejias, *Internet Policy Rev.* 2019, 1 (6).

[60] *Cf* Arora, *Television & New Media* 2019, 366 (369) who argues that the GDPR could 'become a neocolonial entity'.

the adverse impact of 'data colonialism'. Such a 'Race to the General Data Protection Regulation'[61] is currently well underway, as the EU has proclaimed that it aims to 'export' the GDPR's data protection framework across the globe[62]. In order to achieve its goal, it can not only rely on the soft factor of the EU's considerable market power.[63] There are also a number of mechanisms through which the GDPR's hard law works to make itself the global standard for data protection.

One mechanism is the GDPR's territorial scope.[64] Its framework is not only relevant if data are processed by companies seated in the EU (Art. 3(1) GDPR). It also applies to certain processing activities of non-EU companies, most notably where they relate to the offering of goods or services to data subjects in the EU (Art. 3(2)(a) GDPR). While it is not enough that a company's website can be accessed from within the EU for the GDPR to apply, the website does not have to be geared entirely towards EU sales either: It normally suffices if it states that payments may be made in Euro, for example.[65] Due to this broad interpretation, a great number of international corporations operating online have to comply with the GDPR's requirements.[66] 27

Additionally, the GDPR's scope is *de facto* extended through its 'data protection by design' approach, expressed most clearly in Art. 25 GDPR. By adjusting their technology to meet the GDPR's demands in this regard, corporations embed its framework directly into their products and services.[67] While this might legally only be required for data processing activities falling within the scope of the GDPR, some corporations have implemented technical changes across all data, as it would be too burdensome to differentiate between the data of EU data subjects and the data of non-EU data subjects.[68] 28

A third mechanism is the instrument of the adequacy decision (Art. 45 et seqq. GDPR).[69] If a third country is found to ensure an adequate level of data protection, personal data falling within the scope of the GDPR may be transferred from the EU to this country without any further specific authorisation or additional requirements (Art. 45(1) GDPR). This prospect is currently leading some countries in the Global South to adjust their data protection laws to meet the standards set by the EU.[70] 29

2. Honouring Different Values and Realities

The GDPR undoubtedly provides a high level of data protection in the EU. However, its introduction in countries of the Global South would not automatically have the same effect. A legal transplant such as the 'export' of the GDPR can only be successful if the 'exported' law fits into the culture – both legal and otherwise – of the country which imports it.[71] As the GDPR's framework relies on certain cultural, political, and economic assumptions which do not necessarily reflect the values and 30

[61] Hennemann, *RabelsZ* 2020, 864 (870).
[62] *Cf* COM (2017) 7 final, 2.
[63] Hennemann, *RabelsZ* 2020, 864 (876); Vatanparast, *ZaöRV* 2020, 819 (823 and 826).
[64] Hennemann, *RabelsZ* 2020, 864 (878); Mannion, *Vand. J. Transnat'l L.* 2020, 685 (691 f.).
[65] Rec. 23 of the GDPR.
[66] Hennemann, *RabelsZ* 2020, 864 (880); Hennemann/Boshe/von Meding, *ZfDR* 2021, 193 (218).
[67] Vatanparast, *ZaöRV* 2020, 819 (832 f.).
[68] Vatanparast, *ZaöRV* 2020, 819 (832). For example, Microsoft announced in 2018 that its products and processes had been adjusted globally – not only in the EU – to meet the demands of the GDPR (Brill, *Microsoft*, 21 May 2018).
[69] Hennemann, *RabelsZ* 2020, 864 (882).
[70] Hennemann/Boshe/von Meding, *ZfDR* 2021, 193 (219).
[71] *Cf* Hennemann/Boshe/von Meding, *ZfDR* 2021, 193 (196).

realities encountered in other regions of the world,[72] it should not simply be transplanted into the laws of these regions.

31 Firstly, the GDPR holds data subjects responsible for the protection of their personal data. They can consent to or deny their consent to data processing (Art. 6 et seqq. GDPR) and they have several rights against data controllers and processors (Art. 16 et seqq. GDPR), for example the above-mentioned right to be forgotten. It is the European Commission's current position that these rights can only be exercised by the data subjects themselves, and that this exercise cannot be delegated to third parties that might assist them.[73]

32 But to be able to give consent or to exercise one's right to be forgotten against large corporations requires a high level of digital literacy. The GDPR builds on the assumption that all data subjects within its scope conform to this standard. However, a high level of digital literacy cannot be expected across all nations of the Global South[74] (and the South-in-North). Some nations still have to meet more basic challenges such as providing safe housing, clean water and health services to their citizens and cannot focus their efforts on digital education yet.[75] If the GDPR was simply exported to regions with low levels of digital literacy, their inhabitants might in theory be able to deny consent to data processing or to ask for the deletion of their data. In practice, 'data colonialist' practices would nevertheless persist, as they would not necessarily have the knowledge required to exercise these rights.

33 Secondly, one of the GDPR's greatest assets is its strong enforcement framework. For its enforcement, the GDPR relies on one hand on administrative agencies, the so-called supervisory authorities (Art. 51 et seqq. GDPR), with considerable powers. These authorities can, for example, demand fines of up to 20 million Euros or 4 percent of a company's global annual revenue in case of certain data breaches (Art. 83(5) GDPR). On the other hand, the GDPR gives individual data subjects a right to compensation in Art. 82, enlisting the power of private enforcement. Knowing that non-compliance with the GDPR can lead to significant (financial) drawbacks can serve to increase compliance with its framework.[76]

34 However, it cannot simply be assumed that a similar enforcement is possible in the Global South.[77] Not all of its nations have independent and well-funded administrative agencies (yet) which could provide for reliable public enforcement.[78] Similarly, not all of them have a steadfast and easily accessible judicial system which would enable the private enforcement.[79] If the GDPR was simply 'exported' to these countries, 'data colonialist' practices might in theory be prohibited by data protection laws. However, if it could not be ensured that these prohibitions were enforced effectively in practice, they would likely soon be disregarded.

35 Lastly, and most fundamentally, which data should be protected and how far these protections should reach is a question which may elude different answers in different countries.[80] The GDPR has given one answer, but nations in the Global South may give

---

[72] Hennemann/Boshe/von Meding, *ZfDR* 2021, 193 (223); Mannion, *Vand. J. Transnat'l L.* 2020, 685 (705); Vatanparast, *ZaöRV* 2020, 819 (821/824 f./836).

[73] Rec. 24 of the proposed Data Governance Act.

[74] Arora, *Television & New Media* 2019, 366 (369). *Cf* in addition Coleman, *Mich. J. Race Law* 2019, 417 (438).

[75] Curtiss, *Wash. J.L. Tech. & Arts* 2016, 95 (110).

[76] Curtiss, *Wash. J.L. Tech. & Arts* 2016, 95 (104).

[77] Arora, *Television & New Media* 2019, 366 (369); Curtiss, *Wash. J.L. Tech. & Arts* 2016, 95 (107 f.).

[78] *Cf* the examples in Hennemann/Boshe/von Meding, *ZfDR* 2021, 193 (210 ff.).

[79] Curtiss, *Wash. J.L. Tech. & Arts* 2016, 95 (107 f./112); Mannion, *Vand. J. Transnat'l L.* 2020, 685 (702 ff.).

[80] *Cf* Arora, *Television & New Media* 2019, 366 (370 f.); Arora, *Surveill. Soc.* 2019, 717 (718).

a different one. One example from within the EU illustrates how the approach to data protection can vary, depending on a country's history and values: Google Streetview. When the project started in Germany over a decade ago, Google's colourful cars driving around German cities with a camera on their roof caused a public outcry.[81] Google had to introduce a tool allowing the inhabitants of the houses shown on Streetview to demand their pixelation.[82] It soon stopped updating the pictures. Today, Germany is a blind spot on the European Google Streetview map which is otherwise well-populated, as the citizens of other European nations did not voice similar concerns.[83] If such a fundamental difference regarding the protection of data can transpire within the EU, it is likely to be even more pronounced in comparison with other regions of the world.

The focus should therefore be on developing data protection solutions at the local level which are able to take into account each country's values as well as its cultural, political, and economic realities instead of simply 'exporting' the GDPR. While some nations may adopt frameworks similar to the GDPR, others may prefer a different approach. **36**

II. Data Law

Even if the GDPR was introduced on a global scale, the impact of 'data colonialism' would not be fully countered. Presently, the GDPR does not challenge 'data colonialist' practices as such.[84] Instead, it provides a framework which prohibits some of the most excessive datafication, appropriation, and profit generation practices but legitimises others.[85] For example, while automated decision-making is in principle banned if it significantly affects data subjects (Art. 22(1) GDPR), the GDPR does not prevent the generation of the Big Data sets needed for such decision-making, instead providing a number of potential legal bases for it in Art. 6(1) GDPR. **37**

To assert this does not mean to condemn it. How one assesses 'data colonialism' and whether and how one believes it should be regulated depends largely on one's general assessment of capitalist practices. In this chapter it is argued that 'data colonialism' does not need to be eradicated in all its forms. This is where it differs from colonialism's historical manifestation. Instead, the focus of this last subsection lies on a counter-measure which would fundamentally alter the power dynamics underlying 'data colonialist' practices: giving data subjects discretionary power over their data. With the 'nationalisation' of data, the introduction of a property right to data ascribed to the individual data subjects, and the establishment of private data trusts, three possible approaches to implementing this proposal are examined. **38**

1. 'Nationalising' Data

Mejias proposes that states should declare individual data a national resource, nationalise the data and demand a payment for their collection and use from the tech corporations which want to use them for profit generation purposes. The state could **39**

---

[81] Jacobs, *Big Think*, 26 September 2019.

[82] *Cf* Der Hamburgische Beauftragte für Datenschutz und Informationsfreiheit, *Aus den Augen, aus dem Sinn …* available at https://lfd.niedersachsen.de/startseite/themen/wirtschaft/google_street_view/vorab-widerspruchsverfahren-google-street-view-89269.html (last accessed 4 January 2023).

[83] Jacobs, *Big Think*, 26 September 2019.

[84] *Cf* Couldry/Mejias, *Internet Policy Rev.* 2019, 1 (9).

[85] *Cf* Vatanparast, *ZaöRV* 2020, 819 (822, 824, and 840).

then invest these payments in building local software and hardware infrastructure which would eventually provide an alternative to the infrastructures built and controlled by the 'data colonisers'.[86] In fact, China has recently announced plans to nationalise privately-held data which it considers to be a factor of production.[87]

40 This approach could perhaps prevent the appropriation of data by corporations, as these data would already have been appropriated by the state. Likewise, it might prevent corporations from generating profits without passing as least some of them on to the state and thus in effect to the individual data subjects.

41 As previously argued with regard to the phenomenon of 'data colonialism' as such, how one assesses Mejias' proposal therefore depends largely on one's position on 'nationalisation' and on the required expropriation of individual resources in general. However, the 'nationalisation' of individual data in particular poses an (insurmountable) problem: it requires some extent of state control over these data. While such control is questionable in liberal, democratic states, additional potential for misuse exists in illiberal, undemocratic nations which may already use their citizens' data to control them.

2. Introducing a Property Right to Data

42 Another potential countermeasure is the introduction of a property right to data. In the US, Senator John Kennedy has proposed the Own Your Own Data Act which states in Sec. 2(a) that '[e]ach individual owns and has an exclusive property right in the data that individual generates on the internet [...]'. The idea of a 'data dividend' paid to users by tech corporations was also a campaign promise of US presidential candidate Andrew Yang in 2020. He has since founded the 'Data Dividend Project' to make his idea a reality.[88] In contrast, the European Commission initially identified data ownership as one of the 'emerging issues' in the digital single market,[89] but has since appeared to abandon this position, stating that stakeholders do not favour the introduction of such a right[90].

43 A property right to one's data could prevent the corporate appropriation of individual data because these data would no longer be 'terra nullius' but belong to the data subjects who generated them. It might also counteract the practice of generating profits for corporations alone, as they could have to pay data subjects in order to be able to access and use their data. This would lead to the transfer of at least some earnings to the data subjects. However, two of the realities discussed with regard to data protection law cast doubt on the effectiveness of a property right to one's data in countering 'data colonialism' especially in the Global South.

44 Firstly, it does not suffice to have a right to one's own data in theory if the rightsholder does not exhibit the high level of digital literacy which is necessary to wield it against large corporations wishing to appropriate their data for profit generation purposes in practice. For the reasons set out in the previous section, such a high level cannot be assumed across all nations of the Global South. Yet if data subjects do not know that they have a right to their data, or how to enforce it, such a right cannot effectively prevent the appropriation of their data for profit generation purposes.

---

[86] Mejias, *Aljazeera*, 14 December 2019.
[87] *Cf* Yin, *Protocol*, 16 June 2021.
[88] *Cf* Klein, *Slate*, 23 July 2020.
[89] COM(2015) 192 final, 15.
[90] COM(2018) 232 final, 9.

Secondly, having a property right to one's data does not avert 'data colonialist' practices if the rightsholder cannot rely on well-functioning and easily accessible courts or other enforcement agencies to help assert their right. As stated above, not all nations of the Global South provide such robust enforcement opportunities. Introducing a property right to data in these countries would therefore not protect their citizens against 'data colonialism' in practice. 45

3. Establishing Data Trusts

This chapter therefore proposes a different countermeasure: the establishment of privately held data trusts. A data trust is a person or institution that mediates access to data which are provided or held by data subjects in accordance with contractual or statutory data governance regulations in the interest of another, i.e. not in their own interest.[91] 46

Data trusts can – among other purposes – serve two functions which are relevant for countering 'data colonialism': Firstly, a data trust can have a management function. In this capacity, it assists individual data subjects in controlling their data. One example are Personal Information Management Systems (PIMS).[92] PIMS can store personal data and allow data subjects to manage these data and to determine with whom they are shared.[93] If one condition of such sharing is the payment of a 'sharing fee' to the data subject, a data trust with a management function can also help them to monetise their data.[94] 47

Secondly, a data trust can be established with the goal of solving a data access problem in the interest of data subjects.[95] The focus of this type of data trust is less on the individual who wishes to control their data and more on the third party that wishes to access it. Its establishment can, however, benefit the data subjects as well, as it may serve as a stronger version of a PIMS: A data trust of this type can negotiate the conditions of access to the data it holds with the third party that wishes to access it. If it holds large amounts of data, it can conduct these negotiations at eye level and thus achieve better outcomes than the ones which individual data subjects would have been able to attain. After granting access, the data trust can check that the agreed-upon conditions for such access are met, and take collective enforcement action if this is not the case.[96] 48

A data trust which falls into one of these categories could on one hand help unlock the benefits of 'data colonialism': With the datafication of many aspects of human life and the generation of Big Data sets which it enables, it is increasingly possible to solve problems which were previously unsolvable. At the same time, a data trust could counteract the adverse impact of 'data colonialism' in two ways. 49

Firstly, it could prevent the corporate appropriation of data, as it would give data subjects an opportunity to enforce the rights afforded to them by data protection laws more efficiently (where such laws exist). If data subjects lacked the high level of digital literacy needed to take action against corporations, for example, collective enforcement 50

---

[91] Specht-Riemenschneider/Blankertz/Sierek/Schneider/Knapp/Henne, *MMR-Beil.* 2021, 25 (27).

[92] Specht-Riemenschneider/Blankertz/Sierek/Schneider/Knapp/Henne, *MMR-Beil.* 2021, 25 (27).

[93] EDPS, 3 *Tech Dispatch* 2020, 1.

[94] Specht-Riemenschneider/Blankertz/Sierek/Schneider/Knapp/Henne, *MMR-Beil.* 2021, 25 (27). Very critical of such monetisation opportunities in the context of 'data colonialism' Ricaurte, *Television & New Media* 2019, 350 (352 f.).

[95] Specht-Riemenschneider/Blankertz/Sierek/Schneider/Knapp/Henne, *MMR-Beil.* 2021, 25 (28).

[96] Specht-Riemenschneider/Blankertz/Sierek/Schneider/Knapp/Henne, *MMR-Beil.* 2021, 25 (28).

action taken by a data trust could ensure that their rights are nevertheless preserved. Where data protection laws do not exist, the technical ability to preclude third parties from even accessing their personal data could give data subjects a *de facto* protection against the corporate appropriation of their data. This could solve the problems posed by deficient enforcement structures in some nations of the Global South.

51 The use of a data trust could secondly counteract the 'data colonialist' practice of generating profits for corporations alone. If using a data trust enabled data subjects to demand payments from corporations, these individuals could reap at least some of the benefits generated through the corporate use of their data. If data subjects did not wish to enable the generation of profits, putting their data into a data trust would give them a means to effectively preventing corporate access to, and thus corporate profit generation from their data.

Bibliography

52 Alibaba Cloud, CT Image Analytics for COVID-19, available at https://www.alibabacloud.com/de/solutions/ct-image-analytics (last accessed 4 January 2023)

Arora, The Bottom of the Data Pyramid: Big Data and the Global South, 10 *Int. J. Commun.* 1681 (2016)

Arora, Decolonizing Privacy Studies, 20(4) *Television & New Media* 366 (2019)

Arora, General Data Protection Regulation – A Global Standard? Privacy Futures, Digital Activism, and Surveillance Cultures in the Global South, 17(5) *Surveill. Soc.* 717 (2019)

Bloomberg, Apple plans smaller, cheaper iPhone for customers in developing nations, *South China Morning Post*, 10 January 2013, available at https://www.scmp.com/business/companies/article/1123993/apple-plans-smaller-cheaper-iphone-customers-developing-nations (last accessed 4 January 2023)

Brill, Microsoft's commitment to GDPR, privacy and putting customers in control of their own data, *Microsoft*, 21 May 2018, available at https://blogs.microsoft.com/on-the-issues/2018/05/21/microsofts-commitment-to-gdpr-privacy-and-putting-customers-in-control-of-their-own-data/ (last accessed 4 January 2023)

Cohen, The Biopolitical Public Domain: the Legal Construction of the Surveillance Economy, 31 *Philos Technol* 213 (2018)

Coleman, Digital Colonialism: The 21st Century Scramble for Africa through the Extraction and Control of User Data and the Limitations of Data Protection Laws, 24 *Mich. J. Race Law* 417 (2019)

Couldry/Mejias, *The Costs of Connection. How Data is Colonizing Human Life and Appropriating it for Capitalism*, 2019

Couldry/Mejias, Data Colonialism: Rethinking Big Data's Relation to the Contemporary Subject, 20(4) *Television & New Media* 336 (2019)

Couldry/Mejias, Making data colonialism liveable: how might data's social order be regulated?, 8(2) *Internet Policy Rev.* 1 (2019)

Curtiss, Privacy Harmonization and the Developing World: The Impact of the EU's General Data Protection Regulation on Developing Economies, 12(1) *Wash. J.L. Tech. & Arts* 95 (2016)

EDPS, Personal Information Management Systems, 3 *Tech Dispatch* 1 (2020)

Facebook Connectivity, Free Basics, available at https://www.facebook.com/connectivity/solutions/free-basics (last accessed 4 January 2023)

Facebook Investor Relations, FAQ, available at https://investor.fb.com/resources/default.aspx (last accessed 4 January 2023)

Federal Foreign Office, Foreign Minister Maas on the conclusion of negotiations with Namibia. Press Release, 28 May 2021, available at https://www.auswaertiges-amt.de/en/newsroom/news/-/2463598 (last accessed 4 January 2023)

Google Search, *Die Grundpfeiler der Google-Suche*, available at https://www.google.com/search/howsearchworks/mission/ (last accessed 4 January 2023)

GSMA Intelligence, *Connected Society. The State of Mobile Internet Connectivity 2020*, 2020

Der Hamburgische Beauftragte für Datenschutz und Informationsfreiheit, *Aus den Augen, aus dem Sinn ... Informationen zur Umsetzung des Vorab-Widerspruchs gegen Abbildungen im Internetdienst Google Street View*, available at https://lfd.niedersachsen.de/startseite/themen/wirtschaft/google_street_view/vorab-widerspruchsverfahren-google-street-view-89269.html (last accessed 4 January 2023)

Hennemann, Wettbewerb der Datenschutzrechtsordnungen. Zur Rezeption der Datenschutz-Grundverordnung, 84 *RabelsZ* 864 (2020)

Hennemann/Boshe/von Meding, Datenschutzrechtsordnungen in Afrika, 3 *ZfDR* 193 (2021)

Jacobs, Why Germany is a blank spot on Google's Street View, *Big Think*, 26 September 2019, available at https://bigthink.com/the-present/germany-street-view/ (last accessed 4 January 2023)

Jolaso, "Insulting!" Critics slam German-Namibian agreement on Herero genocide, *The African Courier*, 30 May 2021, available at https://www.theafricancourier.de/news/africa/insulting-critics-reject-german-namibian-agreement-on-herero-genocide/ (last accessed 4 January 2023)

Klein, Andrew Yang Wants You to Own and Sell Your Data, *Slate*, 23 July 2020, available at https://slate.com/technology/2020/06/yang-launches-data-dividend-project.html (last accessed 4 January 2023)

Kwet, Digital colonialism: US empire and the new imperialism in the Global South, 60(4) *Race Cl* 3 (2019)

Mann/Daly, (Big) Data and the North-*in*-South: Australia's Informational Imperialism and Digital Colonialism, 20(4) *Television & New Media* 379 (2018)

Mannion, Data Imperialism: The GDPR's Disastrous Impact on Africa's E-Commerce Markets, 53 *Vand. J. Transnat'l L.* 685 (2020)

Marker/Vestergaard/Hendricks, Digital Colonialism on the African Continent, 10(1) *African Statistical Newsletter* 6 (2019)

Mejias, Why the Global South should nationalise its data, *Aljazeera*, 14 December 2019, available at https://www.aljazeera.com/opinions/2019/12/14/why-the-global-south-should-nationalise-its-data (last accessed 4 January 2023)

Milan/Treré, Big Data from the South(s): Beyond Data Universalism, 20(4) *Television & New Media* 319 (2019)

Reuters Staff, Germany apologises for colonial-era genocide in Namibia, *Reuters*, 28 May 2021, available at https://www.reuters.com/article/ozatp-uk-namibia-germany-genocide-idAFKCN2D90JY-OZATP (last accessed 4 January 2023)

Ricaurte, Data Epistemologies, The Coloniality of Power, and Resistance, 20(4) *Television & New Media* 350 (2019)

Segura/Waisbord, Between Data Capitalism and Data Citizenship, 20(4) *Television & New Media* 412 (2019)

Specht-Riemenschneider/Blankertz/Sierek/Schneider/Knapp/Henne, Die Datentreuhand, 6 *MMR-Beil.* 25 (2021)

Thatcher/O'Sullivan/Mahmoudi, Data colonialism through accumulation by disposession: New metaphors for daily data, 34(6) *Environ Plan D* 990 (2016)

Vatanparast, Designed to Serve Mankind? The Politics of the GDPR as a Global Standard and the Limits of Privacy, 4 *ZaöRV* 819 (2020)

Yin, *China is laying the groundwork to nationalize private companies' data*, 16 June 2021, available at https://www.protocol.com/china/china-national-security-data-exchange (last accessed 4 January 2023)

The World Bank, *Data: Population, total*, available at https://data.worldbank.org/indicator/SP.POP.TOTL (last accessed 4 January 2023)

Zuboff, *The Age of Surveillance Capitalism. The Fight for a Human Future at the New Frontier of Power*, 2019

Index

(bold = paragraph, light = margin number)